Aligning Business Processes
and Information Systems

Robert Heinrich

Aligning Business Processes and Information Systems

New Approaches to Continuous Quality Engineering

Foreword by Prof. Dr. Barbara Paech

 Springer Vieweg

Dr. Robert Heinrich
Karlsruhe, Germany

ISBN 978-3-658-06517-1   ISBN 978-3-658-06518-8 (eBook)
DOI 10.1007/978-3-658-06518-8

The Deutsche Nationalbibliothek lists this publication in the Deutsche Nationalbibliografie; detailed bibliographic data are available in the Internet at http://dnb.d-nb.de.

Library of Congress Control Number: 2014943413

Springer Vieweg
© Springer Fachmedien Wiesbaden 2014

Printed on acid-free paper

Springer Vieweg is a brand of Springer DE.
Springer DE is part of Springer Science+Business Media.
www.springer-vieweg.de

Foreword

The quality of business software is determined not only by the functionality and the quality properties of the software, but also by its fitting into the business context. Business processes constitute the major part of this context. Missing alignment between software and context induces disruption, inefficiency and frustration. The design (and thus also the quality) of business processes and of business software are nowadays typically separated in the discipline of business process management and in the discipline of software engineering. Business informatics and information system science study the concurrence of both, but typically focusing on functional aspects and not addressing detailed technical software properties. A precise specification of quality as well as its measurement and prediction is neglected both in practice and in research.

The contribution of this book is to give examples from research and practice for an integrated design of the quality of business processes and software. The first research contribution is a foundation for the integrated specification of quality for business process and software in terms of a business process quality reference model (BPQRM) which is compatible with well known software product quality standards such as ISO/IEC 25000. To apply the BPQRM in practice an extension of typical business process modeling notations such as BPMN is proposed and implemented. The second research contribution is an integrated model of business process and software performance and a corresponding tool for integrated simulation and performance analysis and prediction. The book shows the limitations of a separated but connected simulation of business processes and information systems (BIIS) which could be viewed as a natural solution to the alignment problem. Based on this the intricacies of a true integration are motivated and developed. Important parts of this integration (IntBIIS) are a scheduling policy for human actors as well as the treatment of variable load which does not impact the stability of the simulation.

To support further work on quality specification and alignment this book contains several case studies which show the potential of the integrated approach. The usefulness of the BPQRM for elicitation of quality issues is shown through a study in the medical domain. The usefulness of BIIS and IntBIIS is discussed for the order picking process at a manufacturing and distribution company. This is first published application of performance modeling and prediction in practice and provides several interesting insights on the difficulties and opportunities of such application in industry.

Integration (of the design of business process and software quality as well as of research and practice) is the underlying theme of this book. This is exactly what we need to advance the quality of information technology and its application.

Heidelberg   Prof. Dr. Barbara Paech
                                               Chair of Software Engineering
                                                  University of Heidelberg

Preface

One of the major reasons why information systems encounter problems or fail in the context of an organization is the missing alignment with business processes. This means that information systems are designed without taking the impact of business processes into account, and vice versa. Business processes and information systems mutually affect each other in non-trivial ways. Missing alignment at design-time often results in quality problems at run-time, such as interrupted business processes due to overloaded information systems, or large information system response times due to unexpectedly high workloads induced by business processes.

Aligning business process quality and information system quality at design-time requires the solving of the following problems **(P)**. Business process quality and information system quality have to be characterized. **P1:** In contrast to information system quality, which is specified, e.g. in the ISO/IEC 9126 standard, there is no common and comprehensive understanding of business process quality. **P2:** Beyond that, current business process modeling notations do not aim at representing quality aspects. The impact of a business process on the quality of an information system, and vice versa, is unknown at design-time. **P3:** The mutual impact between business processes and information systems must be predicted at design-time.

In this book, the *Business Process Quality Reference-Model* (BPQRM), a quality model for business processes, is introduced. The model allows for a comprehensive characterization of business process quality (P1). The BPQRM is applied successfully in a case study to identify potentials for process quality improvement in practice. Based on the BPQRM, an existing process modeling notation is extended by model elements to represent quality aspects (P2). Simulation is a powerful means to predict the impact of a business process on the quality of an information system, and vice versa, at design-time. This book proposes two simulation approaches to predict the mutual impact between business processes and information systems in terms of performance (P3). The approach *Business IT Impact Simulation* (BIIS) defines interfaces between the business process simulation and the information system simulation. Performance-relevant information is exchanged via the interfaces between both simulations. When using business process simulation and information system simulation in isolation, workload burstiness is not adequately reflected. This is especially true for occasional, volatile peak loads. Workload burstiness can significantly affect the performance of business processes and information systems. The approach *Integrated Business IT Impact Simulation* (IntBIIS) for the integration of business processes and information systems in a single simulation allows reflecting workload burstiness correctly. The simulation approaches support the comparison of design alternatives and the verification of a certain design against requirements. A case study confirms the feasibility in practice and the acceptance from practitioners' point of view.

This book is equivalent to the dissertation titled "Aligning Business Process Quality and Information System Quality" submitted by me to the Combined Faculty for the Natural Sciences and Mathematics of the Ruprecht-Karls-University of Heidelberg. The degree Doctor of Science (Dr. rer. nat.) has been awarded to me subsequent to the submission and demonstration of my scientific ability by oral defense.

Numerous people supported me in the course of my research for and during writing this book over the last years. Without the support of these people, it would not have been possible to develop the proposed contributions and to apply them in practice.

Taking the risk of forgetting someone, I explicitly want to name the involved people. First, I thank my supervisors, Barbara Paech and Ralf Reussner, for their helpful comments, fruitful discussions, and support during my research. I thank Jörg Henß, Philipp Merkle, Wilfrid Utz, and Franz Brosch for valuable discussions on the properties of business processes and information systems, their mutual impact, the prediction of such impact, and much more. The extension of EventSim for the integrated simulation of business processes and information systems was strongly supported by Philipp Merkle and Jörg Henß.

I had the chance to apply the major contributions of this book in practice. This would not have been possible without the support of practitioners. I thank all the responsible people at the Center of Information Technology and Medical Engineering of University Hospital Heidelberg for their support in the discharge letter study. Special thanks go to Ulrike Kutscha, Antje Brandner, and Björn Bergh for their commitment while creating the questionnaire, and to all participants in the questionnaire survey. Moreover, I thank all the responsible people and all the employees at Thor GmbH for their support in the order picking study. Special thanks go to all the participants in the questionnaire survey.

I thank the Combined Faculty for the Natural Sciences and Mathematics of the Ruprecht-Karls-University of Heidelberg and all its members for providing a pleasant work environment and for supporting my research. Furthermore, I got great support from students, for which I am very grateful. I supervised three master students, as well as bachelor students, internship students, and student assistants. Each of them contributed her/his piece to the puzzle of my research.

Last, but not the least, I thank my family for their support during my studies and the preparation of this book. My parents, grandparents, and sister gave me personal support. Special thanks go to my girlfriend for her encouragement and patience during this time-intensive endeavor.

Mannheim   Robert Heinrich

On www.springer.com (follow the link of this book via ISBN) you may download the *OnlinePLUS* material under "Additional Information".

Contents

List of Figures

List of Tables

1 Introduction

> The scientist is not a person who gives the right answers,
> he's one who asks the right questions.

— Claude Lévi-Strauss, 1908–2009 —

This chapter motivates the alignment of business process (BP) quality and information system (IS) quality. First, the need for new methods for quality modeling and analysis, that take into account the mutual quality impact between BPs and ISs, is revealed in Section 1.1. Then, Section 1.2 points out the specific problems addressed in this book. Afterwards, the scientific contributions are listed in Section 1.3. Finally, Section 1.4 presents the structure of this book and Section 1.5 lists parts of the book previously published in scientific proceedings.

1.1 Motivation

Organizations face the challenge of ensuring that success-critical BPs yield adequate quality[1]. BP quality largely depends on the quality of ISs (covering both, software application and IT infrastructure). For example, it has to be ensured that ISs are continuously available with adequate performance to maintain BP execution. There is mutual impact and alignment between BPs and ISs [Aerts et al. (2004)]. Frequently, innovation in one domain is an enabler or driver for developments in another. For example, new technology, such as cloud computing or smart devices [WinterGreen Research (2012)], is an enabler of organizational change. Thus, ISs can dramatically improve business performance [Davenport (1993)]. Consequently, ISs are of strategic importance to economic organizations (e.g., [Davenport (1993), Mooney et al. (1996), King & Xia (2004)]). Considering this, ISs not only have to

---

[1] Note, cost is not considered as a quality aspect in this book, as justified in Section 3.3

fulfill technical requirements, but also have to fit within the business context [Wieringa et al. (2003)].

Business Process Management [Rosemann & vom Brocke (2010)] is a key factor for long-term organization success. Ever since organizations realized that automating their BPs via ISs is a key to market growth, Business Process Management is creating new market opportunities [WinterGreen Research (2012)]. One of the most important activities in the Business Process Management life-cycle is modeling [Rosemann & vom Brocke (2010)]. BP modeling is applied as a method to increase awareness and knowledge of BP, and to deconstruct organizational complexity [Bandara et al. (2005)]. Gartner Inc. stated that organizations that had best results in establishing their Business Process Management spent more than 40 percent of the total project time on discovery and construction of their initial BP model [Melenovsky (2005), Mendling (2008)].

BP quality is a central aspect of Business Process Management. BP quality is a multi-dimensional concept, as related work indicates [Heravizadeh et al. (2009), Heidari et al. (2011), Guceglioglu & Demirors (2005)]. The same applies to IS quality (e.g., [ISO/IEC 9126-1]). A comprehensive understanding of quality – both, BP quality as well as IS quality – is important to establish a holistic modeling and analysis, which includes various quality aspects. This is a prerequisite to align BP quality and IS quality. It supports the identification of success-critical impact on the BP. Therefore, a comprehensive understanding of quality is of fundamental importance in the marketplace, due to two reasons [Powell et al. (2001)]. First, the organization's effectiveness strongly depends on its BPs. Second, BPs strongly influence the quality of products and services. Thus, BPs affect the satisfaction of the customers.

Frequently, software-intensive ISs do not fail because of technical issues, but, due to inadequate support for, or integration within the organization's BPs [Barjis (2008)]. According to [Standish Group International Inc. (2004)], one major reason for software projects being challenged or completely failing, is poor conceptual modeling, meaning poor definition of requirements. Quality requirements typically arise together with requirements on structure and behavior of BPs and ISs. Consequently, considering quality aspects within conceptual models contributes to a more complete representation of the overall BP [Pavlovski & Zou (2008)] and IS [Rech & Schmitt (2009)].

BP modeling is a starting point in IS requirements elicitation [Adam et al. (2009), Barjis (2008)]. Representing a comprehensive set of quality aspects within the BP model would increase the modeler's focus on quality at the modeling stage, and facilitate the capturing of quality requirements [Saeedi et al. (2010), Pavlovski & Zou (2008)] for both, BPs and ISs.

In the joint development of BPs and ISs, the non-trivial mutual impact between both domains have to be considered, in order to align the corresponding designs in terms of certain quality aspects. In the design phase, alternative designs have to be compared and verified against requirements, which involves several roles.

i. Requirements engineers have to verify, in the design phase, whether an IS quality requirement can be fulfilled by a proposed IS design for a given BP design.

ii. System designers have to compare the quality of proposed IS design alternatives invoked in a given BP, without having the possibility to implement IS prototypes.

iii. Hardware administrators have to check the utilization of hardware resources, such as a CPU or a hard disk drive, for a proposed IS design or BP design, for example, to determine the extent of future hardware acquisition.

iv. Business analysts have to verify, in the design phase, whether a BP quality requirement can be fulfilled by a proposed BP design and a given IS design.

v. Process designers have to compare BP design alternatives, without having the possibility to execute a process in practice, while the IS impact must be included in the comparison.

1.2 Description of the Problems

Aligning BP quality and IS quality at design-time requires to address several problems, which are discussed in this section.

Business process quality (P1): BP quality and IS quality have to be characterized. In contrast to IS quality, which is specified in several standards (e.g., [ISO/IEC 9126-1]), there is no comprehensive understanding of BP quality. Although BP quality is on the focus of research and practice for several decades, mostly, only single quality aspects were investigated. This results in a limited view on BP quality in process analysis and requirements elicitation, which, for example, leads to neglected design and controlling objectives or incomplete quality requirements. A consequence of that is limited acceptance of the BP from the organizational perspective, as well as from the external perspective (e.g., customers).

Quality modeling (P2): In recent years, several notations emerged for annotating quality aspects to IS models (e.g, [SPTP 1.1 (2005), QFTP 1.1 (2008)]). However, current BP modeling notations do not aim to express quality aspects of BPs. They reflect the functional perspective on a BP, but do not provide sufficient insight in related quality aspects [Heravizadeh et al. (2009)]. If considered at all, only few quality aspects are represented in current notations. Consequently, quality is not in the focus of the modelers. This results in an incomplete representation of the overall BP. Moreover, the interrelation between functional aspects and quality aspects is little understood, due to limited integration [Heravizadeh et al. (2009)]. Quality requirements are often not considered at the BP modeling stage, which leads to increased costs and delays in the further development of BPs and ISs, due to rework caused by neglected quality impact.

Aligning BP and IS designs (P3): Business/IT Alignment is commonly understood as a state, in which, business objectives and information technology are in a harmonic relationship. Approaches to establish Business/IT Alignment largely focus on the alignment at strategic level ([Henderson & Venkatraman (1993), Luftman (2000), Hiekkanen et al. (2013)]). Business/IT Alignment activities are considered as management tasks, for example, by improving communication between decision makers. Thus, current approaches to Business/IT Alignment cannot help to answer the question whether a certain IS design is aligned with a BP design, and vice versa. At design-time, the mutual impact between BPs and ISs is unknown. On the one hand, it is not known whether a particular quality requirement can be satisfied by a proposed IS design, because it is not known how the system is used in the BP scenario, and how this usage affects the IS quality. On the other hand, it is unknown whether a particular quality requirement can be satisfied by a proposed BP design, because it is unknown whether involved

ISs adequately support the adherence of the requirement. For example, if an IS is not available to the actors within the process, the process execution may be impeded, so that a BP requirement cannot be satisfied. Moreover, at design-time, it is unknown whether a particular design drives hardware resources into an overload situation or whether human actors are overexerted by the workload induced by the BP. It cannot be foreseen which of the available design alternatives performs best, because it is unknown how they perform taking into account the impact of the other domain. Furthermore, the impact of changes on existing designs – the so called "what-if question" – is hard to foresee, at design-time. For example, organizations have to know in advance how the BP performance will change, if their software components are migrated to another IT infrastructure. Inadequate alignment of BP designs and IS designs result in loss of quality (of the BPs and the ISs), inefficient use of resources, and loss of the organization's productivity.

1.3 Scientific Contributions

This book proposes the following contributions to the body of knowledge in Software Engineering and Business Process Management.

1.3.1 Comprehensive Quality Model for Business Processes

This book presents the *Business Process Quality Reference-Model* (BPQRM), a quality model for BP, that allows for a comprehensive characterization of BP quality in order to addresses **P1**. The quality model defines a set of quality characteristics and allocates them to the components of a BP. Components are the activities of the BP, the actors performing these activities, the objects handled and created by the BP, as well as the resources (information systems for example) necessary for execution. The BPQRM serves as a checklist one can select quality characteristics relevant to a specific application scenario. A multi-level hierarchy of quality aspects is introduced in order to interrelate measures relevant to a particular BP, to the characteristics of the BPQRM. Comparing the BPQRM to related quality models from literature, confirms its comprehensiveness. The BPQRM is a foundation for a comprehensive assessment of BP quality and the elicitation of a holistic set of quality requirements on the process components. Moreover, it is the foundation to analyze the mutual impact between the process components.

Quality models often lack a sufficient operationalization in practice. One possible application scenario of the BPQRM is described in this book. An approach is proposed to develop a questionnaire for identifying process quality problems in an interview study. The BPQRM and the approach are applied in a real-life case study to evaluate the applicability of the BPQRM in practice. The case study demonstrates the ability of the BPQRM to be tailored to a specific process and its applicability in practice.

1.3.2 Quality Modeling Approach

A modeling approach is proposed to represent a comprehensive set of quality aspects related to the BPQRM within a BP model in order to address **P2**. The approach allows for modeling a large set of different quality aspects, as well as for capturing detailed quality aspects, without a major increase of complexity of the BP model. It is compared to related modeling approaches and tools. The comparison showed that other approaches and tools only allow for modeling few or single quality aspects, where the proposed approach enables to represent a comprehensive set of quality aspects. Prototypical tool support is provided. The approach and tooling are applied to model quality aspects of a real-life BP. This demonstrates the applicability of the approach and tool support to a real-life example.

1.3.3 Simulation Approaches to Align BP and IS Design

The alignment of BP designs and IS designs in terms of performance is addressed in this book (**P3**). Performance was chosen, because it is one of the most demanded quality aspects across several domains, including BP [Davenport (1993)] and IS [Smith (1990)]. In contrast to other quality aspects, there are established performance prediction methods and formalisms (e.g., [Lazowska et al. (1984), Rolia & Sevcik (1995), Bause (1993)]) that can be built upon. The performance of an existing BP and IS can be measured fast and easy (e.g., using monitoring techniques), where other quality aspects, such as reliability, may require a long time-frame of observation, e.g., to gather failures with a low probability. Consequently, performance prediction methods can be validated fast and easy, by comparing prediction results to measurements. For that reason, performance is better suited for empirical validation in conjunction with organizations than other quality aspects. Thus, any reference to simulation in the following, means performance simulation.

In order to align BP designs and IS designs, the impact of a BP on the performance of ISs, and vice versa, has to be predicted at design-time. Model-based simulation is a powerful approach to predict the mutual impact between BPs and ISs. Compared to other prediction methods, such as expert estimations, simulation promises a more reliable and explicable prediction. This book proposes two simulation methods to predict the mutual performance impact between BPs and ISs. The method *Business IT Impact Simulation* (BIIS) defines interfaces between existing BP simulations and IS simulations, where the simulations are conducted in isolation and information is exchanged ex-post, via the interfaces. BIIS demonstrates that workload burstiness (cf. Section 5.3.4) is not adequately reflected using isolated simulations. It is proven that workload burstiness significantly affects performance, which results in limited prediction accuracy of simulation methods built upon isolated simulations. The method *Integrated Business IT Impact Simulation* (IntBIIS) for the integrated analysis of BPs and ISs, using simulation, is presented. A holistic simulation is proposed that combines performance prediction on software architecture level and business process level. In contrast to existing approaches, workload burstiness is adequately reflected in simulation. In this way, the alignment of BP designs and IS designs can be supported, by comparing the performance impact of design alternatives and verifying them against requirements. Tool support is provided by extending the Palladio tool chain, a software architecture simulator, by business process concepts.

There is little empirical evidence about the application of prediction methods in practice [Melao & Pidd (2003), Koziolek et al. (2013)]. Applying a prediction method to a real-life example is a challenging task. Often, they are only applied to fictitious examples, which results in little practical experience. Little experience in applying prediction methods may result in limited willingness, or even reluctance, of practitioners, to apply them in the design phase. Although, the methods promise to reduce rework in subsequent development phases. Thus, practitioners would benefit a lot by saving time and costs. In this book, both prediction methods (BIIS and IntBIIS) are validated on a real-life case study. It is described in detail, how the methods were applied to the case. Important decisions and workarounds required to map reality to models, as well as effort required to apply the methods to the case, are described. The validation confirms the feasibility of the methods. The prediction accuracy of the methods is determined by comparing prediction results to measurements from reality, and to results of the other method. The comparison showed that both methods provide adequate performance prediction, where IntBIIS yields higher prediction accuracy. Based on a constructed example, it is demonstrated that IntBIIS correctly reflects workload burstiness in simulation, where it is not correctly represented by BIIS. Moreover, the validation on the real-life example confirms the practicability of both prediction methods. Questionnaires constructed based on the *Technology Acceptance Model* [Davis et al. (1989)] and the *Theory of Reasoned Action* [Fishbein & Ajzen (1975)] are filled in by practitioners, in order to assess the acceptance from the practitioners' point of view. Furthermore, the practicability of the integrated tool support for third-party users is discussed, based on the practicability of the original Palladio tool chain.

Another form of alignment refers to the holistic usage of opportunities of the BP design and the IS design. BPs may be unnecessarily inefficient, due to neglected opportunities of the IS design. This means that the IS provides more opportunities, than considered in the BP design. For example, the IS provides automated execution of a step relevant in the BP. BP design alternatives that use the opportunity to automate the step are more aligned to the IS design than others. Since this is rather a functional alignment, than an alignment in term of quality, it is not addressed in this book. However, the methods proposed in this book allow for evaluating several design alternatives in terms of performance that reflect different IS opportunities. For example, automating the step may be more efficient than executing the step manually by an actor. BP design alternatives that use the opportunity to automate the step may show higher performance than those executing the step manually. By comparing the prediction results of the design alternatives, an adequate BP design can be identified.

1.4 Structure of the Book

The remainder of the book is structured as follows. The book consists of three parts. Part I addresses a comprehensive understanding and modeling of BP quality. Part II is concerned with the prediction of the mutual impact between BPs and ISs in terms of performance. The book concludes with a summary and discussion of future work in Part III.

Part I

- **Chapter 2** presents the basic terminology and definitions related to BPs and ISs.
- **Chapter 3** attends to a comprehensive understanding of business process quality. The chapter starts with a description of foundations in the area of quality specification, and introduces established quality models for software product quality and data quality (Section 3.1). In Section 3.2, the state of the art in BP quality specification is analyzed and it is concluded that a comprehensive understanding of BP quality is missing. Afterwards, the BPQRM is presented (Section 3.3), to establish a comprehensive understanding of business process quality. One possible application of the BPQRM is illustrated in Section 3.4, by describing an approach to create a questionnaire for identifying potentials for process improvement. A case study in which the quality model and the approach are applied to a real-life BP is described, and identified quality-related issues are presented (Section 3.5). The comprehensiveness and practicability of the BPQRM are discussed in Section 3.6. In Section 3.7, the chapter concludes with a summary and a discussion of future work related to the BPQRM.
- **Chapter 4** addresses the modeling of quality aspects within BP models. Section 4.1 analyzes the state of the art, and concludes that current process modeling notations and tools do not adequately support the modeling of quality aspects. In Section 4.2, a modeling approach to reflect quality aspects comprehensively within a BP model is introduced and corresponding tool support is presented. In Section 4.3, the quality modeling approach is compared to related approaches and tools. Moreover, lessons learned

from an application of the tooling are discussed. Finally, the chapter is summarized, and future work related to the modeling approach and the tooling is discussed in Section 4.4.

Part II

- **Chapter 5** describes the BP modeling language and concepts related to the alignment of BP design and IS design. Section 5.1 introduces foundations regarding performance prediction. In Section 5.2, the Palladio Component Model – a meta-model for information system modeling and analysis – is described. The meta-model is extended by new model elements to represent business processes and their organizational environment (Section 5.3). In Section 5.4, performance measures applied in this book are introduced, and the alignment of BP designs and IS designs is defined.

- **Chapter 6** introduces the order picking process and the involved IS, that are used as a real-life application example for demonstration and validation purposes in Part II of the book.

- **Chapter 7** describes the mutual performance impact between BPs and ISs. First, an overview of related work is given in Section 7.1. The BP impact on IS performance is described in Section 7.2. The IS impact on BP performance is presented in Section 7.3. Finally, in Section 7.4, the joint impact on workload burstiness is discussed.

- **Chapter 8** is concerned with the prediction of the mutual impact between BPs and ISs. The chapter starts with a discussion of related work on performance prediction in Section 8.1. The prediction method BIIS is proposed in Section 8.2 to investigate benefits and limitations of isolated simulations. A significant artifact of BIIS is the IS usage profile, which is derived from a BP model, as described in Section 8.3. A discussion of BIIS in Section 8.4 shows that workload burstiness is not adequately represented using isolated simulation. In Section 8.5, three solution alternatives are discussed to adequately reflect workload burstiness. The chapter concludes with a summary of the findings in Section 8.6.

- **Chapter 9** addresses the integration of BP simulation and IS simulation, by introducing the method IntBIIS. In Section 9.1, a novel scheduling policy for human actors is described. A fundamental property of BPs is time-variant workloads, i.e., workloads varying over time. IS simulation is often oriented towards steady-state analyses, where workload is time-invariant. The impact of time-variant workload on steady-state analysis is discussed in Section 9.2. In Section 9.3, the simulator extension for integrating BP simulation and IS simulation is presented. Then, Section 9.4 describes how IntBIIS reflects workload burstiness. The chapter concludes with a summary and discussion of future work related to the prediction method in Section 9.5.

- **Chapter 10** describes the validation of the prediction methods BIIS and IntBIIS. Section 10.1 discusses three types of validation for prediction methods. In Section 10.2, the research questions and hypotheses used in the validation are listed. Decisions and workarounds required to apply the methods in practice, are described in Section 10.3. In Section 10.4, the validation of the feasibility of BIIS and its acceptance from practitioners' point of view is described. Afterwards, in Section 10.5, the validation of the feasibility of IntBIIS and the practicability of the integrated tool support is presented. Finally, threats to validity are discussed (Section 10.6) and the validation results are summarized (Section 10.7).

Part III

- **Chapter 11** concludes the book. It provides a summary of the book's scientific contributions (Section 11.1), describes the benefits of the contributions to the joint development of BPs and ISs (Section 11.2), and discusses assumptions and limitations (Section 11.3). In addition to the future work closely related to the single contributions that is already listed in previous chapters, this chapter presents future work on the alignment of BP quality and IS quality, in a broader sense (Section 11.4).

1.5 Previous Publications

Parts of the concepts, literature reviews, and evaluation results presented in this book were already published in scientific proceedings. The BPQRM was published in an early version in:

Heinrich, R., Paech, B. **Defining the Quality of Business Processes**, In: Engels, G. et al. (eds.), Modellierung 2010, LNI Vol. P-161, pp. 133–148, GI, 2010.

The approach to develop a questionnaire for process improvement and the case study on the practicability of the BPQRM were originally published in:

Heinrich, R., Paech, B., Brandner, A., Kutscha, U., Bergh, B. **Developing a Process Quality Improvement Questionnaire – A Case Study on Writing Discharge Letters**, In: Daniel, F. et al. (eds.), BPM 2011 Workshops, Part II, LNBIP 100, pp. 261–272, Springer, 2012.

The analysis of the state of the art in modeling quality within BP models was published in:

Heinrich, R., Kappe, A., Paech, B. **Modeling Quality Information within Business Process Models**, In: Wagner, S. et al. (eds.), Proceedings of the 4th SQMB'11 Workshop, TUM-I1104, pp. 4–13, TUM, 2011.

The quality modeling approach and the corresponding tooling were published in:

Heinrich, R., Kappe, A., Paech, B. **Tool Support for the Comprehensive Modeling of Quality Information within Business Process Models**, In: Nüttgens, M. et al. (eds.), Enterprise Modelling and Information Systems Architecture, LNI Vol. P-190, pp. 213–218, GI, 2011.

The Palladio Component Model extensions were published in an early version in:

Heinrich, R., Henss, J., Paech, B. **Extending Palladio by Business Process Simulation Concepts**, In: Becker, S. et al. (eds.), Palladio Days 2012 Proceedings, Karlsruhe Reports in Informatics 2012,21, ISSN 2190-4782, pp. 19–27, KIT, 2012.

Here, also parts of the discussion of solution alternatives in Section 8.5 were presented in an early form. The prediction method BIIS was originally published in:

Heinrich, R., Paech, B. **On the Prediction of the Mutual Impact of Business Processes and Enterprise Information Systems**, In: Kowalewski, S., Rumpe, B. (eds.), Software Engineering 2013, LNI Vol. P-213, pp. 157–170, GI, 2013.

The two last-mentioned publications also contain parts of the discussion of the mutual impact between BPs and ISs in an early form. Moreover, further publications on the integrated simulation and the validation of both prediction methods were still under review at the date the book was submitted.

Part I
Business Process Quality

2 Terms and Definitions

Part I of this book addresses a comprehensive understanding of business process quality. Before describing a business process quality model in Chapter 3, this chapter introduces the basic terminology and definitions related to business processes and information systems.

The concept of *business process* gained increasing importance since organizations begun to redesign and optimize their processes in the early 1990s. A variety of definitions for the term BP were presented in the past decades. Some definitions refer to the components of a BP, such as activities, inputs, and outputs. According to [Hammer & Champy (1993)], a BP is "a collection of activities that takes one or more kinds of input and creates an output that is of value to the customer". [Davenport & Short (1990)] define a BP as "a structured set of activities designed to produce a specified output for a particular customer or market". Other definitions also consider the organizational context of the BP. According to [Weske (2007)], a BP "consists of a set of activities that are performed in coordination in an organizational and technical environment". This definition is similar to the established definition by the Workflow Management Coalition (WMC). A BP is a "set of one or more linked activities which collectively realize a business objective or policy goal, normally within the context of an organizational structure defining functional roles and relationships" [WMC (1999)].

This book builds upon the definition of WMC, where the quality of BP components, as well as the organizational environment of the BP, is considered. In analogy to [WMC (1999)], an *activity* is a "piece of work that forms one logical step within a process". Manual and automated parts of an activity are not clearly distinguished in [WMC (1999)]. In contrast to

[WMC (1999)], we do not use the term activity to refer to the smallest unit of work, but introduce the term *step*. Each activity within the BP is composed of a set of linked steps and (sub-)activities, meaning that activities can be hierarchically nested. Steps are either performed completely by a human actor – called *actor steps* – or are performed completely by an IS – called *system steps*.

Each BP is located within an *organizational environment*. An organizational environment comprises the *human actors* in their *organizational roles*, as well as *passive organizational resources*. A *human actor* (hereafter also referred to as actor) is an organizational resource who actively performs actor steps. An organizational role (hereafter also referred to as role) is a grouping of actors "exhibiting a specific set of attributes, qualifications and/or skills" [WMC (1999)]. It is an abstraction of competencies [Caetano et al. (2007)] and properties of concrete actors. Passive organizational resources are non-IT devices or machines, such as a fork-lift. They are required to perform an actor step, but do not actively process the step.

ISs are an enabler of BP redesign and optimization [Davenport (1993)]. They play a critical role in BP innovation, by providing new technology and automation. Therefore, ISs can improve BP efficiency, or enhance their effectiveness and reliability [Mooney et al. (1996)]. However, ISs can also influence BP quality negatively, for example, by hampering actors to execute activities of the BP. A detailed discussion of the mutual impact between ISs and BPs in terms of performance is given in Chapter 7. Consequently, the quality of ISs is considered as an influence factor of BP quality in this book.

According to [O'Brien & Marakas (2010)], an *information system* consists of five basic component types:

- Hardware components, which comprehend all the physical devices of the IS.
- Software components, which comprise all the programs and procedures.
- Data, which includes all the knowledge in the IS.
- Networks, which comprise all the communication channels.
- People, which cover IS specialists and end-users.

In this book, an IS only comprises the four non-human component types, since people are part of the organizational environment.

In modern IS landscapes, where ISs are distributed across several hardware nodes, it is often difficult to distinguish one IS from another. In the context of this book, all the components that interact with each other, either directly or via other components, are part of the same IS. Components that do not interact with each other are part of different ISs.

3 Business Process Quality*

This chapter presents a comprehensive quality model for BPs and demonstrates its application in practice. First, the foundations the model builds upon are described in Section 3.1. Then, Section 3.2 argues that a comprehensive understanding of BP quality is missing, by discussing the state of the art. In Section 3.3, the Business Process Quality Reference-Model is described, which represents the main contribution in this chapter. Based on the quality model, an approach to identify potentials for improvement of BPs is presented in Section 3.4. The quality model and the approach were applied in an interview study to a real-life BP, as described in Section 3.5. The chapter continues with a discussion of the comprehensiveness and practicability of the quality model in Section 3.6. Finally, in Section 3.7, the contributions of the chapter are summarized and future work is discussed.

3.1 Foundation

In the past decades, many experts have tried to make the term quality in an organizational context tangible. It was defined as "conformance to require-

---

* The BPQRM presented in this chapter was originally published in an early version in: Heinrich, R., Paech, B. **Defining the Quality of Business Processes**, In: Engels, G. et al. (eds.), Modellierung 2010, LNI Vol. P-161, pp. 133–148, GI, 2010.
The approach to create a questionnaire for process improvement and the case study on the practicability of the BPQRM were originally published in: Heinrich, R., Paech, B., Brandner, A., Kutscha, U., Bergh, B. **Developing a Process Quality Improvement Questionnaire – A Case Study on Writing Discharge Letters**, In: Daniel, F. et al. (eds.), BPM 2011 Workshops, Part II, LNBIP 100, pp. 261–272, Springer, 2012.

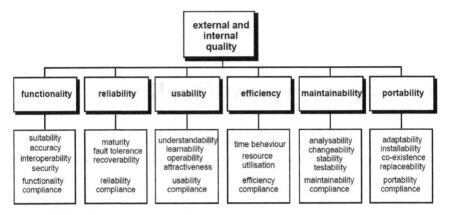

Figure 3.1: Quality Model for External and Internal Quality [ISO/IEC 9126-1]

ments" [Crosby (1979)] or "fitness for use" [Juran (1986)]. [Feigenbaum (1991)] – from a more economic point of view – specified quality as "best for the customer use and selling price". According to [Deming (1982)], "quality should be aimed at the needs of the consumer". [Dale (2003)] gives an overview of several quality definitions and concludes that "they all can be boiled down to either meeting requirements and specifications or satisfying and delighting the customer".

[McCall et al. (1977)] gives a first overview of quality aspects relevant in Software Engineering [Juran & Godfrey (1999)], such as reliability or maintainability. In Software Engineering, quality is considered as a non-functional property of a software product or process. Quality has been researched well in Software Engineering and described in several standards, such as [ISO/IEC 9126-1, ISO/IEC 25012], or [IEEE Std. 1061-1992].

This book builds upon the ISO/IEC 9126-1 software product quality models [ISO/IEC 9126-1] and the ISO/IEC 25012 data quality model [ISO/IEC 25012].

The ISO/IEC 9126-1 standard defines a quality model for external and internal quality, as well as a quality model for quality in use. Both quality models are composed of a set of quality characteristics. A *software quality characteristic* is a "category of software quality attributes that bears on software quality" [ISO/IEC 25000]. Consequently, software quality is defined

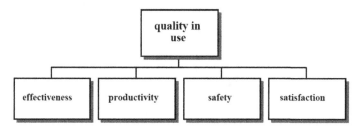

Figure 3.2: Quality Model for Quality in Use [ISO/IEC 9126-1]

as "the totality of characteristics of an entity that bear on its ability to satisfy stated and implied needs". Where "entity" denotes the object (here a software product) to be characterized by its attributes. In the quality model for external and internal quality, software quality is categorized into the six characteristics functionality, reliability, usability, efficiency, maintainability, and portability, as depicted in Figure 3.1. Each characteristic is again segmented into sub-characteristics. The quality model for quality in use is composed of the characteristics effectiveness, productivity, safety, and satisfaction, as depicted in Figure 3.2. A *quality attribute* is an "inherent property or characteristic of an entity that can be distinguished quantitatively or qualitatively by human or automated means" [ISO/IEC 25000]. Attributes are not specified in the quality models, because they may vary from one software product to another. Each attribute is assessed by measures. A *measure* is a "variable to which a value is assigned, as the result of measurement" [ISO/IEC 25000].

Since 2005, the ISO/IEC 9126 standard is replaced by the more extensive ISO/IEC 250xx series of standards. The ISO/IEC 25012 data quality model defines 15 quality characteristics for data kept in a structured format within a computer system. A *data quality characteristic* is a "category of data quality attributes that bears on data quality" [ISO/IEC 25012]. The characteristics are depicted in Figure 3.3. Data quality is defined as the "degree to which the characteristics of data satisfy stated and implied needs when used under specified conditions" [ISO/IEC 25012]. In analogy to ISO/IEC 9126, to each characteristic, attributes are allocated, which are assessed by measures.

Note, in the context of this book, the term *quality aspect* is used as a superset of characteristics, attributes and measures.

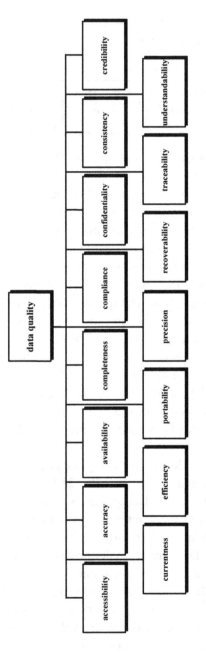

Figure 3.3: Characteristics of ISO/IEC 25012

3.2 State of the Art of Business Process Quality

BP quality is a central aspect of Business Process Management. It is in the focus of research and practice since the early 1990s [Malone et al. (2003), Reijers (2005)]. Frequently, two perspectives regarding BP quality are distinguished – internal quality and external quality [Reijers (2005), Grigori et al. (2001)]. Internal quality refers to the organization's point of view, e.g., in terms of performance of BP execution. External quality is perceived by the customers. It refers to the quality of products or services. For example, the maturity of a product or the time it takes to deliver a service to the customer.

Both perspectives were addressed by related work on BP quality. A lot of quality aspects, such as performance or reliability, were investigated. However, a comprehensive understanding of BP quality is still missing [Heravizadeh (2009)]. In contrast to software product quality, there is no standard definition of what contributes to BP quality.

In the context of this book, comprehensive understanding of BP quality means that

(a) several components of a BP, such as activities or involved resources, are distinguished, and, for each component, specific quality aspects are specified, and

(b) several categories of quality aspects, such as functionality, reliability, or efficiency, are distinguished. This means, the proposed set of quality aspects is equivalent in extent to quality models established in Software Engineering, such as those proposed by ISO/IEC.

In literature, there is a variety of work somehow related to the assessment, improvement, or specification of BP quality. An analysis of several research fields resulted in a categorization of related work into the following six classes:

i. work from strategic planing and management,

ii. work on benchmarking,

iii. work that applies best practices for BP improvement,

iv. work that describes domain-specific quality aspects,

v. quality of service models,

vi. BP quality models

Moreover, there is work concerned with the quality of BP modeling [Vander-feesten et al. (2007), Mendling (2008)] and work that observes the quality of BP execution via process mining [van der Aalst (2007)]. As this is not in the focus of our research, it is not discussed in this book.

In the following, representatives of the six classes of related work are described. It is discussed that work from the five first-mentioned classes does not contribute to a comprehensive understanding of BP quality. Related BP quality models are discussed in detail, in Section 3.6.1, after introducing the proposed quality model.

3.2.1 Strategic Planing and Management

The class strategic planing and management covers related work from two research fields – performance measurement systems and quality-centered management. Performance measurement systems, such as the balanced score card [Kaplan & Norton (1993)] or the performance prism [Neely et al. (2001)], provide guidelines for creating and establishing performance measures on several perspectives in an organization. The balanced score card, for examples, distinguishes the perspectives "financial", "customer", "internal business", and "innovation and learning". The measures are often related to BP and their quality aspects. Note, performance measurement systems have a broader understanding of the term performance, compared to the established meaning, which goes beyond efficiency aspects. Several approaches specific to BP performance measurement are discussed in [Heckl & Moormann (2010)] and [Kueng (2000)]. However, performance measurement systems do not aim to establish a comprehensive understanding of BP quality. They do not give an overview of several BP quality categories, but only handle single quality aspects. Performance measurement systems do not aim to provide a universal set of BP quality aspects. Typically, the measures are designed specifically for a particular organization.

Quality-centered management approaches, such as Six Sigma [Pyzdeh & Keller (2009)], Kaizen [Imai (1986)], or Total Quality Management [Dale

(2003)], assist in improving BPs. They establish quality measures, often specific to a particular organization, but do not contribute to a comprehensive understanding of BP quality.

3.2.2 Benchmarking

Benchmarking [Camp (1989)] is a way to evaluate the quality of a BP by comparison. [Camp (1989)] distinguishes quantitative and qualitative benchmarking. Quantitative benchmarking compares Key Performance Indicators (KPI) between BPs and organizations. The goal of the comparison is to learn from the "class winner".

Qualitative benchmarking compares the as-is BP to established practices, for example, as described in frameworks, such as [COBIT 5 (2012)], to derive ideas for process improvement. Since benchmarking focuses on comparing BPs, it does not provide insights on BP quality.

3.2.3 BP Improvement based on Best Practices

Several related research fields use best practices for BP improvement. Best practices may be related to, or give hints for quality aspects. Business Process Improvement [Harrington et al. (1997)], Process Redesign [Davenport & Short (1990)] and Business Process Reengineering [Hammer & Champy (1993), Johnson et al. (1993), Davenport (1993)] are closely related to the improvement of business process quality. According to [Hammer & Champy (1993)], Business Process Reengineering is a "fundamental rethinking and radical redesign of business processes", and the organization as a whole, to improve critical quality aspects. Reengineering is commonly based on established best practices, such as those described in [Reijers (2005)], not on a comprehensive view on BP quality.

Best practices are also inputs to maturity models, such as the Business Process Maturity Model (BPMM) [BPMM 1.1 (2008)] or the Process and Enterprise Maturity Model (PEEM) [Hammer (2007)]. Maturity models can be used as a kind of benchmark, where organizations can evaluate their BPs relative to the maturity of other BPs in their market segment [BPMM 1.1 (2008)]. Based on certain criteria, a BP is allocated to a specific level, which reflects its maturity. Criteria result from best practices and established knowledge on BPs. Since a maturity model focuses on classifying and comparing BPs, it does not provide a categorization of BP quality aspects. Thus, it does not contribute to a comprehensive understanding of BP quality.

Another approach to improve BP quality, based on existing knowledge, is the process checklist [Fischermanns (2009)]. The process checklist is a collection of typical BP problems. Thus, it relies on the assumption that quality is often threatened by similar problems in different organizations. [Fischermanns (2009)] mainly focuses on time and cost aspects of a BP, but does not present a comprehensive set of quality aspects. However, the process checklist is a good source of practice-oriented measures regarding the aforementioned aspects.

3.2.4 Domain-Specific Quality Aspects

BP quality is often described in the context of a specific domain, such as health care. Two domain-specific collections of quality aspects are mentioned as an example in the following. The process potential screening [Ehlers et al. (2006)] is a screening instrument to identify problems of hospital processes. It uses a matrix that relates quality aspects of a hospital process with criteria to assess the aspects. Quality aspects for the assessment of IT-supported health care processes from the users' point of view are listed in [Ammenwerth et al. (2010)]. Three views on process quality are distinguished: quality of the process in general, quality of data handling, and quality of the used IT-system. Since this work only provides domain-specific quality aspects, it does not contribute to a common understanding of BP quality. However, domain-specific quality aspects may provide hints for general quality aspects.

3.2.5 Quality of Service Models

Quality of service (QoS) is related to BP quality. There are quality models describing different characteristics of service quality. [Cardoso et al. (2004)] specifies a quality model for workflows and web services that comprises the characteristics time, cost, reliability, and fidelity. For each characteristic, measures are described. Another quality model that aims to specify QoS requirements is presented in [W3C (2003)]. This quality model consists of 13 characteristics for web service quality, such as performance, scalability, integrity, or accessibility. QoS models reflect a technical perspective on quality. Therefore, they are not sufficient for BPs.

3.2.6 BP Quality Models

Only few publications try to provide a unifying basis of BP quality. Four quality models were identified in literature [Guceglioglu & Demirors (2005), Heravizadeh et al. (2009), Heidari et al. (2011), Lohrmann & Reichert (2013)]. Except [Lohrmann & Reichert (2013)], these models try to adapt software product quality standards, such as ISO/IEC 9126-1, to BPs. All the models identified only cover a subset of the quality model proposed in this book, as discussed in Section 3.6, after the introduction of the proposed quality model.

3.3 The Business Process Quality Reference-Model

The *Business Process Quality Reference-Model* (BPQRM) was developed to provide a comprehensive understanding of BP quality. Therefore, quality characteristics from software product quality standards were transferred to BPs. This approach is supported by related quality models [Guceglioglu & Demirors (2005), Heravizadeh et al. (2009), Heidari et al. (2011)] and analogies between processes and software products discussed in the following.

[Osterweil (1987)] revealed several analogies between software products and software processes. Both have logical structures comprising inputs, outputs, and operations, whether in the form of software services (cf. Section 5.2) or in the form of activities. Software products, as well as software processes, consist of a structure of linked and hierarchically nested operations, which are performed to achieve a specified result. Software and processes are both executed, either by hardware resources or by human actors. They both address requirements and both must evolve guided by measurement [Osterweil (1997)]. The same is true for BPs in general [Yang (2003), Sánchez-González et al. (2012)].

In this book, a hierarchical structure of quality aspects regarding BPs is proposed, which is defined as follows. The definitions were transfered from the software product quality standard [ISO/IEC 25000]. A *business process quality characteristic* is a category of business process quality attributes. For example, the maturity of an activity is a business process quality characteristic. A *business process quality attribute* is an inherent property of a business process that can be distinguished quantitatively or qualitatively. For example, the error density of an activity is a business process quality attribute. An error in an activity is a deviation from the specified or intended behavior. A *business process quality measure* is a variable to which a value is assigned, as the result of measurement. Measures can be distinguished in base measures and derived measures. A *base measure* is a measure for which the value is directly applicable to the BP. For example, the number of errors or the number of (sub) activities are base measures. A *derived measure* is a measure that is defined as a function of two or more values of base measures. For example, the number of errors per activity size is a derived measure. Abstract characteristics are decomposed to detailed measures, using this multi-level hierarchy.

Considering this, *business process quality* is defined as the totality of characteristics of a BP that bear on its ability to satisfy stated and implied needs.

BP quality refers to the components of a BP, as well as to its context. The context of a BP covers the organization in which the BP is located. For example, it contains the organizational objectives and the conditions of BP execution. Components are the activities of the BP, the actors performing these activities, the information objects handled and created by the BP, as well as the resources (an IS for instance) necessary for execution. As an activity can be subdivided into sub activities, a BP itself is considered as an activity in the BPQRM. A set of quality characteristics is associated to each component of a BP. The ISO/IEC 9126-1 software product quality characteristics are taken for resources and are also adapted for activities. For information objects (e.g., documents or data records used in the BP), the ISO/IEC 25012 data quality characteristics are taken. The actor characteristics were developed based on quality aspects from related work (cf. [Fischermanns (2009), Heravizadeh et al. (2009), Ehlers (2004), Gabriel et al. (2002)]).

Note, cost is not considered as a quality characteristic in the BPQRM. Cost may be an indicator for quality, or for absence of quality. For example, high costs may point to a quality problem. However, it does not provide insights on a quality problem. Cost does not denote a category of quality attributes.

Figure 3.4 shows the BPQRM on characteristic level. The nodes correspond to the components and the characteristics are listed either within the node or on an edge between nodes. If the assessment of a characteristic depends on information of another component, it is located on the edge, where A —> B means that B must be considered to assess A.

3.3.1 Activity Characteristics

A BP consists of activities, where an activity can be atomic or can be a BP itself (this means it contains sub-activities). The following characteristics apply to activities (and by definition also to the BP as a whole). The characteristics were developed based on the ISO/IEC 9126-1 characteristics and sub-characteristics. Mostly, the definitions from [ISO/IEC 9126-1] were taken and only single words were changed. For example, "software product" was replaced by "activity". Sometimes, further parts of the definition had to be adapted or the name of the characteristic had to be changed. These characteristics are marked with "(N)" in the following and an explanation of the adaptation is given.

Suitability (N) is the capability of the activity to be appropriate for a specified context of use. In [ISO/IEC 9126-1] suitability of the software product is focused on "specified tasks and user objectives". We wanted to use uniform terms. Thus, "context of use" was used, instead of tasks. Furthermore, as an actor is a BP component, suitability for user objectives was covered by the characteristic "actor satisfaction". Moreover, the term "set of functions" is improper for activities. Hence, we changed the wording.

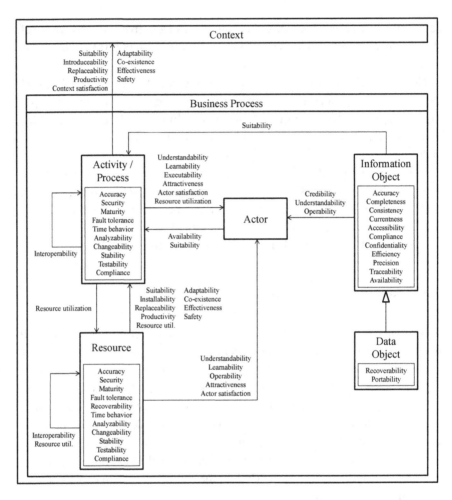

Figure 3.4: Business Process Quality Reference-Model

Accuracy is the capability of the activity to provide the right or agreed results or effects with the needed degree of precision.

Interoperability (N) is the capability of the activity to be executed together with dependent activities. With respect to activities, interaction corresponds to execution dependency. Thus, the definition was reworded. Execution dependencies may be input/output dependencies, resource dependencies or control dependencies.

Security (N) is the capability of the activity to protect information objects and physical objects so that unauthorized actors or resources cannot access them and authorized actors or resources are not denied access to them. An activity should also protect physical objects. Hence, the definition was extended.

Maturity is the capability of the activity to avoid failure, as a result of faults in the activity.

Fault tolerance is the capability of the activity to maintain a specified level of performance in cases of faults, or of infringement of its specified interface.

Note: Regarding activities, recovery is covered by the recovery of its resources and information objects. Hence, the ISO/IEC characteristic recoverability was not adapted for activities.

Understandability (N) is the capability of the activity to enable the actor to understand whether it is suitable, and how it can be executed in a particular context of use. In order to apply uniform terms, "tasks and conditions of use", as stated in ISO/IEC 9126-1, was replaced by "context of use".

Learnability is the capability of the activity to enable the actor to learn its execution.

Executability (N) is the capability of the activity to enable the actor to execute and control it. In our view, "execution" is more appropriate for BPs than "operation". Thus, the naming was changed.

Attractiveness is the capability of the activity to be attractive to the actor.

Time behavior (N) is the capability of the activity to provide appropriate execution times, processing times, and throughput rates when executed, under stated conditions. In ISO/IEC 9126-1, the definition of time behavior covers response time. The term response time is uncommon for activities. Thus, response time was replaced by execution time to fit the terminology established in Business Process Management.

In Section 5.4.1, these performance-relevant terms are defined in more detail, building upon a terminology established in queuing network theory. In the following, a short introduction of the terms is given. Response time is the "interval between user action and system response" [ISO/IEC TR 25021] for a specific system entry call (i.e., a call of a service at system provided roles [Becker et al. (2009)]). Throughput is determined by the number of operations completed in a given time period [ISO/IEC TR 25021]. This definition is applicable to both, system entry calls and activities. Execution time is the overall time it takes to perform an activity. Processing time is the time required, by a hardware resource or a human actor, to actively process an operation.

Resource utilization is the capability of the activity to use appropriate amounts and types of resources when executed under stated conditions.

Analyzability is the capability of the activity to be diagnosed for deficiencies or causes of failure, or for the parts to be modified to be identified.

Changeability is the capability of the activity to enable a specified modification to be executed.

Stability is the capability of the activity to avoid unexpected effects from modifications of the activity.

Testability (N) is the capability of the activity to be validated. In ISO/IEC 9126-1, testability is focused on "modified software" to be validated. We could not see any reason for the restriction to a modification.

Adaptability (N) is the capability of the activity to be adapted for different specified contexts of use. The definition of adaptability was shortened, because the add-on, "without applying actions or means other than those provided for this purpose for the software considered", seemed unnecessarily complex.

Introduceability (N) is the capability of the activity to be introduced, in a specified context of use. In our view, "introduction" is more appropriate for BPs than "installation". Hence, the naming was changed.

Co-existence is the capability of the activity to be executed with other independent activities in a common context of use, sharing common resources.

Replaceability is the capability of the activity to be used in place of another specified activity for the same purpose, in the same context of use.

Effectiveness is the capability of the activity to enable actors to achieve specified goals with accuracy and completeness, in a specified context of use.

Productivity (N) is the capability of the activity to enable actors to achieve specified goals with appropriate efforts, in a specified context of use. The definition of the characteristic productivity was changed, because "enable users to expend appropriate amounts of resources in relation to the effectiveness achieved in a specified context of use" seemed unnecessarily complex.

Safety is the capability of the activity to achieve acceptable levels of risk of harm to people, business, process, property, or the environment, in a specified context of use.

Actor satisfaction (N) is the capability of the activity to fulfill a specific actor objective. **Context satisfaction (N)** is the capability of the activity to fulfill a particular constraint, in a specified context of use. In analogy to related work (e.g., [Reijers (2005)]), the ISO/IEC characteristic satisfaction was split into actor satisfaction, which is focused on a specific actor objective, and context satisfaction, which is focused on contextual constraints, like requirements of the customer, because we want to enable a separate consideration of these characteristics.

Compliance (N) is the capability of the activity to adhere to standards, conventions or regulations in laws, and similar prescriptions. In ISO/IEC 9126-1, for each characteristic, there is a compliance sub-characteristic. These sub-characteristics were generalized in the BPQRM, using the characteristic compliance.

3.3.2 Resource Characteristics

Activities usually need resources to be executed. The BPQRM focuses on IS-supported BPs, where it is not limited to IS-resources, but also enables to consider non-IS resources. The term resource in the BPQRM does not denote a single hardware resource, such as a CPU or a hard disk, as it does in Section 5.3, but more generally denotes an entire IS or machine. The quality of the resources affects the quality of the activities. The context of use of a resource are the activities in which the resource is used. Therefore, the characteristic context satisfaction is omitted for resources. In analogy to related work, the ISO/IEC 9126-1 characteristics were adapted to resources. In the following, definitions of resource characteristics are listed, which differ more substantially from the definition of the activity characteristics, than just replacing "activity" by "resource".

Interoperability is the capability of the resource to interact with one or more specified resources.

Installability is the capability of the resource to be installed, in a specified context of use.

Time behavior is the capability of the resource to provide appropriate response times, processing times, and throughput rates when performing its function, under stated conditions.

3.3.3 Information Object Characteristics

The quality of a BP depends on the quality of the information and data used. Information represented in a structured format and in electronic form, within a computer system, is called data, in the BPQRM. A lot of research on data quality was conducted (e.g., [Wang & Strong (1996), Wand & Wang (1996), Redman (1996), Ballou et al. (1998), Lee et al. (2006)]). Data quality is considered as a multi-dimensional concept, as theoretical and experimental results indicate [Cho (2009)]. This perception is also reflected in the ISO/IEC 25012 standard. The BPQRM is not restricted to data objects, but considers all kinds of information objects used in a BP. Data objects are considered as a subset of information objects. The wide variety of research on data quality was used to adapt characteristics suitable for specifying quality of information objects used in BPs. An information object can contain various information and can be composed of several information objects. In analogy to ISO/IEC 25012, the expression "degree" is used, instead of "capability", for information objects, because information objects are considered as passive. Thus, the expression "capability" is inappropriate. If no other source is mentioned, the characteristic were adapted from [ISO/IEC 25012].

Accuracy (N) is the degree to which the information object represents a concept or event correctly. In ISO/IEC 25012, the definition refers to the value of the data attributes. For information objects in general, this is inappropriate. Thus, the wording was changed.

Completeness (N) is the degree to which the information object includes all expected values. In ISO/IEC 25012, the definition focuses on the values of "subject data associated with an entity". For information objects in general, this is inadequate. Thus, the wording was changed to include all expected values.

Consistency is the degree to which the information object is free from contradiction, and coherent with other information objects.

Credibility is the degree to which the information object is regarded as true and believable by actors.

Currentness is the degree to which the information object is of the right age.

Accessibility is the degree to which the information object can be accessed.

Compliance is the degree to which the information object adheres to standards, conventions or regulations in law, and similar prescriptions.

Confidentiality is the degree to which the information object ensures that it is only accessible and interpretable by authorized actors.

Efficiency is the degree to which the information object can be processed and provides the expected level of performance, by using the appropriate amounts and types of resources.

Precision is the degree to which the information object is exact or provides discrimination.

Traceability is the degree to which the information object provides an audit trail of access and of any changes made.

Understandability is the degree to which the information object is to be read and interpreted by actors, and is expressed in appropriate languages, symbols, and units.

Availability is the degree to which the information object is able to be retrieved by authorized actors and/or resources.

Suitability (N) is the degree to which the information object is appropriate for a specified activity. The definition of suitability was adapted from ISO/IEC 9126-1, because suitability is missing in ISO/IEC 25012, but it is addressed in related work (e.g., *suitability for effective activity execution and achievement of process goals* in [Ehlers (2004)], or *relevancy* in [Wang & Strong (1996)]). It should be noted that "set of functions" was removed, because it is inappropriate for information objects, and "specified tasks and user objectives" was replaced by "activity".

Operability (N) is the degree to which the information object enables the actor to manage and manipulate it. This definition was adapted from [Wang & Strong (1996)], because it is missing in ISO/IEC 25012, but often mentioned in data quality literature (e.g., ease of manipulation in [Pipino et al. (2002), Kahn et al. (2002)]).

Some of the ISO/IEC 25012 characteristics are too much focused on data objects, so it is not possible to generalize all of them for information objects. Next, the ISO/IEC 25012 characteristics are listed that cannot be generalized for information objects.

Portability is the degree to which data has attributes that enable it to be installed, replaced, or moved, from one system to another, preserving the existing quality.

Recoverability is the degree to which data has attributes that enable it to maintain and preserve a specified level of operations and quality, even in the event of failure.

3.3.4 Actor Characteristics

Human actors perform the activities of a BP. The quality of a BP depends on the availability and competency of those who perform it. According to [Caetano et al. (2007)], competencies classify actors with respect to their ability of performing activities in a specific environment. An actor's competency comprises several factors, such as knowledge and skills [Caetano et al. (2007), Harzallah & Lecrere (2002), McClelland (1973)]. Next, the characteristics of the BP component actor are listed. These characteristics were developed to cover attributes and measures mentioned in related work (cf. [Fischermanns (2009), Heravizadeh et al. (2009), Ehlers (2004), Gabriel et al. (2002)]). The BPQRM focuses on the characteristics availability and suitability. The actor characteristics differ from the resource characteristics. Thus, in analogy to [Heravizadeh et al. (2009)], the actor is not treated as a resource in the BPQRM.

Availability is the capability of the actor to be able to perform the activity in the required time-frame.

Suitability is the capability of the actor to perform the activity well.

3.4 Applying the BPQRM to Develop a Process Quality Improvement Questionnaire

BP quality is often assessed by identifying potentials for improvement. This section describes one possible application of the BPQRM in practice. An approach is presented to develop a questionnaire for identifying BP quality problems, from the actors' point of view, in an interview study. Thereby, the BPQRM serves as a checklist to identify quality aspects relevant in a specific BP.

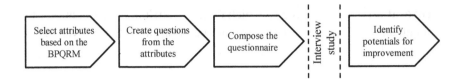

Figure 3.5: Deriving a Questionnaire to Identify Quality Problems

An interview study based on a questionnaire is an effective means to identify BP quality problems from the actors' perspective. However, the selection of the questions is crucial to the success of the study. To support this selection, the BPQRM is applied. Figure 3.5 gives an overview of the four phases of the approach.

Phase 1, select attributes: Attributes that are suitable to identify problems of a specific BP can be selected based on the characteristics in the BPQRM. A set of selection criteria was developed, to select attributes for each characteristic in the BPQRM. The selection criteria are presented in Table 3.1. They are inspired by literature on the selection of Requirements Engineering tools [Pohl & Rupp (2011)] and criteria for selecting measures in [ISO/IEC 15939]. The idea to define different views on the attributes was taken from [Pohl & Rupp (2011)]. The criteria domain, expressiveness, effort, and method were adapted from [ISO/IEC 15939].

In the following, a more detailed description of the views and criteria is given. The views and criteria are not specific to interviews, but can be used to select attributes for an arbitrary elicitation method. An attribute may be highly relevant in one domain, whereas, it may be less relevant in another domain. For example, precision or security has a higher relevance in the medical context, than in a general office context, where it may be neglected for cost reasons. Therefore, the suitability or relevance of an attribute to a specific domain is considered in the domain view. In the outcome view, the expressiveness of the attributes' measures, with respect to the ability to derive potentials for improvement, is considered. Note, that in this section, we abbreviate base measure by using the term measure. There are measures with high expressiveness, which directly provide information about problems in the BP. For example, measures that

Table 3.1: Criteria for Attribute Selection

View	Criterion	Description
Domain View	Domain	Is the attribute suitable or relevant for the domain?
Outcome View	Expressiveness	How high is the expressiveness of the attribute's measures?
	Knowledge added	Does the attribute promise to provide new information?
Operational View	Effort	How high is the effort to capture the attribute's measures?
Method View	Method	Can the attribute's measures be captured using the available method?
Customer View	Importance	How high is the attribute's importance to the customer?
	Constraints	Are there any constraints from the customer regarding the attribute?

detect inadequate IS support. Furthermore, there are measures with lower expressiveness that result from observations, for example, execution time values of an activity. Time values must be compared to other time values or requirements to interpret the value and decide whether improvements are needed. In the outcome view, it is also considered whether the elicitation of the attribute promises to provide new information, in comparison to the current state of knowledge. Although an attribute is relevant, expressive, and provides new information, there may be high effort required to capture the attribute's measures. For example, diagrams or other auxiliary means have to be created in case of an interview. Thus, effort is considered in the operational view. The method view is concerned with the methods available to capture the attributes' measures. Examples of methods are process mining, data analysis or interview. For attribute selection, one must consider that the attributes' measures can be captured by the available method. For example, consistency of a data object can be determined easier using the method data analysis, than using an interview. The customer's opinion should be considered, too. In the context of this approach, the customer is the organization whose BPs are analyzed. In the customer view, the importance of an attribute to the customer is considered. Moreover, constraints from the customer should also be considered. For example, the assessment of employees of the customer might be problematic. Since this approach creates a questionnaire for an interview study, the generally applicable views and criteria are restricted. In the method view, only attributes whose measures can be captured in an interview are selected.

For each characteristic in the BPQRM, a variety of attributes are available in related work, such as those described by representatives of the six classes of related work in Section 3.2 or those listed in quality standards, e.g [ISO/IEC TR 25021]. Moreover, domain specific knowledge, in the form of standards, guidelines, and policies, should be considered as a source of attributes. Aforementioned related work is also a source of measures related to the attributes. Attributes can be analyzed and appropriate ones can be identified, using the selection criteria. For each criterion, a justification should be recorded to support the reproduction of the analysis. We propose to use a matrix form, with the selection criteria on one axis, and the attributes on the other axis to document the justification.

Phase 2, create questions: After the selection of the attributes, the questions have to be created. As questions created ad-hoc from the attributes may be relatively abstract, the questions are related to a specific BP model. Thus, before creating the questions, the BP to be evaluated has to be documented in a graphical model. Therefore, one of the established BP modeling notations, such as [BPMN 2.0 (2011)], can be used. The BP model helps the interviewees to understand the questions, by visualizing the activities they perform, the objects they handle, the ISs they use (in some modeling notations), as well as the interfaces between the components of a BP. The questionnaire should first request the interviewer to explain the BP model to the interviewee. Then, the questionnaire should contain a question about activities the interviewee performs, and a request to mark these activities in the BP model. In this way, the context of the interview

Table 3.2: Example of a Questionnaire

B1	Questions on activities	
Now, present the process model to the interviewee.		
	General questions on activities	
1	Which activities in the process do you perform? (Please mark your activities in the process model)	
	Are there any activities you perform in the process that are not contained in the process model? If yes, please add these activities to the model.	
	Questions on actor satisfaction and attractiveness of the process	
2		Which of your activities in the process do you like to perform?
	Attractiveness	What bothers you about the activities you do not like to perform?

is made clear to the interviewee. Section B1.1 in Table 3.2 presents an example.

For the creation of the questions regarding the attributes, it is important to consider how to measure the attributes. As a measure, per definition (see Section 3.3), is used to assess the related attribute, it gives a good idea of what to ask for. However, further adaptations are necessary to create concrete and useful questions for an interview situation.

Based on the attributes, two types of questions can be derived – qualitative and quantitative questions. A qualitative question, for example, is "what is the problem?". A quantitative question, for example, is "how many problems are there?" or "how much time does it take?". The answers to qualitative questions directly describe quality problems, but are not presented in a measurable manner. The answers to quantitative questions are measurable. They can be used to compare one BP to another, or BP components with each other, and, thereby, identify the problems. For each attribute, qualitative questions, as well as quantitative questions, are possible. Answers to quantitative questions are hard to estimate by the interviewees. It is recommended to avoid them, where possible, and, instead, to ask a qualitative question from which a quantitative statement can be derived. In other words, one should avoid asking for the number of BP components (e.g., activities) that have a specific property. Instead, one should better ask the interviewee to name BP components which have a specific property. Thus, the number is provided implicitly. For example, the attribute attractiveness of the BP may be determined by the measures *number of activities which are considered as attractive by the actors* and *total number of activities*. In Table 3.2, the interviewees were asked for the activities they like to perform. The first question in Section B1.2 is a qualitative question, however, one can derive a quantitative statement from it. The total number of activities can be determined from the BP model. The second question in B1.2 is a qualitative question, which leads to a qualitative statement. Here, the interviewees describe the problems with the activities.

For estimations, a good granularity of the measure (e.g., output per day, per week, or per month) is important to help the interviewees to give meaningful answers. Therefore, typical frequencies of execution, error rates, and amounts of objects in the BP should be considered. This information has to be captured before creating the questionnaire. In case of questions on errors , it is recommended to ask also for the frequency and the severity of the errors, in order to prioritize the errors.

Phase 3, compose the questionnaire: The questionnaire is composed by arranging the questions in a meaningful manner. Guidelines for this can be found in literature from psychology and social sciences, such as [Oppenheim (2000)]. An example of a questionnaire structure is presented in Section 3.5.

Phase 4, identify quality problems: As described in phase 2, potentials for improvement either directly arise out of the interviewees' answers (in case of a qualitative statement), or are derived by comparison (in case of a quantitative statement).

The proposed approach provides a systematic way of selecting attributes, based on the characteristics in the BPQRM. For the derivation of the questions from the attributes, heuristic support is provided, as this includes context-specific adaptations. The results of the interviews, of course, depend on the interviewer and the interviewees. Expertise is still required in all the phases. It is not the goal of the approach to enable a non-expert to create a meaningful questionnaire. However, the approach aims to provide a methodical support that can be used by experts.

3.5 A Case Study on the Practicability of the BPQRM

A case study was conducted in cooperation with the University Hospital Heidelberg, to demonstrate the applicability of the BPQRM in practice. Therefore, the approach introduced above was applied. The case study was conducted in the hospital context as, especially in the medical domain, BP quality plays an important role [Ehlers et al. (2006)].

The process of writing discharge letters at the hospital was analyzed. A discharge letter is a summary of the performed patient treatment and is used for communication between physicians, for follow-up treatments. The process of writing discharge letters is chosen, because all the BP components of the BPQRM are contained in the process, and there is a large number of quality aspects to be elicited. In the case study, the people were interviewed separately. We did not conduct group interviews.

At the beginning of the case study, the current state of the process was documented in a BPMN model. The BP model was created based on documents provided by the hospital, and on interviews with experts of the Center of Information Technology and Medical Engineering (ZIM) of the hospital. The BP model consists of 15 activities, 5 information objects, 4 actors, and 1 IS (hospital information system, HIS). Figure 3.6 shows a representation of the process of writing discharge letters on an abstract level. BP starting points and end points are represented by circles. Activities are visualized by rectangles with rounded corners. Arrows represent the control flow in the BP, where diamonds visualize XOR path branches. Lanes represent roles of human actors. The complete BP model is contained in the *OnlinePLUS* material of this book on www.springer.com. As mentioned in phase 2 in Section 3.4, the BP model is used as a basis for the interviews.

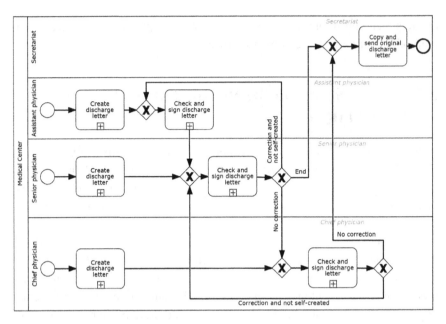

Figure 3.6: Process of Writing Discharge Letters

In the case study, the effort to create a questionnaire based on the BPQRM, and the adequacy of the questions to identify problems, were examined. Thus, the following research questions (RQ) were used.

RQ1: How much effort is necessary to develop a questionnaire based on the BPQRM?

The effort is measured in person hours. Because the effort is unknown prior to the study, the hypothesis regarding RQ1 is that the effort required is adequate in the opinion of the ZIM experts.

RQ2: Are the questions adequate to identify BP quality problems?

The questions are considered as adequate, if the ZIM experts assess the identified problems as useful input for BP improvement. Regarding RQ2, the hypothesis is that the ZIM experts assess the identified problems as relevant.

3.5.1 Effort to Develop a Questionnaire

First, RQ1 is answered by describing the development of the questionnaire based on the BPQRM and presenting the effort required.

The BPQRM was presented to experts of the ZIM who had knowledge regarding the process of writing discharge letters. In addition, a list of more than 200 attributes and related measures, collected from Business Process Management literature and ISO/IEC standards, were provided to the experts. The experts were asked to select characteristics from the BPQRM they consider as relevant for the process of writing discharge letters. After the characteristics were selected, in conjunction with the experts, attributes related to the characteristics were chosen from the list of attributes, using the selection criteria introduced in Table 3.1. The experts selected 21 attributes, which fit best the selection criteria. Further characteristics and attributes may be relevant in the study. However, because of a time restriction of a maximum of one hour for the interview, the number of characteristics and attributes had to be limited. Table 3.3 presents the selected characteristics and attributes per BP component. The characteristics are presented in bold, and the attributes are listed below.

In the medical domain, attributes of characteristics, such as maturity or precision, are highly relevant. This was considered in the domain view. In the outcome view, attributes whose measures are not sufficiently expressive were excluded. For example, the attribute help accessibility (cf. [ISO/IEC TR 25021]) was not chosen to assess learnability, as it was considered as less expressive than the frequency of faulty operations (correct execution). Moreover, attributes, which do not promise to bring additional knowledge, were excluded. For example, the attribute actor documentation (derived from [ISO/IEC TR 25021]) was not chosen, as it was already known that there is no documentation available. In the operational view, attributes that can be captured without additional auxiliary means were selected. Therefore, and because time values were considered as hard to estimate by the interviewees (method view), questions on time were excluded (transport time efficiency focuses on transport means and routes). However, the questionnaire contains a general question whether the entire BP takes too long. This is the only question on quality which is not

Table 3.3: Selected Characteristics and Attributes

	Maturity: Error density, Callbacks	Time behavior: Transport time efficiency	Interoperability: Freedom of collision
Activity	Attractiveness: Attractiveness	Resource utilization: Adequate resource usage, Capacity of the resource	Actor satisfaction: Problems of the actors, Challenging work
	Suitability: Significance	Understandability: Understandable purpose	Safety: Media disruption
Res.	Maturity: Error density	Interoperability: Freedom of collision	Attractiveness: Ergonomics
	Understandability: Understandable purpose	Learnability: Correct Execution	
IO	Availability: Availability	Operability: Ease of manipulation	Currentness: Currency
	Compliance: Conformity		

directly related to an attribute. The ZIM experts put high emphasis on characteristics like maturity and actor satisfaction, and less emphasis on characteristics like changeability or adaptability of the BP. This was considered in the customer view. Moreover, on request of the hospital, attributes, which directly or indirectly allow the assessment of the quality or capability of the actors involved in the BP, were excluded. For example, the questionnaire does not contain a question on the precision of the discharge letter, as this may allow for assessing the capability of its author.

After selecting the attributes for the case study, the questions for the interview were created based on measures related to the selected attributes.

The questionnaire comprises qualitative as well as quantitative questions. Altogether, 43 questions on quality were created for the study. The row IO in Table 3.3 shows the selected attributes related to information objects. Owing to the time restriction, only the questions related to the attribute availability were asked for all the objects within the BP. Questions related to other attributes are asked solely for the discharge letter.

The resulting questionnaire is contained in the *OnlinePLUS* material of this book on www.springer.com. The questionnaire consists of two parts (A and B) and five sections. Part A asks for personal details of the interviewee, such as her/his role in the BP, or contact details for possible further queries. Part B contains the questions to assess the quality of the BP and consists of 4 sub sections. Section B1 contains questions on the actor satisfaction and the attractiveness of the BP. The quality of the HIS involved in the BP is evaluated in Section B2. Section B3 contains questions on the quality of the information objects used in the BP. Finally, Section B4 contains questions regarding errors within activities, the HIS, and the discharge letter. Note: the questionnaire is in German and the interviewees also answered in German. For this book, the interviewees' answers were translated into English.

The selection of the characteristics and attributes lasted about 20 person hours. The compilation of the list of more than 200 attribute is not included, since this list was an input to the study. The creation of the questions required about eight person hours. The final arrangement of the questionnaire required further two person hours. The effort to create a questionnaire for the example BP from the BPQRM is, therefore, about 30 person hours. Additionally, the composition of the BP model required about six person hours.

3.5.2 Adequacy of the Questions

In order to answer RQ2, the adequacy of the derived questions to identify quality problems, in practice, was evaluated. The case study was conducted with three employees of the ZIM, who, in the past, were involved as actors in the process of writing discharge letters, but who were not involved in creating the questionnaire. Although these employees of the ZIM, currently, are not involved in the BP, they can provide meaningful answers, since they were involved in the past, and they have good knowledge of the current BP and the HIS.

The goal of the case study is to identify problems directly, not to compare the discharge letter process to another one. Consequently, only those questions of the questionnaire were analyzed which lead to qualitative statements (30 of the 43 questions).

The questions were answered in interviews and the answers directly lead to the bullet points in the list below. Altogether, 12 quality problems were identified.

- The entire process of writing discharge letters is considered as boring and annoying by the physicians. It is considered as additional bureaucratic effort that does not contribute to their core activities. More automation of the BP is required by the interviewees. This was identified by asking for attractiveness of the activities (attribute attractiveness).
- The entire BP is considered as too time-consuming. This was the answer to the general question on time, as mentioned in Section 3.5.1.
- The step "documentation of diagnosis" is performed twice in the activity create discharge letter. Once for clinical purpose, and, again, for billing. The purpose of the repetition is not understood by the interviewees that results in refusal regarding the repetition. This was identified by asking for activities whose purpose is not understood by the actors (attribute understandable purpose).
- The HIS used for writing discharge letters provides a Microsoft Word integration, as a so called Word container. Data can be moved from the HIS to the Word container, however, there is no integration in the other direction. Data once contained in the Word container cannot be moved back to the HIS in a structured way. Thus, the actors often have to use the copy and paste function to transfer information between discharge letters. Moreover, data contained in the Word container cannot be updated. This was identified by asking for activities not adequately supported by the HIS (attribute adequate resource usage).

- The questions on learnability and ergonomics of the HIS showed that the HIS is complex and hard to handle (attributes correct execution and ergonomics). The actors often do faulty operations or there are navigation problems, because there is no consistent menu guidance. Especially, diagnostic findings are hard to access, as the actors have to switch between single parts of the findings. An overview of the findings is missing in the HIS.

- The actor has to set a status to forward the discharge letter in the system. However, the interviewees prefer to send the letter directly to a person or a group of persons. Thus, setting the status is not used. This was identified by asking for activities not adequately supported by the HIS (attribute adequate resource usage).

- Our question on availability of information objects showed that after 9 months, the access to findings is locked. However, the interviewees stated that sometimes they require old information (attribute availability).

- The presence file contains information about the patient and is only available for the time the patient is in the hospital. Frequently, it happens that information from the presence file is needed, but it is no longer available. For example, when the patient took the presence file to another hospital. This was another result of the question related to the availability of information objects.

- Discharge letters can be transported digitally or in a paper folder between the physicians. The interviewees consider the paper folder as inappropriate for transport, because the letter can get lost, sometimes the letter is classified in the storage compartment of the wrong physician, there is additional effort, and there is a delay for transport. This was identified by asking for the attribute transport time efficiency.

- A problem identified by asking for interoperability is conflicting access to the letter (attribute free of collision). During the correction of the letter, there may be conflicts when one physician requires a letter which is currently edited by another physician. Conflicts are very common for paper-based letters.

- The question regarding safety discovered several media disruptions in the BP. Owing to the media disruptions, information can be distorted (e.g., transposed numbers), or can get lost. The interviewees mentioned that this happens while dictating, writing, and correcting the letter.

- Frequently, callbacks are necessary in the BP, due to unavailable or incomplete information. For example, when an assistant physician has to correct a letter on request of a senior physician. This was identified while asking for the maturity of activities (attribute callbacks).

3.5.3 Summary

The ZIM experts were closely involved in all the steps required to create the questionnaire and the BP model. The effort for creating the questionnaire was about 30 person hours. The creation of the BP model lasted about six person hours. The ZIM experts confirmed that the overall effort required in the case study is adequate in their opinion. Thus, the hypothesis regarding RQ1 is confirmed.

We received positive feedback from the ZIM experts regarding the findings of the case study. The identified problems are relevant from the experts' point of view. The findings are assessed as useful input for BP quality improvement. The ZIM experts consider the derived questions as an adequate means to identify quality problems of the example BP. Thus, the hypothesis regarding RQ2 is confirmed.

However, there are also some limitations of the study to report on. Note that the results of the interviews are not representative, due the fact that the interviewees were not involved in the process of writing discharge letters at the time the study was conducted. Moreover, the study included only a small number of interviewees. While interviewing a larger amount of people, further potentials for improvement might be identified. Nevertheless, major weaknesses of the BP and the HIS were identified in the interviews.

Further evaluations are required, before the questionnaire can be applied in a broad study in the hospital. For example, strict regulations in the hospital claim the comparison of a new method to a gold standard. This goes beyond the scope of this book. Although the time-frame for the interviews was already restricted to a maximum of one hour, it was still considered as relatively high by the interviewees. Therefore, the number of questions has to be reduced in future studies.

3.6 Discussion of the BPQRM

In this section, first, the comprehensiveness of the BPQRM is elucidated by comparing it to related quality models. Then, the practicability of the BPQRM is discussed.

3.6.1 Discussion of the Comprehensiveness of the BPQRM

The BPQRM creates a comprehensive understanding of BP quality by providing quality characteristics for each component of a BP. The comprehensiveness of the BPQRM is justified by the related work, such as ISO/IEC standards and BP quality literature, it is built upon. In the following, related BP quality models are discussed. A comparison of related quality models to the BPQRM in tabular form is given in the *OnlinePLUS* material of this book on www.springer.com.

The BP quality model by [Heravizadeh et al. (2009)] associates several so called quality dimensions, which are based on ISO/IEC 9126-1 and other related work, to different components of a BP. The components are similar to those represented in the BPQRM. However, this model only covers a subset of the BPQRM. Quality characteristics, such as interoperability, stability, executability, co-existence, or context satisfaction, are missing. Altogether, 13 quality characteristics of the BP component activity are not considered by [Heravizadeh et al. (2009)]. Moreover, also characteristics of other BP components are only partly covered. In contrast to the BPQRM, [Heravizadeh et al. (2009)] do not describe a hierarchical structure of quality aspects. Thus, quality aspects on different levels of abstraction are presented on the same level in the model. For example, reliability is a super-characteristic in ISO/IEC 9126-1 comprising the various sub-characteristics maturity, fault tolerance, and recoverability. [Heravizadeh et al. (2009)] only mention the super-characteristic, but do not consider the different sub-characteristics. In contrast, "amount of data" rather seems to be an attribute than a characteristic. Nevertheless, both are presented as a quality dimension on the same level. In the BPQRM, the abstract characteristics are decomposed to detailed measures using a multi-level hierarchy, as described in Section 3.3.

[Heidari et al. (2011)] present a quality model that covers the BP components activity, input, output, and event. These components reflect a close relationship to BP modeling, where the BPQRM is designed to represent quality independent from modeling. The model comprises the characteristics performance, efficiency, reliability, security, and availability. Therefore, it only covers a subset of the BPQRM characteristics. Moreover, the model does not consider the impact of resources, such as ISs, on BP quality. Especially, ISs can have various impact on BP quality [Davenport (1993)]. Although this model distinguishes between quality dimensions and factors, the granularity of the factors differs. For example, throughput, which is commonly accepted as an attribute of performance, is a factor, as well as maturity, which is commonly accepted as a characteristic.

[Guceglioglu & Demirors (2005)] present a quality model for measuring IS effects on BP quality, based on ISO/IEC 9126-1. This model also covers only a subset of the BPQRM. [Guceglioglu & Demirors (2005)] adapt the ISO/IEC characteristics, as well as related measures, to BPs. However, they do not consider the ISO/IEC characteristics efficiency, portability, as well as all the characteristics of the quality in use model. Moreover, they do not distinguish different BP components.

The framework for BP quality in [Lohrmann & Reichert (2013)] provides a foundation to guide the development of specific quality aspects, for example, with regard to particular application cases. This objective is similar to those of the BPQRM. The framework is based on the so called effectiveness criteria "congruence to organizational targets", "perceived fairness", and "cost effectiveness", which are derived from a management perspective on analysis and control. For each criteria, several detailed quality aspects are listed in a quality model. The model comprises the assessment of the quality of the BP model and the quality of human effort during BP enactment. Both are assessed with respect to their impact on organizational targets on efficacy and efficiency. The authors mention that the model is not yet completed and is presented in an early and simplified state. The BPQRM does not focus on quality of BP modeling, since this was already analyzed in prior research [Vanderfeesten et al. (2007), Mendling (2008)]. With respect to quality of process enactment, the quality model in [Lohrmann & Reichert (2013)] only covers a fraction of the BPQRM. Moreover, in contrast to other quality models discussed here, the model does not bundle related quality aspects to categories that enable an overview of different characteristics of quality.

Related BP quality models only provide a subset of the characteristics of the BPQRM. The three first-mentioned quality models, to some extent, build upon the ISO/IEC 9126-1 standard. However, it is not explained which adaptations were made and why they were made. In contrast, in Section 3.3, all the adaptations made for the BPQRM are described. The last-mentioned quality model is in a too early stage to make a statement on its expressiveness.

The BPQRM serves as a checklist, where one can select quality characteristics relevant to a specific BP. Thus, it prevents overlooking of important quality characteristics. Similar to ISO/IEC quality models, it is not our aspiration to provide a comprehensive quality model on attribute level and measure level, since attributes and measures depend highly on a specific context.

3.6.2 Discussion of the Practicability of the BPQRM

The case study in Section 3.5 demonstrated the applicability of the BPQRM in practice, and its ability to be tailored to a concrete BP. Thus, the practicability of the BPQRM is confirmed in the case study. The BPQRM is a foundation for the three activities described in the following.

As demonstrated in the case study, the BPQRM contributes to a comprehensive quality assessment of BPs and their components. Detailed measures derived via the multi-level hierarchy from the characteristics of the BPQRM can be used for the analysis of as-is BPs. This enables the identification of quality problems, which serves as an input for quality improvement.

A common objective of quality models is to support the identification of quality requirements (e.g., [ISO/IEC 9126-1]). The BPQRM is a foundation for a comprehensive elicitation of quality requirements for BPs and their components. Requirements related to all components have to be considered, to enable a quality-aware development of the BP. BPs are often a starting point in IS requirements elicitation [Adam et al. (2009), Barjis (2008)]. Based on a comprehensive understanding of BP quality, a more complete set of quality requirements on BPs and ISs can be identified. Moreover, precise requirements can be specified, based on detailed measures derived from characteristics of the BPQRM, via the multi-level hierarchy. Requirements are specified, for example, in the form of mean values or thresholds and are related to expressions constructed from base measures. For example, a requirement on the maturity of a BP may be formulated in terms of error density (e.g., *the error density must be below 0.1*). Thus, it is easy to determine whether the requirement is satisfied if the base measures (*number of errors* and *activity size*) can be gathered. Elicited quality requirements have to be documented, which is supported by the modeling approach presented in Chapter 4.

The BPQRM reveals quality-relevant dependencies between the components of a BP. Thus, the BPQRM is a foundation to analyze the mutual impact between the BP components. Especially, the mutual impact between BPs and ISs is important, since it is in the focus of activities such as Business Process Reengineering. Simulation and analysis methods can be applied to predict measures derived from the characteristics of the BPQRM. By comparing the predicted measures to quality requirements, one can determine whether a BP design and an IS design are aligned. The alignment of BP designs and IS designs is addressed in Part II of this book.

3.7 Summary and Future Work

In this chapter, the BPQRM was introduced to provide a comprehensive understanding of BP quality. The model allocates quality characteristics derived from related quality standards to the BP components activity, resource, information object, and actor. While comparing the BPQRM to related BP quality models from literature, its comprehensiveness was confirmed. One possible application of the BPQRM was presented by describing an approach to create a questionnaire applicable in interview studies for BP improvement. The BPQRM and the approach were applied in a case study to evaluate the applicability of the BPQRM in practice. In the case study, potentials for improvement of the process of writing discharge letters at the University Hospital Heidelberg were identified. The case study demonstrated the ability of the BPQRM to be tailored to a specific BP. Experts of the hospital consider the effort required to create the questionnaire as adequate, and confirm the usefulness of the interview findings for BP improvement. Thus, the practicability of the BPQRM was confirmed.

One topic of future work is the integration of the quality characteristics of the BPQRM into a formal quality definition. This could support the specification of relationships between the single quality characteristics. Therefore, a formal quality definition could contribute to a formal justification of the comprehensiveness of the BPQRM.

Further research on the operationalization of the BPQRM is required. A first application of the quality model was presented in this book. We received positive feedback from experts familiar with the application case. However, the application case presented in Section 3.5 provides potential for further investigation. Measures derived from the BPQRM could be compared to gold standards, in the medical domain for instance, which may provide further insights on the operationalization of the BPQRM. Further applications of the BPQRM have to be evaluated, such as the identification of quality requirements on BPs and ISs. Therefore, case studies based on a real-life BP, in cooperation with organizations, seem to be appropriate. Moreover, further quality-relevant dependencies between BP components may be investigated based on the BPQRM.

4 Quality Modeling within Business Process Models[*]

> The sciences do not try to explain, they hardly even try to interpret,
> they mainly make models.
>
> — *Johann von Neumann, 1903–1957* —

BP modeling is widely used within organizations as a method to increase awareness and knowledge of BPs, and to deconstruct organizational complexity [Bandara et al. (2005)]. A BP model typically visualizes activities and their dependencies, involved actors, and their communication with one another and external parties. In some cases, BP models also capture information about data and resources involved in the BP. Therefore, a BP model is a commonly used means to express structure and behavior of a BP.

Current BP modeling notations do not aim to express quality aspects of a BP [Korherr (2008), Pavlovski & Zou (2008), Saeedi et al. (2010), Adam et al. (2009), Heravizadeh et al. (2009)]. Hence, quality requirements are often not considered at the BP modeling stage, which results in increased costs and delays in the further development of BPs and involved IS. Annotating the BP model with quality aspects contributes to a model that provides a more complete representation of the overall BP [Pavlovski & Zou (2008)]. A (graphical) expression of quality aspects, together with information on

---

[*] The literature and tool review presented in this chapter was originally published in:
Heinrich, R., Kappe, A., Paech, B. **Modeling Quality Information within Business Process Models**, In: Wagner, S. et al. (eds.), Proceedings of the 4th SQMB'11 Workshop, TUM-I1104, pp. 4–13, TUM, 2011.
The quality modeling approach and tooling were originally published in:
Heinrich, R., Kappe, A., Paech, B. **Tool Support for the Comprehensive Modeling of Quality Information within Business Process Models**, In: Nüttgens, M. et al. (eds.), Enterprise Modelling and Information Systems Architecture, LNI Vol. P-190, pp. 213–218, GI, 2011.

structure and behavior, within a single model would increase the modeler's focus on quality at the BP modeling stage. Therefore, as stated in related work (cf. [Saeedi et al. (2010), Pavlovski & Zou (2008)]), it facilitates the elicitation of quality requirements and results in a more complete set of requirements. Although the benefits of quality aspects represented in a BP model for early requirements elicitation were already identified by other authors, current approaches only focus on single quality aspects.

This chapter describes an approach to represent the quality aspects of the BPQRM within a BP model. First, the results of an extensive literature and tool review on the state of the art in modeling quality aspects within BP models is presented in Section 4.1. As we want to model quality aspects graphically, the review focuses on graphical modeling notations. The review revealed deficiencies of current approaches, in comparison to quality aspects represented in the BPQRM. Then, a modeling approach to reflect the quality aspects of the BPQRM within a BP model and prototypical tool support are described in Section 4.2. Section 4.3 compares the proposed modeling approach to the review results and discusses lessons learned from an exemplary application. The chapter concludes with a summary and discussion of future work in Section 4.4.

4.1 State of the Art of Modeling Quality Information

This section provides an overview of approaches and tools for modeling quality aspects within BP models, resulting from a literature and tool review. The review was conducted by Alexander Kappe, as a part of his Master's thesis [Kappe (2011)]. The literature review is described in Section 4.1.1, where the tool review is described in Section 4.1.2.

4.1.1 Approaches to Model Quality Information

The literature review included the digital libraries of ACM (http://portal. acm.org), IEEE (http://ieeexplore.ieee.org), and SpringerLink (http://www.springerlink.com), because they give a reasonable confidence of covering the most relevant publications. Moreover, Google Scholar (http://scholar.google.com/) and the online catalogue of the Heidelberg University Library, which provides a variety of eBooks and eJournals, were utilized. The following query was used:

> *['business process (model)' OR model OR graph OR diagram OR visualise OR visualize OR illustrate OR display OR picture OR depict OR represent OR capture]*
> *AND*
> *['quality aspects' OR 'quality characteristics' OR 'quality requirements' OR 'quality information' OR 'quality properties' OR 'quality attributes' OR constraints OR 'process characteristics' OR 'process properties' OR 'non-functional requirements' OR 'NFR' OR goals OR 'business rules' OR metric OR measure OR ratio]*

As a result from 129 relevant matches, 9 publications that describe approaches, which graphically represent quality aspects within a BP model, were selected. In the following, a short description of 6 out of these 9 approaches is given. Then, the approaches are compared in Table 4.1. We limit to these 6 approaches because [Rodríguez et al. (2006)] and [Rodríguez et al. (2007)] present quality aspects similar to [Jensen & Feja (2009)]. The approach in [Pavlovski & Zou (2008)] allows for modeling arbitrary information, but does not provide guidelines or makes regulations to the quality aspects to be modeled. Thus, it is not considered in comparison. However, it is discussed separately in Section 4.3, following the description of our approach.

In [Saeedi et al. (2010)], the authors propose an extension to the BPMN meta-model [BPMN 2.0 (2011)]. The extension comprises the quality aspects time, cost, and reliability (see Figure 4.1). This approach enables to capture quality aspects quantitatively in tabular form as an extension to the activity model element (shown as rounded boxes).

The approach presented in [Gulla (2007)] introduces a concept to represent performance-relevant information within BP models, using a mix of graphical and textual notation (see Figure 4.2). For each activity, a set of performance indicators is calculated and visualized. The area of the circular icon at the lower left corner of the activity box is an average measure of the number

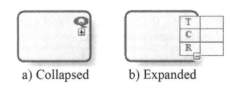

a) Collapsed   b) Expanded

Figure 4.1: Representation of Time, Cost, and Reliability [Saeedi et al. (2010)]

of executions, per month, for the corresponding activity. The size of the dark pie of the circular icon is an average measure of the duration of the corresponding activity. The latest trends of throughput and duration are shown as arrows pointing upwards or downwards.

Figure 4.2: Extension of Activity Elements by Performance Indicators [Gulla (2007)]

[Korherr (2008)] presents extensions to the BPMN, EPC (Event-driven Process Chain), and UML Activity Diagram for modeling BP goals, cost, several quality aspects on time, and quality of activities in general. In the case of the UML Activity Diagram, the quality aspects are only represented textually inside the diagram. However, within a BPMN and EPC model, the quality aspects are also graphically represented inside the model, by a circular icon besides the textual description, as shown exemplarily in Figure 4.3.

In [Mevius (2008)], a concept for modeling performance indicators is proposed. It uses low-level Performance nets which extend traditional low-level

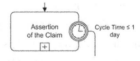

Figure 4.3: Graphical Representation of Quality Aspects in [Korherr (2008)]

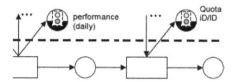

Figure 4.4: Modeling Performance Indicators as Places [Mevius (2008)]

Petri nets by the representation of performance indicators as places (see Figure 4.4). Once performance indicators are defined, they can be refined to machine-readable high-level Performance nets.

The modeling notation Time-BPMN is described in [Gagne & Trudel (2009)] as an extension to the BPMN. Time-BPMN allows for specifying diverse temporal constraints and dependencies that may be relevant while describing real-world BPs. Figure 4.5 presents an example of this notation by showing the activity "Complete Final Exam", which has a defined starting time, a Finish No Later Than constraint of three hours, and a Start-to-Start dependency to the subsequent activity.

An approach to model security aspects is presented in [Jensen & Feja (2009)] as an extension to the ARIS SOA Architect. The extension enables the description of access control, data integrity, and confidentiality within a BP model. In [Jensen & Feja (2009)], the approach is applied to EPC models, but it can also be applied to any other modeling notation. Figure 4.6 shows the security model symbols for each of the security aspects. In [Rodríguez et al. (2006)] and [Rodríguez et al. (2007)], an approach to visualize similar security aspects is proposed. This approach is applied to

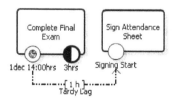

Figure 4.5: Modeling Temporal Constraints and Dependencies [Gagne & Trudel (2009)]

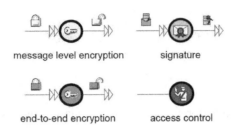

message level encryption   signature

end-to-end encryption   access control

Figure 4.6: Modeling Security Aspects [Jensen & Feja (2009)]

UML Activity Diagrams respectively BPMN models, and uses a padlock symbol.

Table 4.1 shows a comparison of the presented approaches. The approaches extend existing BP modeling notations by few or single quality aspects, such as time or security. However, they do not model a comprehensive set of quality aspects as described in the BPQRM. Altogether, regarding activities, the approaches contain quality aspects covered by 5 of the 26 quality characteristics for activities in the BPQRM, namely time behavior, maturity, understandability, context satisfaction, and security. Regarding information objects, quality aspects covered by accuracy and confidentiality (2 of the 17 characteristics for information objects) can be expressed by the approaches. Regarding resources, the approaches can only express security (1 of the 26 characteristics for resources). There is no actor characteristic expressible by the approaches. The approach in [Saeedi et al. (2010)] only allows the modeling of coarse-grained quality aspects within the BP model, e.g., time or reliability, whereas, the other approaches allow the specification of much finer-grained quality aspects, e.g., waiting time or throughput of an activity. In [Mevius (2008)], a formal approach is proposed, while all others are semi-formal. The maturity of the approaches is another topic of comparison, because there already might be hints on the appropriateness of the notation, the user acceptance, or the benefit of applying the approaches in practice. However, as most of the approaches are rather new, there are no significant experiences to refer to. Only [Gulla (2007)] conducted a case study, including a prototypical implementation of the concept and [Mevius (2008)] provides prototypical tooling.

Table 4.1: Comparison of Current Approaches to Model Quality within Process Models

Approach/ Criterion	[Saeedi et al. (2010)]	[Gulla (2007)]	[Korherr (2008)]	[Mevius (2008)]	[Gagne & Trudel (2009)]	[Jensen & Feja (2009)]
Basic notation	BPMN	Arbitrary BP modeling notation	BPMN, EPC, UML Activity Diagram	Petri nets	BPMN	EPC
Way of expression	Graphical + textual	Graphical + textual	Graphical + textual	Graphical + textual	Graphical + textual	Graphical + textual
Expressible quality aspects	Response time and reliability of activities	Average duration and number of executions per time unit (throughput) of activities	Cycle time, working time, waiting time, goals, complaints	Performance indicators for activities	Start/end time points, durations, temporal constraints and dependencies	Access control for resources, encryption on message exchange, digital signature for information objects (integrity)
Related quality characteristics of the BPQRM	Time behavior, maturity (reliability[1]) (activity)	Time behavior (activity)	Time behavior, understandability, context satisfaction (activity)	Time behavior (activity)	Time behavior (activity)	Security (activity + resource); confidentiality, accuracy (information object)
Granularity of the quality aspects	Coarse-grained	Fine-grained	Fine-grained	Fine-grained	Fine-grained	Fine-grained
Formality	Semi-formal	Semi-formal	Semi-formal	Formal	Semi-formal	Semi-formal
Maturity of the approach	New approach	Case study and tooling	New approach	Tooling	New approach	New approach

[1] According to ISO/IEC 9126-1, in the BPQRM reliability is subdivided into the characteristics maturity and fault tolerance, and, in the case of resources, additionally, recoverability. As in [Saeedi et al. (2010)] for reliability only failures are considered, we only allocate maturity.

4.1.2 Tools for Modeling Quality Information

In addition to the literature review on research approaches to model quality aspects, current tools are analyzed to understand the state of practice.
Restricting the review only to BP modeling tools did not lead to satisfying
results. These tools comply with a standardized BP modeling notation (like
BPMN or UML Activity Diagram), and, as none of these notations allow for
the modeling of quality aspects, the tools do neither. Therefore, the review
was extended to include Business Process Management (BPM) systems and
tools for Enterprise Modeling (EM). These tools usually include a BP modeling component, and additionally provide utilities to support other activities
of BPM respectively EM, such as execution, monitoring, optimization, or
data modeling. The corresponding components are closely interconnected.
Thus, the associated data is also more interconnected. That is the kind of
data we want to visualize within BP models.

We finally analyzed[2] 42 BPM, EM and BPMN tools currently used in
practice, which we obtained from lists published by independent BPM-related
organizations [3]. From these tools, 16 enable the description of some kind of
quality aspects for BPs. However, none of the tools satisfactorily enables the
(graphical) modeling of quality aspects within BP models. This means that no
tool was found which enables the modeling of a broad range of quality aspects,
comparable to those represented in the BPQRM. Note that prototypical
tooling of approaches presented in Section 4.1.1 was not considered, since
these were already discussed in the previous section. Moreover, we are
rather interested in tools used in practice than in research prototypes. In
most cases, quality aspects can only be captured textually, as a property of a
model element in a tabular structure with predefined or free-text fields, or
in separate views, which are not visible in the BP modeling view. In few
cases [ABACUS 3.2, ARIS Design Platform 7.1, MEMOCenterNG], the
quality aspects can be visualized as labels to the corresponding element. In

---

[2] Analyzed means that the tools were installed and executed, and associated white papers,
tutorials and all sorts of published information material were consulted.

[3] An overview of current BPM- and BPMN-tools is available under http://www.
bpm-netzwerk.de respectively http://www.bpmn.org

[ARIS Design Platform 7.1], quality aspects furthermore can be presented by a freely selectable graphical symbol.

Table 4.2 gives an overview of five exemplary tools, which allow the expression of quality aspects. Further tools can be found in [Kappe (2011)]. For each tool, the functional range, the supported BP modeling notations, the expressible quality aspects and the related characteristics of the BPQRM, the way of expression, and the granularity of the quality aspects is represented.

Similar to the research approaches, the tools only allow the documentation of few quality aspects and are not suitable to model quality comprehensively. Altogether, regarding activities, quality aspects covered by 6 of the 26 quality characteristics for activities, namely time behavior, maturity, fault tolerance, understandability, actor satisfaction, and context satisfaction were found. For resources, quality aspects covered by 5 of the 26 characteristics, namely resource utilization, suitability, maturity, fault tolerance, and recoverability were identified. Regarding actors, quality aspects covered by availability and suitability (2 of the 2 characteristics) were found. Regarding information objects, the tools are not able to express any characteristic.

4.1.3 Summary

As shown in the literature review, there are some approaches that are able to express few or single quality aspects. However, none of the approaches were able to express a larger set of quality aspects, which is necessary for capturing quality requirements or doing BP assessment comprehensively. Tools from practice also do not enable the capturing of quality aspects satisfactorily. In fact, most of the tools were not able to capture quality aspects at all. Some of the tools were able to model few quality aspects, but, mostly, these are not visible in the BP modeling view. The literature and tool review showed that there is a gap between the capability of current approaches and tools to represent quality aspects and the quality aspects in the BPQRM, which we want to represent within a BP model.

The tools, as well as the research approaches, do not support a hierarchical structure of quality aspects, such as described in Section 3.3. This means that they do not distinguish between characteristics, attributes, and measures.

Table 4.2: Comparison of Current Tools from Practice

Tool/Criterion	[ABACUS 3.2]	[ADONIS 3.9]	[Kern Process 2.6]	[GRADE 4.1]	[Horus 1.2.1]
Functional range	IT strategy, planning and EM	BPM	BPM	CASE	BPM
Modeling notation	BPMN	BPMN and own notation	Own notation	Own notation	Own notation
Expressible quality aspects	• Process: processing time, frequency of execution, reliability, availability • Resource: utilization, business fit, reliability, availability, etc. • Actor: reliability, availability, etc.	Own notation: • Process: quantity of execution per time unit (throughput), tolerance waiting time (before canceling) • Activity: processing-, waiting-, resting-, transport time	• Process: service time, customer satisfaction, employee satisfaction • Actor: qualification	• Activity: duration, goals	• Activity: error rate, processing- and transport time, execution frequency per time unit (throughput)

Related quality characteristics of the BPQRM	Time behavior, maturity, fault tolerance (because of reliability and availability[4]) (activity); resource utilization, suitability, maturity, fault tolerance, recoverability (because of reliability and availability) (resource); availability (actor)	Time behavior (activity)	Time behavior, context satisfaction, actor satisfaction (activity); suitability (actor)	Time behavior, understand-ability (activity)	Time behavior, maturity (activity)
Granularity	Fine- & coarse-grained	Fine-grained	Fine- & coarse-grained	Fine-grained	Fine-grained
Way of expression	Textual	Textual	Textual	Textual	Textual
Visibility within the diagram	One property per model element (optional)	Not visible	Not visible	Not visible	Not visible

[4] According to ISO/IEC 9126-1, availability (just like reliability) is a combination of maturity, fault tolerance and recoverability.

This may lead to confusion regarding the concrete measures that are to be applied. For example, reliability cannot be specified by a single measure, as it is proposed by [Saeedi et al. (2010)], since reliability comprises a variety of different attributes.

4.2 Extending a Process Modeling Notation by Quality Aspects

The deficiencies identified in the literature and tool review motivated us to develop an approach to model quality aspects comprehensively within BP models, and to provide a new tool support. The approaches and tools discussed in the previous section provide first ideas on documenting quality aspects within BP models. They model small sets of quality aspects that are easy to capture by minor extensions to present notations. [Gagne & Trudel (2009)] and [Gulla (2007)] visualize different quality aspects of the same characteristic using different graphical symbols. Owing to the large number of possible attributes per characteristics of the BPQRM, this will not scale to a large number of attributes or characteristics. Modeling a large set of different quality aspects within a BP model will quickly reduce the clarity. Consequently, the proposed solutions have to be revised to model a relevant set of quality aspects.

The research question, thereby, is how to enable the modeling of a large set of different quality aspects without a major increase of complexity of the modeling notation. To keep the complexity manageable, small graphical symbols were added to already existing model elements. Each characteristic in the BPQRM is represented by a graphical symbol, as depicted in Figure 4.7. To each symbol, related attributes, derived measures, base measures, and the corresponding values are associated.

Based on this initial idea, Alexander Kappe specified a mapping of graphical symbols to the characteristics of the BPQRM, in his Master's thesis [Kappe (2011)]. Moreover, he prototypically implemented the concept as an extension to the Eclipse-based CASE tool UNICASE [5]. In this way, for

---

[5] UNICASE is available online http://unicase.org/

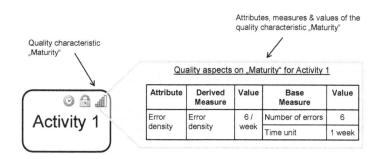

Figure 4.7: Modeling Concept

each BP component of the BPQRM, quality aspects can be represented comprehensively in a BP model.

Figure 4.8 shows a screenshot of the tooling [6]. The BP model is presented in a split screen view together with the corresponding tables of attributes and measures. Therefore, – in contrast to the reviewed tools – information on structure and behavior, as well as information on quality, can be presented in a single view. In the BP modeling view (Business Process Model), the modeler can specify information on structure and behavior of the BP as a BPMN model, and can additionally specify the quality characteristics of the BPQRM. The modeler can add quality characteristics to a BP model element by dragging and dropping the characteristic icons from the toolbar beside the model to the corresponding BP model element. By clicking a characteristic icon in the BP model, the table of attributes and measures related to the selected characteristic appears in the Details view below. Here, the modeler can specify the attributes, measures, and their values. Thus, it is possible to model a large set of different quality aspects (in the form of characteristics), as well as to capture detailed quality aspects (in the form of attributes and measures), without a major increase of complexity of the BP model.

Note that in our view, it is important to model quality aspects simultaneously with information on structure and behavior, because quality is often

---

[6] the Process Modeling Editor is available online
`http://code.google.com/p/unicase/wiki/BusinessProcessEditor`

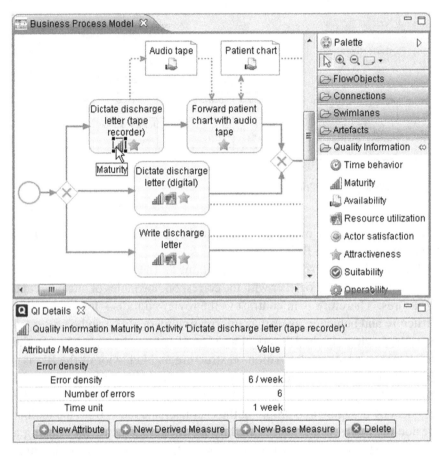

Figure 4.8: Screenshot of the Process Modeling Editor

elicited together with information on structure and behavior. We think it is not sufficient to enter quality aspects, ex-post, into the model, as quality may influence the structure and behavior of a BP.

The proposed modeling approach is applicable to an arbitrary graphical modeling notation. The BPMN was chosen as an example, as it is an up-to-date and established modeling notation for BPs. Moreover, the BPMN is well suited to be extended [BPMN 2.0 (2011)]. The extension to the BPMN meta-model is described in detail in [Kappe (2011)].

4.3 Discussion and Application Example

This section first discusses how the proposed approach fits the comparison criteria of the literature and tool review. Afterwards, lessons learned by applying the approach and tool support are presented.

4.3.1 Discussion

Table 4.3 shows a comparison of the supersets of the approaches and tools discussed in Section 4.1 to our approach. The comparison criteria way of expression, related quality characteristics, and visibility within the diagram were already discussed while introducing the approach. In the following, criteria not already mentioned in the previous section are described.

As the approach supports a hierarchical structure of quality aspects, it allows the modeling of fine-grained quality aspects in the form of attributes and measures. The approach is applicable to an arbitrary graphical modeling notation. To give an example, the BPMN was extended. As the BPMN is a semi-formal modeling notation, the extension is semi-formal, too. Although tool support was provided and the approach was applied to an example from practice (see Section 4.3.2), the approach is still in an early stage of development. Additional evaluation will be necessary to make a final statement on the maturity of the approach. The prototypical implementation of the approach is an extension to the CASE tool UNICASE. Thus, the functional range of the tooling is CASE.

Now that the approach has been described, it is compared to [Pavlovski & Zou (2008)]. The approach in [Pavlovski & Zou (2008)] proposes the artifacts "operating condition" and "control case" to model constraints associated with a BP. The "operating condition" denotes a BP constraint and the "control case" defines controlling criteria to mitigate risks associated with an "operating condition". This approach aims to assist in the mitigation of risk and the early discovery of non-functional requirements during IS development. However, this approach enables the modeling of arbitrary quality aspects and does not provide guidance to the quality aspects to be modeled. In contrast, the approach proposed in this book is based on the BPQRM. Therefore, it provides a broad range of quality characteristics the

Table 4.3: Comparison of Current Approaches and Tools to the Proposed
Approach

Superset/ Criterion	Approaches of Section 4.1.1	Tools of Section 4.1.2	Proposed approach
Basic notation	BPMN, EPC, UML Activity diagram, Petri nets	BPMN, own notations	Arbitrary graphical modeling notation
Way of expression	Graphical + textual	Textual	Graphical + textual
Related quality characteristics of the BPQRM	Time behavior, maturity, understandability, context satisfaction, security (activity); security (resource); confidentiality, accuracy (information object)	Time behavior, maturity, fault tolerance, context satisfaction, actor satisfaction, understandability (activity); resource utilization, suitability, maturity, fault tolerance, recoverability (resource); availability, suitability (actor)	All the characteristics of the BPQRM
Granularity of the quality aspects	Mostly fine-grained	Mostly fine-grained	Fine-grained
Formality	Mostly semi-formal	/	Semi-formal
Maturity of the approach	Mostly new approach	/	Tooling and application example
Functional range	/	EM, BPM, CASE	CASE (tool support)
Visibility within the diagram	Visible within the diagram	Mostly not visible	Characteristics visible

modeler can select from. The approach in [Pavlovski & Zou (2008)] is limited to constraints related to activities. The proposed approach allows the modeling of quality aspects for all the BP components represented in the BPQRM. Moreover, as the approach in [Pavlovski & Zou (2008)] introduces two separate model elements, the modeling of a larger number of constraints (especially for a single activity element) will quickly reduce the clarity. Thus, this approach is not adequate to model a larger amount of quality aspects.

The proposed approach aims to model a comprehensive set of quality aspects within a BP model. However, it may not provide the optimal form of expression for specific quality aspect. Approaches designed to model specific quality aspects may provide better forms of expression, but they will not scale for a large set of different quality aspects. As the proposed approach aims to present the characteristics of the BPQRM and related attributes and measures, it does not express temporal constraints and dependencies (cf. [Gagne & Trudel (2009)]) or trends (cf. [Gulla (2007)]).

4.3.2 Application Example

In order to get feedback whether the modeling approach and tool support are adequate to model the quality aspects of a BP, they are applied to a real-life process. As an application example, the process of writing discharge letters is chosen, because all the components of the BPQRM are contained in the BP, and several quality aspects relevant to the BP were already elicited as a result of the interview study in Section 3.5.

As an application example, 12 different characteristics of the BPQRM and related attributes and measures identified in the interview study were modeled. Note, the quality problems described in Section 3.5.2 were identified from the answers of all interviewees. Moreover, not all the quality aspects elicited in the study represent quality problems. In the application example, the results of a single interview are modeled, because the answers may differ from one interviewee to another which would result in different models. For activities, quality aspects related to the characteristics maturity, time behavior, interoperability, safety, attractiveness, resource utilization, and understandability, were elicited in the interview. For resources, the interview results in quality aspects related the characteristics maturity, attractiveness, and learnability. For information objects, quality aspects related to current-ness, compliance, availability, and operability, were elicited. Quality aspects related to actors could not be elicited, since these were excluded on request of the hospital.

Figure 4.8 depicts an excerpt of the BP modeled in the process modeling editor. The diagram shows four activities and two data objects annotated with characteristic icons, which are relevant in the BP. This demonstrates that the proposed approach and tool support can be applied to model quality aspects of a real-life BP. In the following, lessons learned by the application are discussed.

The application example showed that the approach is a valid and practically applicable means, to model the 12 different characteristics that were elicited in the interview. In general, annotating a large set of characteristics to a single model element (the worst case is 26 characteristics per model element for the BP components activity and resource) very likely will reduce the clarity of a model developed using the approach. It turned out, however, that in the application example the number of modeled characteristics per model element was much lower (1 to a maximum of 5 characteristics per model element), because not all of the characteristics were relevant to every model element in the specific BP.

In the BP model, only the quality characteristics are visualized. One characteristic icon may represent several attributes and measures. The limitation to characteristics is a useful means to allow a compact overview of the quality aspects. However, the modeler cannot access a specific attribute or measure directly. Instead, s/he has to click on the corresponding characteristic icon. For example, if the modeler wants to view the value of the measure *number of errors*, s/he first has to click on the *maturity* icon (see Figure 4.8).

The split screen view is a useful means to show details of a single characteristic together with the BP model element the characteristic is annotated to. This is an advantage compared to the tools found in the review. Moreover, the tool allows the switching between characteristics quickly. However, selecting single characteristic icons may be cumbersome, if the modeler wants to view quality aspects aggregated over different characteristics or model elements.

4.4 Summary and Future Work

In this chapter, a modeling approach was introduced to represent a comprehensive set of quality aspects related to the BPQRM within a BP model. The proposed approach was compared to related modeling approaches and tools. The comparison showed that other approaches and tools only allow for modeling few or single quality aspects, where the proposed approach enables to represent a comprehensive set of quality aspects. Prototypical tool support was implemented. The approach and tool support were applied to model quality aspects of the process of writing discharge letters. The application demonstrated the applicability of the approach and tool support to a real-life example, and exposes topics of future work.

In the future, the tool support may provide additional functionality to support the modeler and to increase usability. The tool support may enable the direct retrieval of a specific attribute or measure, for example, by searching for its name, in addition to the access via clicking the corresponding characteristic icon. Moreover, the tooling may support the aggregation of quality aspects over different characteristics (e.g., for depicting security while considering performance) or model elements (e.g., for depicting the performance or reliability of a sequence of activties). Views on the BP model specific to certain quality aspects may also increase the usability. Extending the tool support by additional functionality, such as automatic calculation of derived measures, is also desirable.

The formalization of the quality modeling approach is another topic of future work. Prerequisite to this is a formal quality definition based on the BPQRM, as mentioned in Section 3.7. Formalizing the modeling approach will be facilitated while building upon a formal modeling notation, such as Petri nets, instead of the BPMN, as proposed in this chapter. Moreover, further evaluation is required to assess the maturity of the approach and its acceptance from the users' point of view. This can be done in a case study or controlled experiment, involving third-party users.

Part II
Aligning Business Process Design and Information System Design

5 Foundations and Definitions*

> Prediction is very difficult, especially about the future.
>
> — *Niels Bohr, 1885–1962* —

Part II of this book addresses the alignment of BP designs and IS designs in terms of performance. Therefore, the mutual impact between BPs and ISs is characterized and new prediction methods are proposed. To bridge the gap to Part I of this book, it is important to note that performance is covered by the BPQRM characteristics time behavior and resource utilization.

This chapter introduces the BP modeling language and basic concepts related to the alignment of BP design and IS design. In Section 5.1, foundations regarding performance prediction are introduced. Then, the Palladio Component Model, a meta-model for IS modeling, is described in Section 5.2. The Palladio approach, so far, supplies comprehensive support for modeling and simulating IS designs. In this book, Palladio is extended by new model elements, to represent BPs and their organizational environment, as well as by new simulation behavior. The extensions to the Palladio Component Model are described in Section 5.3. In Section 5.4, performance measures are introduced, and the alignment of BP designs and IS designs in terms of performance is defined.

5.1 Foundations on Performance Prediction

This section introduces foundations on performance prediction. First, the queuing network formalism is described. Then, simulation is introduced as an

---

* The PCM extensions proposed in the chapter were originally published in an early version in: Heinrich, R., Henss, J., Paech, B. **Extending Palladio by Business Process Simulation Concepts**, In: Becker, S. et al. (eds.), Palladio Days 2012 Proceedings, Karlsruhe Reports in Informatics 2012,21, ISSN 2190-4782, pp. 19–27, KIT, 2012.

approach to performance prediction, based on queuing networks. Finally, this section distinguishes two types of simulation and motivates the application of discrete-event simulation for predicting the performance of BPs and ISs.

5.1.1 Queuing Network

An established formalism for performance prediction is queuing network theory [Lazowska et al. (1984)]. In queuing network theory, a model is constructed that represents a system of processing resources. A system may not necessarily be a technical system, but may also be a system of human actors. A *processing resource* (i.e., service center) is composed of a waiting queue and its server, as depicted in Figure 5.1. "Customers", which, for example, represent users of an IS, transactions, or orders handled in a BP, are processed by the resources. They arrive at a resource, wait in the queue if necessary, receive service, and depart. Processing resources can be composed to a network, as visualized in Figure 5.2 for instance. The queuing network model is traversed by "customers", each of them arriving and departing at one resource after another, on a certain path through the network. The figures are taken from the corresponding figures in [Lazowska et al. (1984)].

Queuing network models have basically two types of parameters. The workload intensity at the model and the service demands at the processing resources. Workload can be specified in several forms, such as the rate at which the "customers" arrive at the model, by specifying a fixed number of "customers" traversing the model continuously, or by determining the number of "customers" and an average time that each of them "spends thinking" before traversing the model again. The service demand of a "customer", at a specific processing resource, is the amount of work to be done by that resource. It is typically specified by the time required to process the "customer".

Based on the parameter specification, the queuing network model can be evaluated to predict the following performance measures for each processing resource in the model [Lazowska et al. (1984)].

- *residence time*: "the time spent at the service center by a customer, both queuing and receiving service".

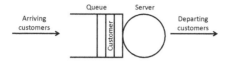

Figure 5.1: A Single Processing Resource

- *queue length*: "the number of customers at the service center, both waiting and receiving service".
- *utilization*: "the proportion of time the server is busy."

The time required by a "customer" to traverse the queuing network model is then determined by adding up the residence time spent at the corresponding processing resources on a certain path through the network. This time is called *response time* to comply with the intuitive notion of perceived system response time.

Note, most performance measures obtained from a queuing network model are average values (e.g., average residence time). Thus, in [Lazowska et al. (1984)] the definitions concentrate on average performance measures. As this book is as well interested in the entire performance measure distribution, the implicit average assumption is discarded and the definitions are adapted accordingly. This means that from the two first-mentioned definitions, the word "average" was removed, compared to the definitions of [Lazowska et al. (1984)].

5.1.2 Simulation

For the evaluation of a model basically two different kinds of methods are available – analysis and simulation [Law & Kelton (2000)]. Analysis is a mathematical method, which leads to an exact solution. However, it is only applicable to simple models. There are analytical methods to solve queuing network models. Queuing networks that have a product-form [Chandy & Martin (1983)] are computationally tractable. However, product-form queuing networks rely on strong assumptions that are typically not met in realistic settings. For example, scheduling policies like priority queues cause queuing

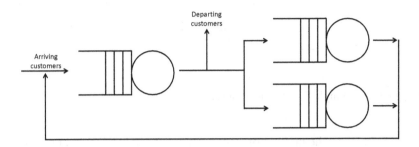

Figure 5.2: A Network of Processing Resources

networks that are not in product-form, as stated in [Becker (2008)]. Queuing networks with weaker assumptions that reflect real-life BPs or ISs are typically computationally intractable. This means that their output measures cannot be calculated using an analytical method.

Simulation is a numerical method, which is an imitation of a real-world phenomena. It does not lead to an exact solution, but can be applied to complex models. In simulation, a model is evaluated using a computer, where it is exercised for the inputs in questions to see how they affect the output measures [Law & Kelton (2000)]. Data, such as residence times at processing resources, are gathered, in order to estimate the desired output measures, such as the average response time of the model. Consequently, simulation techniques are applied in this book to examine models, which reflect real-life BPs and ISs, and determine related performance measures.

5.1.3 Discrete-Event Simulation

In simulation, two alternatives are distinguished for describing the behavior of a system that changes its state over time – discrete-event simulation and continuous simulation [Law & Kelton (2000)]. In discrete-event simulation, a system is described by a finite sequence of system states as it evolves over time. This means that the state of a *discrete-event system* can change at only a "countable" number of separate points in time. At a certain point in time, an event can occur that may change the system state. No changes to the system state can happen between two points in time. In contrast, some systems cannot be described by a finite number of states, as there is an indefinite number of states between two points in time. The state of such a system changes continuously with respect to time. An air plane moving through the air is an example [Law & Kelton (2000)], since the position of the air plane changes continuously over the duration of flight. For these systems a continuous simulation is appropriate.

The state of a BP changes as a discrete sequence of events (i.e. stepwise), for example, when an order is placed or when the processing of an order is finished. Likewise, the state of an IS changes whenever a user enters the system or leaves the system. Therefore, BPs and ISs are typically modeled as discrete-event systems. In this book, discrete-event simulation is applied to evaluate BPs and ISs as they evolve over time.

5.2 The Palladio Component Model

The Palladio Component Model (PCM) is a meta-model designed for the description of component-based software architectures [Becker et al. (2009)]. It was developed for the prediction of software architecture quality characteristics, especially performance. The PCM is based on a development process that distinguishes five types of developer roles depicted in Figure 5.3.

i.   Component developers specify and implement the components of a software architecture.

ii. System architects arrange components in order to create applications.

iii. System developers specify the hardware environment and allocate components to hardware nodes of the environment.

iv. Business domain experts specify the system usage profiles, as they have knowledge about customers and users, and critical usage scenarios of the system.

v.   QoS analysts (not depicted in the figure) elicit quality-relevant information, conduct QoS analysis, and assist the system architect in interpreting the results of the QoS analysis [Koziolek (2008)].

The roles in the Palladio development process partly overlap with the roles introduced in Section 1.1. The system designer covers the roles system

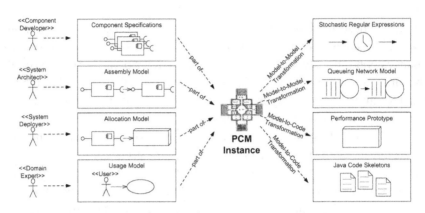

Figure 5.3: The PCM Developer Roles [Becker et al. (2009)]

architect and system developer, because s/he is responsible for the IS design. The hardware administrator overlaps with the hardware-specific tasks of the system developer. The requirements engineer covers the role business domain expert, due to his/her knowledge about requirements from customers and users, regarding a specific IS. Moreover, the requirements engineer covers parts of the QoS analyst, because s/he is also responsible for IS requirements verification. The business analyst is also related to the role business domain expert, because s/he has knowledge about requirements on business-level. Business-related requirements may affect several BPs and ISs. In contrast to the requirements engineer, which is focused on a certain IS, the business analyst manages and verifies requirements that may span several ISs.

Each developer role in the Palladio development process is responsible for the specification of a certain partial model in a domain-specific modeling language. The partial models are introduced in the following.

In the *repository model*, software components are specified via provided and required interfaces, modeled by ProvidedRoles and RequiredRoles. Components implement *services* that are described by the corresponding interfaces. The relationship between a required and a provided service of a component is described in the *service effect specification*. The service effect specification determines the behavior of a component service as a sequence of internal actions, control flow constructs, and external calls. Internal actions comprise

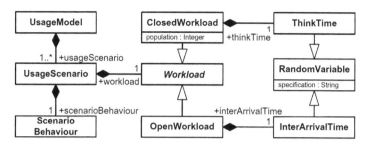

Figure 5.4: The PCM Usage Model: Usage Scenario and Workload [Becker et al. (2009)]

quality-relevant annotations, such as resource demands on CPU or hard disk resources. Moreover, a software component may declare passive IS resources used by the services it implements, such as threads in a thread pool or database connections. In the *system model*, software components are connected via their interfaces to build the software application. The *resource model* specifies the hardware environment of the software system. Processing resources (e.g., a CPU) are grouped in resource containers (e.g., a server) and resource containers are connected via communication resources (e.g., a computer network). A communication resource is also represented by a processing resource in the PCM. In this book, the term *hardware resource* is used to refer to hardware-based processing resources, such as a CPU or a computer network. In the *allocation model*, software components are allocated to a specific resource container. The system's usage profile is described in the *usage model*, by specifying the workload the system has to handle and the control flow of user actions (e.g., system entry calls). Figure 5.4 shows the meta-model for PCM usage models as a class diagram [UML 2.0 (2005)]. The usage model is explained in detail in the following, because it is extended by BP model elements in this book.

A UsageModel contains a number of UsageScenarios. Each UsageScenario consists of a Workload specification, which reflects the usage intensity of the scenario, and a ScenarioBehavior, which describes the control flow of user actions. The PCM distinguishes two types of workload – open and closed workload. This is in analogy to workload specifications in queuing networks [Lazowska et al. (1984)]. A closed workload specifies a fixed number of

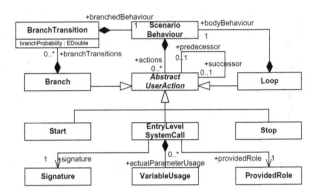

Figure 5.5: The PCM Usage Model: Scenario Behavior [Becker et al. (2009)]

users circulating within the system. In contrast, an open workload does not
determine the number of users, but specifies an inter-arrival rate of users at
the system, in the form of an InterArrivalTime between subsequent users as a
RandomVariable. The inter-arrival time denotes the time that passes between
two subsequent users arrive at the system. A ScenarioBehavior consists of
several AbstractUserActions, visualized in Figure 5.5, which are interconnected by a predecessor-successor relationship. Besides the basic control
flow elements Start, Stop, Branch, and Loop, the call of services at the system's provided roles can be specified in the form of EntryLevelSystemCalls.
Therefore, EntryLevelSystemCalls refer to a Signature and a ProvidedRole specified in the repository model. All the services modeled in the usage model
have to be delegated to the system's provided roles.

There are two specialized software architecture simulators available for
the PCM – SimuCom [Becker et al. (2009)] and EventSim [Merkle & Henss
(2011)]. The simulators rely on queuing network theory, in order to estimate
the operation of a software system at different layers, as depicted in Figure 5.6.
The figure is adapted from [Becker (2008)]. The layers refer to the partial
models of the PCM. The simulators are applied to predict performance
measures, such as response times and resource utilizations.

The representation of an IS by the original PCM model elements is called
IS design, hereafter. The representation of a BP by the new model elements
introduced in the next section is called BP design in the following.

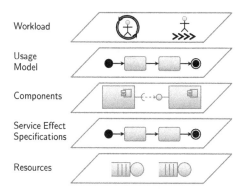

Figure 5.6: Simulation Layers Used in the PCM

5.3 Business Process Modeling Concepts

The PCM is extended by new model elements to represent BPs and their organizational environment. Thus, the process designer can use the extended PCM to specify alternative BP designs for which performance measures are predicted. This section introduces the new modeling language.

5.3.1 Business Process Model

A *business process model* represents a set of BPs. The existing PCM usage model is extended by meta-classes for BP modeling and an additional workload specification type (described in Section 5.3.3). The extensions are visualized in Figure 5.7. If meta-classes are taken from the original PCM usage model, this is mentioned in brackets. A business process model consists of one or more ScenarioBehaviours. While a ScenarioBehaviour in a regular PCM usage model represents the behavior of a certain class of system users (i.e., a usage scenario), it represents a BP in the context of this book. A BP is specified by a sequence of AbstractUserActions and their predecessor-successor relationships. All types of actions that can be used in a regular PCM usage model are also allowed within a business process model. For BP modeling, four additional actions are introduced – ActorStep, Activity, AcquireDeviceResource and ReleaseDeviceResource.

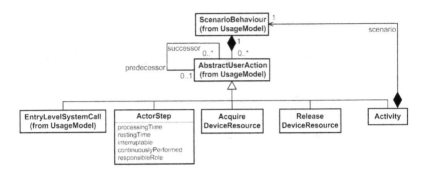

Figure 5.7: Meta-Model Extension for Business Processes

An ActorStep denotes a step within the BP to be completely performed by a human actor in a specified role (responsibleRole). Each actor step requires a certain time to be processed by the assigned actor (processingTime) and may be followed by a time of resting (restingTime). These attributes are explained in detail while describing the performance measures in Section 5.4.1. The interruptible attribute indicates whether the actor step may be interrupted. Interrupting an actor step is desirable when one of the following conditions holds: (i) the corresponding actor stops working, for example, due to a lunch break or to prevent working overtime, or (ii) the corresponding actor gets assigned an actor step with higher priority. Non-interruptible actor steps are given preferential treatment in that they always "overtake" interruptible steps waiting for processing by the same actor. The scheduling policy defining how human actors process steps is described in Section 9.1. The continuouslyPerformed attribute indicates that a sequence of actor steps for which the attribute is set true, is performed by the same actor, if the same responsibleRole is allocated for all the actor steps. A modeling alternative may be the introduction of two additional actions used in conjunction to specify a sequence of actor steps similar to the acquisition and release of device resources (described in the following). This would allow for a better encapsulation of simulation behavior via traversal strategies in EventSim, as described in Section 9.3. However, selecting an actor is required for each actor step within the business process model. The corresponding simulation behavior is closely related to ActorStep. The continuoslyPerformed attribute indicates a small modification to the standard behavior. This does not justify the introduction of additional actions in the model. The PCM usage model already enables the modeling of steps completely performed by the IS (i.e., system steps) in the form of EntryLevelSystemCalls. Thus, system steps are represented by EntryLevelSystemCalls in the business process model. A system step creates the link between the BP design and the IS design by referring to a ProvidedRole within the IS design. It denotes the invocation of the corresponding service specified within the IS design.

An Activity serves as a container for AbstractUserActions, encapsulated in a ScenarioBehaviour, to allow for modeling hierarchically nested BPs. The actions AcquireDeviceResource and ReleaseDeviceResource are used in conjunction to specify a sequence of actions for that a particular non-IT device or machine is required. Alternatively, the amount of required device resources may be specified as an attribute of ActorStep (like continuouslyPerformed). Since passive resources are not required for each actor step within the business process model, a separate modeling of actions is chosen to allow for a better encapsulation of the simulation behavior.

5.3.2 Organization Environment Model

The *organization environment model* represents the organizational context of the BPs in terms of resources involved in the BPs. Resources encompass human actors and their equipment – devices or machines, for example a fork-lift used by a warehouser. In this sense, an organization environment model is the counterpart of a PCM resource model, which specifies available hardware resources, such as CPUs.

Figure 5.8 shows the meta-model for organization environment models. ActorResources represent human actors. Like with regular PCM processing resources (i.e., hardware resources), actor resources have a waiting queue (also called worklist [WMC (1999)] for human actors) that lines up work to be done. In contrast to regular PCM processing resources, which provide continuous operation, actor resources may interrupt operation for a certain time span. Thus, an actor resource is called a *suspendable* resource. They adhere to working hours determined by one or more working periods (WorkingPeriod), each defined by a periodStartTimePoint and a periodEnd-

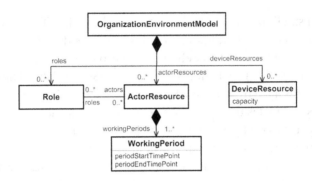

Figure 5.8: Organization Environment Meta-Model

TimePoint. For example, a working day split by a lunch break would be represented by two successive working periods – one before and one after lunch. Each human actor is assigned to one or more organizational Roles, as introduced in Chapter 2. It is common in BP modeling that BPs do not refer to actors directly, but point to roles instead. A DeviceResource is a non-IT device or machine, which is required to perform an actor step, but does not actively process the step. Thus, it is called a passive resource. Device resources are available in a limited capacity in the organization and are shared among the actors for processing steps. The attribute capacity determines the number of resources of the corresponding type available to be shared. In contrast to actor resources, which may differ due to different working periods specified, in this book, it is assumed that one device resource of a certain type equals another of that type. Thus, the device resource type and the capacity is modeled, instead of the single device resources, to avoid unnecessarily increasing the model complexity.

5.3.3 Business Process Workload

In addition to the workload types described above, a further type of workload is introduced to reflect workload properties of BPs.

In [WMC (1999)], an *instance* is a "representation of a single enactment" of a BP. It represents a "separate thread of execution" of the BP. In the context of this book, a *business process instance* is the representation of a single enactment of a BP design. Consequently, a BP instance is a synonym for "customer" in traditional queuing network models. A *step instance* is the representation of a step within a single enactment of a BP design (i.e., within a BP instance). BP instances successively instantiate all the actor steps and system steps on a certain path, through the business process model. Having the picture of "customers" traversing a queuing network model in mind, this can be seen like the BP instances *traverse* the BP design. At a particular point in time, each BP instance has its own *position* relative to the business process model, which represents its progress towards completion. A position is a model element in the business process model, such as an ActorStep, an EntryLevelSystemCall, a Start, or Stop element.

A *business process workload* specifies the intensity of BP execution. The meta-classes for workload specification are shown in Figure 5.9. They are part of the BP meta-model introduced in Section 5.3.1. The ProcessWorkload is an open workload whose intensity changes over simulation time, i.e., the inter-arrival time is specified as a function of time. In analogy to the original PCM, the inter-arrival time denotes the difference in time, in which, two subsequent BP instances come into the process Start position. The simulation time-frame can be decomposed into a sequence of non-overlapping, but not necessarily adjacent periods (ProcessTriggerPeriod), in which, BP instances come into the process start position. Each ProcessTriggerPeriod is specified by a periodStartTimePoint and a periodEndTimePoint, along with the interArrivalTime valid in between. Thus, the BP workload is a mapping of process trigger periods to a number of BP instances that come into the process start position in the course of the simulation.

An alternative way of modeling BP workload is to represent workload as a time series of BP instance arrival rates, which represents the workload in the course of a day, or a week, for example. The arrival rates can easily be measured in practice. Moreover, a time series can be decomposed into the components – trend, season and noise [Verbesselt et al. (2010), Box et al. (2008), Shumway (2011)]. The shapes and relative weights of these three components describe the corresponding workload. Consequently, decomposition could allow for further analysis of BP workloads. However, since time series result from measurements, they are not feasible for early design evalu-

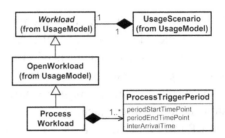

Figure 5.9: Meta-Model Extension for Business Process Workloads

ation as there is often no workload profile available to be measured. Time series are hard for people to read. Thus, they are hard to initially specify and adapt for predicting the impact of workload changes. Process trigger periods are much more intuitive for people. Consequently, workload is represented by a sequence of process trigger periods in this book. The tooling created in the context of this book supports the modeler by automatically generating process trigger periods from a calendar user interface, in order to reduce modeling effort.

A BP workload is *time-invariant* if (a) all process trigger periods are adjacent, and (b) all process trigger periods have the same inter-arrival time, i.e., the inter-arrival time does not change over time. A BP workload is *time-variant* if the inter-arrival changes over time. This means that either the periods are interrupted by a break, in which, no BP instances come into the process start position, or the inter-arrival time changes from one period to another.

For each BP, a corresponding workload specification is part of the business process model. As introduced in Section 5.2, workload specifications are also part of original PCM usage scenarios. These workloads, however, do not change over simulation time. This reflects Palladio's orientation towards steady-state analyses, where the focus is on predicting certain quality measures, as simulation time approaches infinity. Workload variations, however, are a fundamental property of BPs. Especially when studying how performance measures evolve over simulation time, it is vital to consider workloads as a function of time. Figure 5.10 shows a workload varying over the course of a day and its effects on the queue length of a processing resource. It is seen

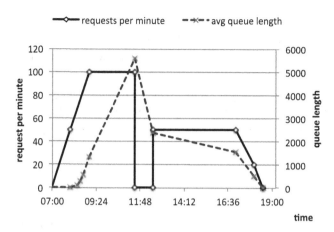

Figure 5.10: Example: Time-Variant Workload on a Resource and Resulting
Queue Length

how the workload variation leads to temporary overload conditions at peak
load, which might be interesting to examine, using simulation. Therefore, the
PCM usage model is extended by time-variant workloads. Thereby, changed
intensities of BP execution over the course of a day, a month, or even a year
and more can be reflected. Consequently, analysis techniques different to
those currently used in Palladio have to be applied which are discussed in
Section 9.2.

5.3.4 Workload Burstiness

Workload burstiness refers to the difference in time, in which, subsequent
BP instances come into a specific position in the business process model.
The difference in time is called *distance* in this book. For example, three BP
instances come into a specific position, e.g., an ActorStep, within a minute.
In the following, two exemplary cases are distinguished. In one case, the
BP instances come into the position at a constant distance (30 seconds) to
each other. In another case, they occur in a burst. For example, the distance
between the first and second instance is 1 second, and that between the second
and the third instance is 5 seconds. In the remaining 54 seconds, no further

BP instance comes into this position. In both the cases, the workload is three BP instances in one minute, where the burstiness differs.

Workload burstiness is of "paramount importance for queuing prediction" [Mi et al. (2008)], because it reflects whether load is dispersed equally, or in bursts, in the BP scenario. This is performance-relevant, because high workload burstiness often leads to increasing mean residence times at the resources (cf. [Mi et al. (2008)]). While traversing the BP design, the distance between BP instances (i.e., workload burstiness) can vary. Occasional bursts of BP instances can emerge, which results in temporary overload situations of resources, as discussed in more detail in Section 7.4.

5.4 Performance Requirements and Alignment

This section first introduces performance measures applied in this book and describes the requirement specification based on the performance measures. Then, the alignment of BP designs and IS designs in terms of performance is defined.

5.4.1 Performance Measures and Requirements

Performance measures applied in this book are built upon performance measures of traditional queuing network models. For each performance measure, a definition is given in the following.

Waiting time of a single resource demand of a step instance is the time the instance spends in the waiting queue of the corresponding resource before receiving service. Depending on the individual waiting queue length, waiting time may differ from one instance to another instance of the same step within the BP design. As described above, an EntryLevelSystemCall can contain several resource demands on different hardware resources, for example, one demand on a CPU resource and another demand on a hard disk resource. An ActorStep contains exactly one resource demand on an actor resource.

Processing time of a single resource demand of a step instance is the time required by the corresponding resource to actively process the demand. Processing time is not dependent on the individual waiting queue length, but given in the design. Consequently, it does not change from one instance to another instance of the same step within the BP design.

The total residence time of a system step instance at hardware resources is called *response time* to address the intuitive notion of perceived IS response time from the user's perspective [Lazowska et al. (1984)]. Thus, response time of a system step instance is the sum of waiting time(s) of the instance and processing time(s) of the corresponding resource demand(s). The response time values of the single system step instances result in the response time distribution of the corresponding system step in the BP design.

The residence time of an actor step instance at an actor resource is called *execution time* to address the terminology established in Business Process Management. It is the sum of the instance's waiting time and the processing time of the corresponding resource demand. In addition, the execution time of an actor step instance may comprise a certain resting time (as explained in the following). The execution time values of the single actor step instances result in the execution time distribution of the corresponding actor step in the BP design. The total time required by a BP instance to traverse a BP, or an activity within the BP design is called execution time, too. Like with actor step instances, the execution time distribution results from the single execution time values of the BP instances.

Resting time is the timespan between the processing of one actor step instance has been finished and the instantiation of its successor by the BP instance. It is the time the BP instance rests. For example, after mixing chemicals, one might have to wait a certain time before further processing. Otherwise, there is a risk of explosion. Resting time is given in the BP design.

Resource utilization is the proportion of time a resource (either actor resource or hardware resource) is busy.

These performance measures are predicted in simulation. The performance measures are also applied to specify performance requirements on a BP design or an IS design. A performance requirement on a BP design is either

- an execution time requirement on an actor step within the BP design, or
- an execution time requirement on an activity within the BP design, or

- an execution time requirement on the entire BP, or
- a utilization requirement on an actor resource within the BP design.

A performance requirement on an IS design is either

- a response time requirement on a system step (i.e., EntryLevelSystemCall that refers to a ProvidedRole within the IS design), or
- a utilization requirement on a hardware resource within the IS design.

The requirements may be specified in the form of mean values, thresholds or intervals, for example. Comparing the predicted performance measures to the requirements allows for determining whether a certain requirement is satisfied or not.

5.4.2 Alignment

A central concept of this book is the alignment of BP designs and IS designs in terms of performance, which is defined as follows.

A set P of BP designs and a set S of IS designs are *aligned* in terms of performance, if

i.   each EntryLevelSystemCall in a $P_i \in P$ refers to a ProvidedRole of an $S_j \in S$.
ii. each EntryLevelSystemCall that refers to a ProvidedRole of an S_j is contained in an element of P.
iii. all the S_j satisfy all their performance requirements in simulation.
iv. all the P_i satisfy all their performance requirements in simulation.

Alignment is defined on design-level so that the designs satisfy the requirements in simulation. It is assumed that the proposed prediction methods yield adequate prediction accuracy, which is validated in Chapter 10. Consequently, if the designs are aligned in simulation, the implementations of the designs in reality are expected to be aligned, too.

6 The Order Picking Process and Involved Information System[*]

Delay always breeds danger and to protract
a great design is often to ruin it.

— *Miguel de Cervantes, 1547–1616* —

In this chapter, the order picking process and the involved IS are introduced as an application case from practice, which is used in the following chapters for illustration and validation purposes. The process was elicited at Thor Gmbh, a multinational manufacturer and distributor of specialty chemicals, in the context of the case study described in Chapter 10.

A simplified representation of the order picking process is shown as a BPMN model in Figure 6.1. For a better understanding, loops and path branches included in the process are not depicted in the figure. The complete model is contained in the *OnlinePLUS* material of this book on www. springer.com.

Steps within the BP are visualized by rectangles with rounded corners. "AS:" denotes actor steps. "ISS:" denotes system steps of the IS. In the order picking process, goods requested by an order are taken out of the stock

---

[*] The order picking process was presented in an early form in:
Heinrich, R., Henss, J., Paech, B. **Extending Palladio by Business Process Simulation Concepts**, In: Becker, S. et al. (eds.), Palladio Days 2012 Proceedings, Karlsruhe Reports in Informatics 2012,21, ISSN 2190-4782, pp. 19–27, KIT, 2012.
and
Heinrich, R., Paech, B. **On the Prediction of the Mutual Impact of Business Processes and Enterprise Information Systems**, In: Kowalewski, S., Rumpe, B. (eds.), Software Engineering 2013, LNI-Vol. P-213, pp. 157–170, GI, 2013.

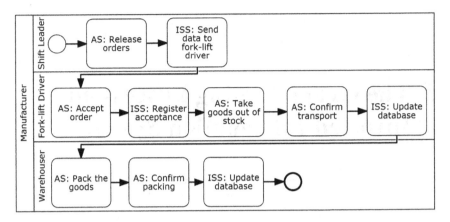

Figure 6.1: The Order Picking Process

and packed for transportation by truck. Orders can be processed concurrently in the BP. First, the shift leader releases an order for packing. The IS inserts the order data into a database (cf. Oracle database in the next paragraph) and afterwards transfers the order data from the database to a mobile client of the fork-lift driver. The fork-lift driver accepts the order, which is registered in the database by the IS. The fork-lift driver takes the goods out of the stock and carries them to a location where they are packed for transport. Afterwards, the fork-lift driver confirms the transport. The IS updates the database and informs the warehouser. Then, the warehouser packs the goods for transport, takes them to a location where they are collected by a truck later, and confirms the packing. Finally, the IS updates the database.

Figure 6.2 shows a simplified representation of the IS involved in the BP, on software component level, as a deployment diagram [UML 2.0 (2005)]. Logical software components are represented by rectangles marked with a component symbol. The software components are deployed on several hardware nodes that are depicted as cuboid. Interface symbols with a half circle at the end represent an interface that a component requires. Interface symbols with a complete circle at the end represent an interface that a component provides. Thus, they mark the source and target of call-dependencies between the software components. PPS is a German abbreviation for the

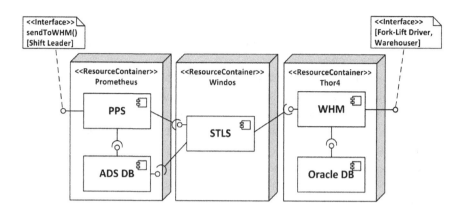

Figure 6.2: Software Component Deployment Model (as-is state)

production planning and controlling component. ADS stands for Advantage Database Server. WHM is an abbreviation for Ware House Manager, and STLS is a German abbreviation for the fork-lift control component. The PPS component and ADS database are deployed on the server Prometheus. The WHM component and the Oracle database are deployed on the Thor4 server and the STLS is deployed on the Windos server.

The PPS component is used to present all the order-related information to the shift leader. The PPS uses the ADS database component for data storage. The ADS database contains all the information of an order, such as ordered goods, amounts, and pricing. The WHM component communicates with the mobile clients located in each fork-lift and with the warehousers' clients. All movements of packing units are sent to the WHM component. The WHM component uses the Oracle database component to store all the information related to the processing of the released orders, such as storage places, movements of packing units, and the status of each order. When the release of an order is triggered in the PPS, via the service sendToWHM, the order data is transferred from the ADS database to the Oracle database. Thereby, the STLS component is responsible for data exchange between the ADS database and the WHM. The STLS reads data from the ADS database and writes it into a text file that is read by the WHM component. The WHM then inserts the order data into the Oracle database. An extended software component deployment model that shows all interfaces relevant in the order picking process is contained in the *OnlinePLUS* material of this book on www.springer.com.

There are strict time constraints in the BP, since requested orders must be available for transport, as soon as the trucks arrive. As delays are very expensive in the logistics business, it is a time-critical process. Based on interviews with experts of the organization, we identified the following requirements.

R1: The order data must be available for the fork-lift driver within one minute on average, at the latest, after the order has been released by the shift leader.

R2: All orders scheduled for pick-up on the actual day, or the following day, must be released and processed. This means that at least 19 orders have to be processed per day, on average.

R3: Delays in the order picking process are to be minimized.

The actors of the order picking process complain that the transmission of order data from the shift leader to the fork-lift driver can last up to 40 minutes and more. Hence, R1 is not satisfied. The actors have to wait a long time before they can continue handling the orders. IS performance significantly impedes the execution of the BP. Thus, the order picking process is an adequate example of IS impact on BP performance, which is discussed in detail, in the following chapter.

7 Mutual Performance Impact between Business Processes and Information Systems[*]

> We are stuck with technology when what we really want
> is just stuff that works.

— Douglas Noel Adams, 1952–2001 —

BPs and ISs mutually impact each other in non-trivial ways, which are discussed in this chapter. Section 7.1 gives an overview of related work. Then, three types of mutual performance impact between BPs and ISs are distinguished. First, the BP impact on IS performance is described in Section 7.2. Second, the IS impact on BP performance is presented in Section 7.3. Third, the joint impact on workload burstiness is discussed in Section 7.4.

7.1 Related Work

In related work, the impact of ISs on BPs was analyzed, which results in several categorizations. [Davenport (1993)] proposes nine different categories of IS impact on BPs – automational, informational, sequential, tracking,

---

[*] Parts of the discussion of the mutual impact were published in an early form in:
Heinrich, R., Henss, J., Paech, B. **Extending Palladio by Business Process Simulation Concepts**, In: Becker, S. et al. (eds.), Palladio Days 2012 Proceedings, Karlsruhe Reports in Informatics 2012,21, ISSN 2190-4782, pp. 19–27, KIT, 2012.
and
Heinrich, R., Paech, B. **On the Prediction of the Mutual Impact of Business Processes and Enterprise Information Systems**, In: Kowalewski, S., Rumpe, B. (eds.), Software Engineering 2013, LNI-Vol. P-213, pp. 157–170, GI, 2013.

analytical, geographical, integrative, intellectual, and disintermediating. According to [Mooney et al. (1996)], these categories are all covered by their more parsimonious model, which proposes three complementary categories of IS impact on BPs – automational effects, informational effects, and transformational effects. However, the model does not describe how to measure the specified impact. The IS Success Model [DeLone & McLean (1992)] classifies IS success into six perspectives that result from a comprehensive literature review on IS success measures. The model comprises the perspectives system quality, information quality, use, user satisfaction, individual impact, and organizational impact. For each perspective, measures are presented and the interdependencies between perspectives are specified. The last perspective considers the IS impact on organizational performance, which is described by measures, such as service effectiveness, productivity gains, or operating cost reduction. Because many of these measures are related to BPs, the IS Success Model reflects aspects of the IS impact on BPs. [King & Xia (2004)] investigated the IT infrastructure impact on the organization, based on a survey incorporating both, direct and indirect impact. They conclude that although there was little direct impact, IT infrastructure significantly affects organizational performance indirectly through its impacts on IS functional effectiveness and BP effectiveness. Because the IT infrastructure either enables or inhibits ISs and BPs, it is of strategic importance to organizations.

There is little explicit description of the BP impact on ISs in literature. As mentioned in the previous chapters, BPs serve as a starting point in IS requirements elicitation [Adam et al. (2009), Barjis (2008)]. Consequently, BP changes have to be propagated to the IS, where they again trigger changes. [Melling (1994)] stated that business process reengineering "is a key element in the factors driving IT architectural change". [Tsai et al. (2010)] conducted a questionnaire survey on the impact of BPs on Enterprise Resource Planning (ERP) system effectiveness, based on the IS Success Model. They conclude that (i) the perspectives user satisfaction and organizational impact are affected by the relationship between system and business process, and that (ii) business process reengineering consideration affects the perspectives information quality, user satisfaction, and individual impact of the IS. In IS performance prediction approaches (e.g., [Becker et al. (2009)]), the BP impact on IS performance is considered implicitly in the form of an IS usage profile, which describes the behavior of system users. Typically, the system users are actors in BPs. Consequently, the IS usage profile is derived from BPs. Merely, some simulation approaches, discussed in detail in Section 8.1, reflect a more explicit consideration of the BP impact on IS performance.

In this book, we focus on the mutual impact between BPs and ISs in terms of performance, which is described in detail in the following section. The adequate representation of the mutual impact is a requirement on the simulation approaches discussed in Chapter 8 and Chapter 9.

7.2 Process Impact on Information System Performance

The BP design represents the usage profile of the IS on an abstract level. The IS performance is affected by the steps and control flow elements in between, as well as by the BP workload. Steps and control flow elements within the BP design determine which and when a specific service of the IS is invoked. They also determine which services are invoked concurrently. Given a BP that includes two system steps, both demanding the same hardware resources of an IS. The IS performance may differ depending on whether the corresponding services are invoked sequentially or concurrently. The BP workload determines the amount of BP instances that traverse the actor steps and system steps in the BP design. Thus, the BP workload also determines the usage intensity of the IS. For example, IS performance may differ depending on whether the system is invoked once or 100 times per second.

7.3 Information System Impact on Process Performance

The IS performance affects the BP performance twofold. First, permanent overloaded hardware resources or permanent exhausted passive IS resources impede the BP execution. If one or more resources of an IS are permanent overloaded or exhausted by too many actor requests, the IS may no longer be available for actors in the BP. As a result, the execution of the BP is impeded or even interrupted. For example, if the order data cannot be transferred to the mobile client of the fork-lift driver (e.g., because a hardware resource is overloaded), the goods may not be available for loading the trucks in time. Second, for each system step instance, its response time may significantly affect the execution time of the enclosing BP instance. Often, IS response times are in a millisecond range. However, large database requests, complex calculations, or data transmission to mobile systems may result in response times of several minutes. Thus, the mean response time of a system step (i.e., the mean value of the response time distribution of all step instances) may be in its extent comparable to the mean execution times of actor steps within the BP, or may be even longer. In this case, the response time may significantly increase the mean execution time of the entire BP or of single activities within the BP. For example, in the order picking process, the transfer of order data to the mobile client of the fork-lift driver may last up to 40 minutes and more, which heavily impairs the process execution time, as it extends accordingly.

7.4 Joint Impact of BP Resources and IS Resources on Workload Burstiness

Workload burstiness is affected by BP resources, as well as by IS resources. The term BP resources is used hereafter, as a shortened form, to refer to actor resources, as well as device resources within a BP design. The term IS resources is used in the following, as a shortened form, to refer to hardware resources, as well as passive IS resources within an IS design.

BP instances traverse the BP design by successively instantiating the steps, as introduced in Section 5.3.3. Given the FCFS (first-come, first-served) scheduling principle as an example. If an actor is already busy when an actor step instance has to be performed by this actor, the execution of the actor step instance is blocked, until the actor is ready to perform it. If a hardware resource is already busy when it is demanded by a system step instance, the instance must wait until the resource is ready for processing. In both cases, the enclosing BP instance is blocked until the resource is ready to provide service, which results in waiting times.

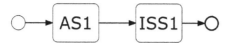

Figure 7.1: Minimum Business Process Example

Waiting times hinder the BP instances in traversing the BP design. For each step in the BP design, waiting times may differ from one BP instance to another, depending on the waiting queue length of the corresponding resources. It is common in a BP that several instances are processed concurrently by several actors of the same role, whose waiting queue length may differ. Frequently, hardware resources are also available in multiple replications, each of them having a different waiting queue length. Consequently, the distances between the BP instances in the BP design may vary, during the process execution.

Figure 7.1 depicts a minimum example of a BP that demonstrates how the distance between BP instances is decreased, which may then result in an occasional burst. The process under observation consists of an actor step (AS1) succeeded by a system step (ISS1). There are two actors A1 and A2 available to perform AS1. ISS1 is executed by an IS that contains one hardware resource, the CPU. The processing time (i.e., actor resource demand) of AS1 is 2 time units. The hardware resource demand of ISS1 is 1 time unit. Each actor also performs another step, which has a processing time of 6 time units. This step is part of a concurrent BP, which is not depicted in the figure. The BP instances start traversing in several non-adjacent intervals, with an inter-arrival rate of 2 time units. At the beginning of each interval, the waiting queues of the actors have a length of 5 time units, due to the other step performed by the actors.

Table 7.1 shows the expected behavior during process execution on the example of two BP instances P'1 and P'2. For the sake of clarity, only the enclosing BP instances are depicted in the table, the step instances are not shown. The cells exhibit the pending resource demand in time units at the corresponding point in time. It is seen that in the waiting queue of the actor resources, the distance between the BP instances shrink.

At the point in time t_0, the process instance P'1 is allocated to the actor A1, because the queues of both actors have the same length, but A1 is the first

Table 7.1: Example: Decreasing the Distance

Time	t_0	t_1	t_2	t_3	t_4	t_5	t_6	t_7
Actor A1	5 (+2 from P'1)	4 (+2)	3 (+2)	2 (+2)	1 (+2)	P'1	P'1	–
Actor A2	5	4	3 (+2 from P'2)	2 (+2)	1 (+2)	P'2	P'2	–

in line. At the point in time t_2, the process instance P'2 is allocated to the actor A2, because its waiting queue is the shortest, now. The processing of P'1 is completed at the point in time t_7. The processing of P'2 is completed at the point in time t_7, too. P'1 and P'2 reach the system step ISS1 at the same time, although they had a distance of 2 time units before AS1. Thus, occasional bursts of BP instances can emerge, which results in temporary overload situations of the corresponding resources.

One BP instance receives service from the CPU immediately, which results in a response time of one time unit, because there is no waiting time. The other BP instance has to wait until its predecessor has been processed, before receiving service, which results in a response time of two time units. The expected mean response time of ISS1 is 1.5 time units.

According to [Mi et al. (2008)], high workload burstiness often leads to increasing mean response times of system steps. In an experiment, they observed bursts in the workload of an IS. They compared the response time distribution of a system step in the case of a random workload burstiness, to the response time distribution of the system step in the case that all the requests are compressed into a single large burst. In case of the burst, they observed that the mean response time is approximately 40 times longer than in random burstiness. The 95th percentile of the response times is nearly 80 times longer in bursts. Although it is an extreme example, the experiment in [Mi et al. (2008)] demonstrates the impact of workload burstiness on performance. Human actors exhibit a similar behavior as hardware resources. They both own a waiting queue, which lines up step instances (either actor step instances or system step instances) to be executed by them, as introduced in Section 5.1 and Section 5.3.2. Enqueued step instances carry an amount of work to be done (the demand of either an actor step or an internal system action). They both process the demands induced by the step instances from their waiting queue in a certain order, for example in FIFO (first-in, first-out) order, or in a priority-based order. Consequently, increasing mean execution time of actor steps can be expected in the case of high workload burstiness. An example of job processing by human actors is described in detail in Section 9.1.

Likewise, passive resources may affect workload burstiness by blocking BP instances. In a BP, a passive resources may be a non-IT device or a machine, as introduced in Section 5.3.2. In an IS, a passive resources may be a thread in a thread pool or a database connection, as described in Section 5.2. They are available in a limited capacity and shared among all BP instances. If more passive resources are requested by the BP instances than currently available, the requesting BP instances have to wait, until passive resources are released again. This affects the distance to other BP instances traversing the BP design. For example, the distance to preceding BP instances that were not blocked may increase, whereas, the distance to succeeding BP instances may decrease, due to moving up while waiting.

Moreover, suspension of resources affect workload burstiness. Actors may interrupt their work in a lunch break, for example. Actor step instances are stuck in the waiting queues of the actors. The enclosing BP instances are blocked, which affects the distance to other BP instances traversing the BP design. For example, the distance to preceding BP instances that were not blocked may increase, whereas, the distance to succeeding BP instances may decrease, due to lining up in the waiting queue.

8 Predicting the Mutual Performance Impact between Business Processes and Information Systems[*]

> To invent, you need a good imagination and a pile of junk.

— Thomas Alva Edison, 1847–1931 —

In this chapter, the prediction of the mutual performance impact between BPs and ISs is discussed. First, the state of the art of mutual impact prediction is examined in Section 8.1, which shows that existing approaches rely on isolated BP and IS simulation. In Section 8.2, the approach BIIS is presented. BIIS was developed to analyze isolated simulation in detail. A significant artifact of BIIS is the IS usage profile, which is derived from a business process model, as described in Section 8.3. Benefits and limitations of BIIS are discussed in Section 8.4. It is argued that workload burstiness is not adequately represented using isolated simulation. In Section 8.5, three solution alternatives are discussed, to adequately reflect workload burstiness

---

[*] The approach BIIS and the discussion of related work presented in this chapter were originally published in:

Heinrich, R., Paech, B. **On the Prediction of the Mutual Impact of Business Processes and Enterprise Information Systems**, In: Kowalewski, S., Rumpe, B. (eds.), Software Engineering 2013, LNI-Vol. P-213, pp. 157–170, GI, 2013.

Parts of the discussion were originally published in:

Heinrich, R., Henss, J., Paech, B. **Extending Palladio by Business Process Simulation Concepts**, In: Becker, S. et al. (eds.), Palladio Days 2012 Proceedings, Karlsruhe Reports in Informatics 2012,21, ISSN 2190-4782, pp. 19–27, KIT, 2012.

in simulation. The chapter concludes with a summary of the findings in Section 8.6.

8.1 State of the Art of Mutual Performance Impact Prediction

Simulation approaches are widely used in the BP domain, as well as in the IS domain. BP simulation is applied to predict BP performance or the organizational impact of the BP (e.g., [Gladwin & Tumay (1994), Warren et al. (1995), Herbst et al. (1997), Hlupic & Robinson (1998)]). Computer network simulation is used to predict the performance of network topologies (e.g., [Varga & Hornig (2008)]). Software architecture simulation is applied to predict the performance of software systems (e.g., [de Miguel et al. (2000), Balsamo & Marzolla (2003), Becker et al. (2009)]) or for design optimization [Koziolek et al. (2011)].

Nevertheless, BP simulation and IS simulation are not adequately integrated in current approaches. Consequently, mutual impact between BPs and ISs is neglected in simulation.

Some approaches in literature predict the impact of ISs on BP performance, namely the ASSESS-IT framework [Eatock et al. (2002)], the BPISS framework [Paul & Serrano (2004)], respectively ISBPS framework [Serrano & den Hengst (2005)] (the framework was published under different names), the approach applied in the case study in [Giaglis et al. (2005)], as well as the approach by [Tan & Takakuwa (2007)]. These approaches merely conduct BP simulation, where the IS is considered as a black box. Because these approaches do not consider the impact of BPs on IS performance, they are not further discussed in the following.

There are few approaches in literature that address the prediction of the mutual performance impact between BPs and ISs. The BPR-II methodology [Painter et al. (1996)] uses BP simulation and computer network simulation in isolation, in order to predict BP and IS performance. A hierarchical three-layered structure is proposed to describe the relationship between BPs, software applications, and computer networks. IDEF3 [Mayer et al. (1992)] models describe behavior at all three layers. Software applications that run on the computer networks are considered as a middle layer and used to create the connection between BPs and computer networks. [Giaglis et al. (1999)] present an approach to support the concurrent engineering of BPs and ISs, and to facilitate investment evaluation. BP simulation is used to predict BP performance. Computer network simulation is used to depict several alternative network architectures and topologies. They recognized that the hierarchical structure proposed by [Painter et al. (1996)] is not sufficient to represent the complex interrelationships between BPs, software applications, and computer networks. Thus, "IT level analysis" is proposed to provide the link between the BP and computer network layers considering mutual impact. However, similar to [Painter et al. (1996)], the "IT level" (i.e., the software applications) itself is not included in the simulation models. [Betz et al. (2012)] sketch a framework to integrate the lifecycles of BPs and business software for requirements coordination and impact analysis. Still, they use BP simulation and component-based software architecture simulation in isolation. Although the approaches are not described in detail, it can be seen that each of the three approaches: (a) considers the BP impact on IS performance, as described in Section 7.2, and (b) IS performance is considered as a factor of BP performance, as described in Section 7.3.

The identified approaches do not clearly define interfaces between BPs and ISs. Merely [Painter et al. (1996)] gives an example of the derivation of a network topology model based on a refined BP model. However, insides on the derivation are not described. The presented approach is limited to control flow aspects, but neglects the derivation of workloads. This means that it is not described how the IS workload is determined. For mutual impact prediction, the IS workload should be derived from the BP workload. Using isolated simulations requires the specification of an IS usage profile based on the BP. This is needed in IS simulation to reflect the impact of the BP design on IS performance. However, none of these approaches describe the specification of an IS usage profile. Performance measures supported by the approaches are rarely described. The approaches do not provide enough details to understand how the mutual impact between BP and IS is represented in simulation. Moreover, it is hard to assess their applicability in practice, due to insufficient description, and because they are not validation with respect to their practicability. Thus, we decided to develop our own approach to analyze how isolated simulations represent the mutual impact between BPs and ISs. The approach is described in the following.

8.2 The BIIS Approach

In line with the approaches discussed in Section 8.1, the simulation-based approach BIIS was developed to predict the impact of a BP on the performance of involved ISs, and vice versa, using isolated simulations. Based on BIIS, it is discussed how the mutual impact between BPs and ISs is reflected by isolated simulations and limitations of the approach are analyzed.

The prediction of the mutual impact between BPs and ISs, using isolated simulations, requires well-defined interfaces between both domains, in order to transfer information from one domain to the other. The interfaces are visualized in Figure 8.1. The central artifact of BIIS is the *business process model*, as specified in Section 5.3.1. It describes the behavior of the human actors involved in the BP, and the interaction between human actors and the IS. The *organization environment model* is specified in Section 5.3.2. The IS design is reflected by the software architecture model and the hardware environment model. The *software architecture model* comprises the software component-specific parts of the PCM. The *hardware environment model* covers the hardware-specific parts of the PCM. However, BIIS is not specific to the Palladio approach. BIIS can be applied to arbitrary BP and IS simulation approaches that are based on similar meta-models and predict the required performance measures. From the business process model, an IS usage profile for the IS performance simulation is derived. The IS usage profile specifies the usage of the IS in the BP scenario. The results of the IS simulation are written back to the business process model to be available for the BP performance simulation. Thus, the IS usage profile and the extensions of the business process model characterize the impact of the BP design on the IS performance, respectively, the impact of the IS design on the BP performance, in simulation.

BIIS consists of two parts that are used for different purposes. Part 1: The performance of an IS is predicted based on a specific IS usage profile derived from a business process model. The prediction output can be used by requirements engineers to verify a proposed IS design against requirements,

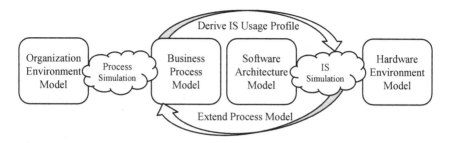

Figure 8.1: Interfaces between BP Simulation and IS Simulation

and by system developers to compare alternative IS designs. Moreover, hardware administrators can check the utilization of hardware resources for a proposed IS design or BP design. Part 2: The performance of a BP is predicted considering the performance of the involved ISs. The prediction output can be used by business analysts to verify a proposed BP design against requirements, and by process designers to compare alternative BP designs. Figure 8.2 gives an overview of BIIS as modified BPMN diagrams. The single steps of BIIS are depicted by rectangles with rounded corners and are annotated by a number. The steps of BIIS are described in the following, ordered by their number.

Step 1, an IS usage profile, which contains information about the usage of the IS, is derived from the business process model (Interface I in Figure 8.1). This step consists of three substeps detailed in Section 8.3.

Step 2, IS performance simulation: The derived IS usage profile, as well as the existing software architecture model and hardware environment model, are used for IS performance simulation. The models include performance-specific annotations, such as hardware resource demands or processing rates of hardware resources. Based on queuing network concepts, the IS performance simulation predicts the utilization of hardware resources and the response times of the system steps. The simulation result indicates one out of two possible cases:

a. One or more hardware resource(s) are permanent overloaded for the given usage profile. In this case, a stable mean response time of the system steps that demand the overloaded resource(s) cannot be predicted. The

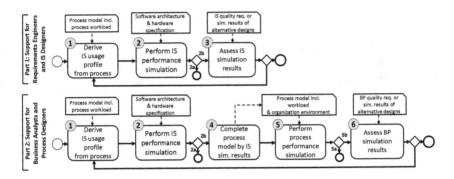

Figure 8.2: Overview of BIIS

procedure ends. The BP design or the IS design has to be adapted to handle this case. For example, the workload induced by the BP may be reduced by revising the BP design (if it is acceptable to change this) or the deployment of software components to hardware nodes may be revised.

b. The IS is not permanent overloaded. In this case, the simulation predicts the response time distribution per system step and the utilization of the hardware resources.

Step 3, the output of the IS performance simulation is compared to IS requirements for requirements verification. For example, for each system step, the predicted mean response time is compared pairwise, to a mean response time requirement. If the requirement is not satisfied, the IS design, the BP design, or the requirement has to be adapted. In the case of design changes, the approach (steps 1-3) has to be repeated. Moreover, the simulation output can be used to compare design alternatives based on the predicted performance measures. Part 1 of BIIS is necessary, as requirements may be missed on the IS level, even if all requirements on the business level are satisfied. For example, all orders were packed in time, but the actors are not satisfied, because they had to wait several minutes for each system response.

Step 4, the business process model is completed by the IS simulation results. The execution time of a single actor step instance typically last several minutes, which is why the entire execution time distribution of an actor step is also typically in a minute range. The response time of a single system step instance often lasts several milliseconds, which is why the entire response time distribution often also lies in a millisecond range. In this case, there is no need to consider the response time of the system steps in the BP simulation, as they have only negligible impact on the BP performance. In the case that the mean response time of a system step is comparable to the mean execution time of an actor step, or is even larger, it must be considered in the BP simulation. For example, large database requests, complex calculations, or data transmissions to mobile systems, as in the order picking process, may have a response time of several minutes. Thus, the response times are annotated to the corresponding system steps in the BP design, for example, in the form of a mean value or probability distribution.

Step 5, BP performance simulation: The completed business process model is used for BP performance simulation, together with information about the organizational environment. Based on queuing network concepts, the BP performance simulation predicts the utilization of human actors and the execution times of each actor step within the business process model. The response times of the system steps, if annotated to the business process model, are used as predicted in step 2. The simulation result indicates one out of two possible cases:

a. One or more actor(s) cannot handle the assigned actor steps as there are too many steps assigned. A stable mean execution time of actor steps assigned to these actors cannot be predicted. The procedure ends. The BP design has to be adapted to handle this case. For example, the steps may be rearranged, or more actors may be allocated. In some cases, where the IS is a performance bottleneck, also an adaptation of the IS design may be useful.

b. The actors can handle the assigned steps. The simulation predicts the execution time distribution per actor step and the utilization of each actor. It also predicts the execution time distribution of the entire BP and of the single activities within the BP design.

Step 6, the output of the BP performance simulation is compared to BP requirements, in order to verify the design against requirements. If the

BP requirements are not satisfied, the BP design, the IS design, or the BP requirements have to be adapted. In case of design changes, BIIS has to be applied again, to predict the impact of the changes. The simulation output can also be used to compare BP- and/or IS design alternatives, based on the predicted performance measures.

The six steps can be mapped to three activities that support the roles in the joint development of BPs and ISs, as introduced in Section 1.1.

1. *Impact prediction* comprises step 1 and step 2 from the IS perspective, as well as step 4 and step 5 from the BP perspective. It is the foundation of the following activities.

2. *Decision support* is represented by step 3 from the IS perspective and from the BP perspective by step 6. It provides support to the IS designer, the hardware administrator, and the process designer, since they can compare predicted performance measures among several design alternatives.

3. *Requirements verification* is also represented from the IS perspective by step 3 and from the BP perspective by step 6. It provides support to the requirements engineer and the business analyst, since they can compare predicted performance measures to requirements.

8.3 Deriving an IS Usage Profile from a BP Model

In this section, step 1 of BIIS is discussed in detail, using the example of the original PCM and the related simulation behavior. The BP can be specified in an arbitrary process modeling notation, as long as it encompass actor steps, system steps, and a workload specification similar to those described in Section 5.3.

Three substeps necessary to create an IS usage profile, based on a business process model, are described in the following. The substeps are not specific to Palladio, but generally applicable in a similar form. As introduced in Section 5.2, in the PCM, the interaction between users and the IS is described in the form of one or more usage scenarios contained in a usage model. For each usage scenario, a time-invariant workload specifies the usage intensity of the IS. In BIIS, an open workload is applied, which is determined by a certain inter-arrival time. Each simulation refers to one usage model. The challenge of step 1 is to create usage scenarios and related workload specifications based on a business process model.

As a first substep 1.1, a business process model is segmented into subprocesses so that each subprocess can be traversed by BP instances without interruptions, and has a time-invariant workload approximation. Only an approximation of the workload can be given, due to two reasons detailed in Section 8.4. The segmentation highly depends on the specific BP. One has to consider when a specific part of the BP is performed. It must be taken into account which parts of the BP are performed concurrently. Concurrent process parts may create concurrent access to resources. Thus, they must be simulated concurrently. It must be considered which parts of the BP exclude each other (e.g., one part is performed during the day, another part is performed at night). Parts that exclude each other have to be simulated separately. The segmentation of a business process model is illustrated by an example in the following. Given a business process model that consists of a sequence of three IS-supported activities A, B and C. Each day, 1000 BP instances start the execution of the process. Two different cases are discussed in this example.

First case: A is performed during the day (8 a.m. to 10 p.m.). B consists of steps exclusively performed at night (10 p.m. to 8 a.m.) within another shift, for example. C is performed the next day (8 a.m. to 10 p.m.). Thus, the business process model is segmented into three subprocesses. Each subprocess covers one of the activities A, B, or C. Two separate IS simulation studies are required to analyze this case. The first simulation study covers A and C as two concurrent subprocesses (the day simulation). Although A and C are performed on different days, except for the first and the last day of process execution, every day, A and C are traversed by BP instances concurrently. The workload of each subprocess in this simulation is approximated as 1000 BP instances in 14 hours, or, on average, one BP instance every 50.4 seconds (which is specified as the inter-arrival time). The second simulation study covers the subprocess B (the night simulation). The workload of this simulation is approximated as 1000 BP instances in 10 hours. The simulation study has to be split, since B is executed during the night, and A concurrent to C (A ∥ C) is executed during the day. B and A ∥ C exclude each other. Thus, there are no concurrent hardware resource demands between B and A ∥ C.

Second case: B is not executed at night, but also executed during the day, however, only from 8 a.m. to 1 p.m. Concurrent resource demands are possible. Thus, B is a subprocess concurrent to A ∥ C, which has to be considered in a simulation concurrently to A and C. The workload of the subprocess of B is approximated as 1000 BP instances in 5 hours. The second case has to be investigated using the two separate IS simulation studies A ∥ B ∥ C from 8 a.m. to 1 p.m., and A ∥ C from 1 p.m. to 10 p.m. There is no activity performed during the night. The two separate simulation studies may result in different mean response times of the same system steps of A and C depending on the workload induced at corresponding time of the day. The result of substep 1.1 is a set of subprocesses which have a time-invariant workload and can be traversed without interruptions.

In substep 1.2, the workload (in the form of a certain inter-arrival time) at each system step in the subprocess is determined based on the workload of the subprocess and the control flow of the subprocess (e.g., probabilities of path branches or number of loop iterations). The determination of the workloads at the single system steps is based on the assumption that BP instances continuously arrive at the system step in a certain distance (i.e., that there is no permanent overload of the hardware resources or the actors, and that passive resources are not permanent exhausted). If the assumption is incorrect, it will become apparent in the course of the investigation (see step 2 and step 5 in Section 8.2). Depending on the control flow of the subprocess, the workload at each system step within the subprocess is calculated as demonstrated in Figure 8.3.

For example, there are three system steps in the subprocess. The subprocess workload is specified in the form of an average inter-arrival time (t) of 40 seconds. Moreover, there is a branch. The probability of one path is 70 percent. The probability of the other path is 30 percent. Based on the probability of the path branch, the totality of the BP instances split up on the paths. This means that a certain BP instance either takes on path or another, which results in the inter-arrival times depicted in Figure 8.3. In the case of

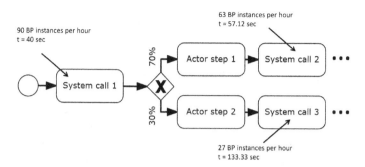

Figure 8.3: Determining the Inter-Arrival Time

parallel steps, there is no split-up. In the case of a loop, the workload adds up depending on the number of loop iterations, because the BP instances pass the system steps several times.

Finally, in substep 1.3, each system step in the subprocess is represented by a usage scenario in a PCM usage model, which only contains a EntryLevel-SystemCall and which is annotated by the system step's specific workload. Moreover, for usage model creation, one has to consider which subprocesses are performed concurrently and which exclude each other, as described above. All the system steps of concurrent subprocesses have to be represented by usage scenarios within the same usage model, since they are evaluated in the same simulation study.

8.4 Discussion of the BIIS Approach

In contrast to related approaches, a detailed description of BIIS was elaborated, as presented in the previous sections. This was required to analyze how the mutual impact is represented using BP simulation and IS simulation in isolation. In this section, it is discussed how the three types of mutual impact described in Chapter 7 are reflected by BIIS. Benefits and limitations, identified while elaborating the approach, are presented.

In BIIS, the IS performance is considered as a factor of the BP performance, since the business process model is extended by IS simulation results (i.e., predicted response time measures of system steps) before BP simulation. Thus, using BIIS, the IS performance influences the BP performance. For IS simulation the behavior of IS users has to be specified. Using BP simulation and IS simulation in isolation requires deriving an IS usage profile for IS simulation from the BP specification. The derivation of an IS usage profile is considered in BIIS, as described in Section 8.3. Thus, also the BP impact on IS performance is addressed in BIIS.

However, two limitations of BIIS were identified, which are discussed in the following. The first limitation is that, for IS usage profile creation, the IS workload can only be approximated. Approximation in workload specification usually results in reduced accuracy of the predicted IS performance measures. Limitation in workload specification is due to two reasons.

(a) There may be changes in the workload during the BP execution, which have to be represented in simulation. For example, from 9 a.m. to 11 a.m., the BP is triggered 100 times per minute, and from 1 p.m. to 5 p.m., it is triggered 50 times per minute. From 11 a.m. to 1 p.m., the BP is not triggered at all, due to a lunch break. As shown in the example, inter-arrival time changes over time. Consequently, the workload at the system steps induced by the BP also changes over time. IS simulation approaches typically rely on the strong assumption of time-invariant workloads. Thus, also the proposed procedure for deriving IS usage profiles is only valid for time-invariant workloads. Workloads changing over time cannot be mapped to a time-invariant workload specification without approximation. For example, the workload induced by an inter-arrival time, changing over the course of a day, cannot be represented by a time-invariant inter-arrival time valid for the entire day. The time-invariant inter-arrival time would not reflect temporary peaks in workload.

(b) IS simulation approaches typically rely on the assumption that, continuously, BP instances traverse the BP design, where simulation time approaches infinity. They do not consider that a BP instance may be blocked by suspended resources (e.g., if an actor stops working at the actual day) and continued later (e.g., if the actors resumes the next day). In the example in Section 8.3, BP instances that cannot completely traverse the BP on one day, increase the workload of the following day, as they continue traversing. Considering (a) and (b), the proposed procedure can only deliver an approximation to the workload.

The second limitation refers to the representation of workload burstiness during simulation. BIIS demonstrates that using isolated simulations, workload burstiness within the BP is not correctly represented in the simulations. This limitation is independent of supported modeling concepts, such as time-variant workload or suspendable resources, but a fundamental limitation of isolated simulations. System steps affect workload burstiness only in IS simulation, but not in BP simulation. Actor steps affect workload burstiness only in BP simulation, but not in IS simulation.

The impact of steps of the other domain on workload burstiness is neglected in both simulations as the resources demanded by the steps are not simulated. Thus, in the example in Table 7.1, the distance between both BP instances would not decrease in IS simulation, which results in a distorted prediction of performance measures. For the same reason, exhausted passive IS resources affect workload burstiness only in IS simulation and exhausted device resources affect workload burstiness only in BP simulation. Workload burstiness may impact the performance significantly, as discussed in Section 7.4. Thus, the prediction accuracy of approaches using isolated simulations is limited.

Note, in the previous discussion, the impact of a varying delay on workload burstiness was excluded for a better understanding. Applying BIIS, workload burstiness in BP simulation may be affected by a system step, if the business process model is extended by a response time distribution, instead of a constant mean value (cf. step 4 in Section 8.2). Owing to the response time distribution, the delay at the corresponding system step may vary from one BP instance to another. Consequently, the distance between BP instances may vary. Since the response time, however, does not result from a simulation considering the current system state, but was specified prior to the simulation, the impact of IS resources on workload burstiness is not adequately represented.

Given a system step whose response time is increasing steadily from one BP instance to another, in some situations. For example, due to temporary overloaded hardware resources or exhausted passive resources. In BP simulation, the response time would not increase steadily in temporary overload conditions, but evolve according to the specified distribution that results from the entire IS simulation time-frame. This means that for a low utilization of the IS resources the probability for a large response time is equal to that for a high utilization of the IS resources. Moreover, the response time distribution of the system step may not have been predicted accurately, due to neglected impact of BP resources on workload burstiness in IS simulation.

Isolated simulations cause higher effort for exchanging information compared to more integrated forms of simulation and engender duplication of information in different models. The usage of the IS is already specified in the business process model. However, applying BIIS, the business process model is not considered in IS simulation. Consequently, an IS usage profile has to be derived which requires additional effort and contains redundant information. The extension of the business process model by IS simulation results also causes effort. This is not required using more integrated forms of simulation.

8.5 Discussion of Solution Alternatives

Although the impact of workload burstiness on performance is easily comprehensible, to the best of our knowledge, the joint impact of BP resources and IS resources on workload burstiness was not discussed in literature before. All the related approaches presented in Section 8.1 do not consider the joint impact on workload burstiness, as they use isolated simulations.

Nevertheless, in performance prediction, often a rough estimation is sufficient. For example, one wants to check whether a system step lasts a few milliseconds or minutes, or whether process execution is impeded, because too many steps are assigned to the actors. For these purposes, approaches based on isolated simulations may be helpful, although they have limited prediction accuracy. Thus, BIIS is adequate for performance prediction in many cases. In cases where higher accuracy is needed, more integrated simulation approaches have to be applied. More integrated approaches are required, for example, if it cannot be clearly decided whether a requirement is satisfied, or in cases where high workload burstiness is expected.

There are several solution alternatives that promise to take into account the open issues of BIIS. In this section, three alternatives are discussed. First, the coupling of existing simulation tools is analyzed. Then, the transformation of BP design and IS design to an existing formalism for simulation is discussed.

Finally, the integration of BP design and IS design in a single simulation is described.

For comparing the solution alternatives, three criteria are applied. These criteria are derived from the discussion in the previous section.

I.   Modeling concepts: refers to relevant modeling concepts, especially time-variant workloads and suspendable resources, that have to be supported by the domain modeling languages and the corresponding simulators.

II. Workload burstiness: refers to the capability of the solution alternative to reflect the joint impact of BP resources and IS resources on workload burstiness.

III. Realizability: refers to the capability of the solution alternative to satisfy prerequisites necessary for realization.

In the following, the solution alternatives are discussed based on these criteria. The comparison is summarized in Table 8.1.

8.5.1 Coupling of Simulations

By coupling, we understand that two or more simulations interact during run-time. The coupling of multi-domain models for the usage in simulation is a common problem found in many engineering disciplines. For example, while evaluating a braking system for a car, several domain models, such as wheel model, road model, and air dynamics model must be considered in simulation (e.g., [Lin & Song (2011)]).

BPs, as well as ISs, are usually modeled as discrete-event systems, as described in Section 5.1.3. Relevant modeling concepts are considered by the corresponding domain-specific modeling languages. For example, [Herbst et al. (1997)] allows for the modeling of time-variant BP workload and suspendable resources. IS-specific modeling concepts are covered by the PCM, for example. Consequently, the coupling of simulations fulfills criterion I (modeling concepts).

In order to adequately reflect workload burstiness (criterion II), the BP simulation and the IS simulation have to interact at run-time, which is discussed in the following. Problems that have to be addressed to enable coupled simulation and possible solutions are analyzed.

Time management: One of the major problems when talking about interacting simulations is the synchronization of simulated time, also called time management. Both simulations have to agree on the same notion of time. Furthermore, at run-time, the simulations require a strict monotonic time; i.e., once a time point has passed, no event can be scheduled prior to this point. Hence, simulation time needs to be synchronized between the interacting simulations for time-consistent simulation results. This synchronization has to be conducted at least at every point in time, when an interaction is done. This leads to the problem that knowledge on when the next interaction will happen, is required a priori. For example, a BP instance reaches a system step at time t_n in the BP simulation, and is forwarded to the IS simulation. In the latter, the traversal of the internal actions of the system step starts at time t'_n, which is time-equivalent to t_n. As the simulations continue to run in parallel, one simulation might "overtake" the other simulation and lead to inconsistencies in terms of the simulation time. For example, when the IS simulation finishes simulating the system step instance at t'_{n+1}, the simulation time t_{n+1} might have already been passed in the BP simulation. Thus, the time inconsistencies lead to a wrong response time of the system step instance just simulated.

A solution to the problem is to synchronize simulation time on each time increment. This can be implemented in a coordinator component, which ensures unique time in both simulations by stopping and restarting single BP instances or entire simulations. Before one simulation is allowed to advance its simulation time, it has to wait until all other simulations also agreed on the time advance. A drawback of this solution is that the coordinator causes a lot of message exchanges between the simulations. Moreover, parallel execution of simulation is impaired.

More sophisticated approaches allow for higher parallelism by limiting synchronization to the points in time when interaction between simulation is happening. *Lower Bound on the Timestamp* (LBTS) [Liu (2011), Fujimoto (1990)] is a conservative synchronization approach, where each simulation has to specify the minimum time, until an outgoing interaction will occur. A coordinator component then calculates the next point in time when a synchronization is required. *Time Warp* [Liu (2011), Fujimoto (1990)] is an example for an optimistic synchronization approach. Optimistic time management approaches can further reduce communication overhead needed for synchronization. Thus, they may speed up simulations. However, they require that simulated actions can be undone when a time conflict is detected.

Interfacing between simulations: There are three issues regarding the interfacing between simulations for coupling at run-time. First, in order to enable simulations to interact, there must be a way to establish interaction points. Basically, interaction points define how one simulation can trigger events in the other simulation. Second, this interaction definition is usually accompanied by a mapping of model entities across the different domains. Third, information has to be transported across simulation borders. Therefore, a common understanding of parameters and values has to be established. In the context of this book, interaction can only occur when executing a system step instance in the BP simulation and when processing a service in the IS simulation. Moreover, the system steps in the BP design have to match system provided roles of the IS design. Furthermore, BP and IS simulation have to use a uniform notion for required parameters and return types of calls.

Many approaches that support the coupling of simulations are based on hierarchic composition [Zeigler (1984), Pidd & Castro (1998)]. This means, a simulation is constructed by combining smaller simulation parts. From this point of view, two simulations to be coupled can be seen as simulation components that are interacting over defined interfaces. These interfaces can be specified on different levels, according to the *Levels of Conceptual Interoperability Model* (LCIM) introduced by [Tolk & Muguira (2003)]. Interaction between simulations can then be realized using inter-process communication. In the context of this book, an interface between the BP simulation and the IS simulation could enable to consider the joint impact of BP resources and IS resources on workload burstiness.

A more sophisticated way of interfacing between simulations is described in the *High-Level Architecture* (HLA) standard [IEEE Std. 1516]. The HLA uses a separately defined object model to describe shared objects along with possible interactions. These descriptions are domain specific and have to be created in coordination with the simulations. Information exchange is done using a publish-subscribe pattern on the object model. This means, whenever a simulation creates or changes an object, other simulations can register to be informed on these changes. HLA provides a central component (Run-Time-Infrastructure, RTI), which controls the simulation execution and manages the data transfer between simulations. An advantage of the HLA approach is that simulations do not have to know each other, as the coupling is done using the shared object model. In the context of this book, the federate object model would include, for example, active BP instances, and interactions for starting and finishing IS simulation jobs. The IS simulation, for example, would then subscribe to the interaction to be notified when a BP instance in the BP simulation reaches a system step.

For both problems – time synchronization and interfacing – approaches are available, which promise to support the interaction between simulations at run-time. Consequently, the coupling of simulation can fulfill criterion II (workload burstiness).

Both problems regarding coupling require that existing simulations are adapted to meet the conceptual and technical prerequisites of the chosen coupling method. Modifications are not always feasible, especially in case of commercial software. Building upon third-party tools implies a strong dependency on the capabilities of these tools and on third-party support. In the context of this book, existing BP simulations as well as existing IS simulations would require major changes, as they typically neither have simulation components, interfaces, and time synchronization, nor support the HLA standard. A BP simulation tool that fulfills criterion I and could be adapted in an extent required for coupling was not readily available. Considering this, criterion III (realizability) cannot be fulfilled for the coupling of existing simulations without implementing an entire BP simulation. While implementing a BP simulation, coupling is not required any longer, because an integrated simulation (cf. Section 8.5.3) could be realized.

8.5.2 Transformation

By transformation, we understand the translation of elements of one modeling language into elements of another. A single target model, capable of representing both, BP design and IS design, would be used for simulation. In this way, the joint impact of BP resources and IS resources on workload burstiness can be reflected. Consequently, criterion II can be fulfilled.

Petri nets and queuing networks have a long tradition as a modeling language and formalism to describe ISs as well as BPs. They are popular, since they allow for the specification of complex system processes and BP workflows, and simultaneously allow for a fast analysis of their performance (e.g., [Kounev (2006)]). Since they are general-purpose formalisms, they do not provide modeling elements for representing constructs specific to ISs or BPs like software components or human actors. There are transformations for translating IS designs to the *Layered Queueing Networks* (LQNs) [Rolia & Sevcik (1995)] and the *Queueing Petri Nets* (QPNs) [Bause (1993)] formalisms. The transformations and corresponding formalisms were successfully applied, for example in [Kounev & Dutz (2009)] and [Koziolek & Reussner (2008)]. There are also approaches to translate BP designs to the LQN or QPN formalism, [Graupner et al. (2008)] for example. However, current transformation approaches for ISs, e.g as described by [Meier et al. (2011), Meier (2010)], have strong restrictions on supported modeling concepts, such as parametric dependencies, stochastic expressions, loop iterations, and mapping of synchronized forked behavior. Moreover, they exhibit lower accuracy, compared to dedicated simulation tools. The restrictions of transformation approaches for ISs are expected to apply to transformation approaches for BPs, too, since they rely on similar modeling concepts. A compatible transformation for BPs supporting all the modeling concepts proposed in Section 5.3 was not readily available. No support for time-variant workload is integrated in widespread LQN and QPN simulators (e.g., lqsim [Franks (2011)] or QPME [Kounev et al. (2011)]). Criterion III (realizability) cannot be fulfilled without major modification to transformation and simulation approaches. The feasibility of these modifications is doubtful.

Moreover, LQNs as well as QPNs do not have support for modeling concepts, such as suspendable resources, and complex scheduling strategies related to them. Consequently, criterion I also cannot be fulfilled.

8.5.3 Integrated Simulation

By integration, we understand that BPs and ISs are part of the same model or components of a modular model, which is used for simulation. In the PCM, IS designs can be represented which are then used for automated performance prediction. In contrast to other software architecture simulators, Palladio provides comprehensive modeling and simulation capabilities. Palladio seems to be an adequate foundation to be extended by BP modeling concepts (such as described in Section 5.3) to enable an integrated simulation. The PCM is already structured in several partial models on different layers, such as hardware layer or software component layer. Thus, the PCM can easily be extended by a business process model and an organization environment model that cover all required BP modeling concepts. Consequently, criterion I can be fulfilled.

An integrated simulation seems to be a promising approach, as there are several analogies when abstracting from the different semantics of BP simulation and IS simulation. Both kinds of simulation

i.   can be built upon queuing network theory,
ii. simulate the utilization of resources (human actor resources or hardware resources),
iii. use a specification of a sequence of actions to be processed by the resources (either in the form of a BP model or in the form of an IS usage profile),
iv. use hierarchical compositions of actions,
v.   use a specification of workload, and
vi. acquire and release shared passive resources.

In contrast to the coupling of two simulations via an interface, a unified simulation can predicts performance measures of an integrated BP and IS model. Thus, there is no message exchange between simulations required. An integrated simulation enables the reflection of the joint impact on workload burstiness, since both BP resources, as well as IS resources, are considered in simulation. Consequently, criterion II can be fulfilled.

Table 8.1: Comparison of Solution Alternatives

Criterion/ Alternative	BIIS	Coupling	Transfor- mation	Integrated Simulation
Modeling concept	no	yes	no	yes
Workload burstiness	no	yes	yes	yes
Realizability	yes	no	no	yes

A lot of the existing simulation infrastructure can be reused or easily be adapted for the new BP elements, since actors and hardware resources often behave similarly, while processing jobs. Complex scheduling strategies of human actors can be realized building upon existing Palladio concepts. Consequently, criterion III can be fulfilled.

8.5.4 Comparison

The discussion in the previous sections is summarized in Table 8.1. The cells represent whether a criterion is expected to be fulfilled or not (yes/no). The table clearly shows that an integrated simulation is the best alternative, since only the integrated simulation fulfills all three criteria.

8.6 Summary

In this chapter, the state of the art in simulating the mutual performance impact between BPs and ISs was discussed. Analyzing existing approaches showed that they use BP simulation and IS simulation in isolation. Since existing approaches were not described in sufficient detail, the approach BIIS was developed to examine benefits and limitation of isolated simulation. The examination showed that workload burstiness is not adequately reflected using isolated simulations. Three solution alternatives were discussed to adequately represent workload burstiness in simulation, namely the coupling of simulations, the transformation of IS designs and BP designs into a common formalism (LQN or QPN) used for simulation, and the integration of IS designs and BP designs in a single simulation. The discussion showed that the integrated simulation is the best solution, since this avoids open topics in realizing simulation coupling as well as limited expressiveness of the formalisms. Moreover, the integrated simulation enables to build upon existing simulation infrastructure of the Palladio tool chain.

9 Extending Palladio by Business Process Simulation Concepts to Enable an Integrated Simulation

> Beauty will result from the form and the correspondence of the whole, with respect to the several parts, of the parts with regard to each other, and of these again to the whole; that the structure may appear an entire and complete body, wherein each member agrees with the other, and all necessary to compose what you intend to form.

— Andrea Palladio, 1508–1580 —

For integrating BP and IS simulation, this book builds upon the Palladio approach. While Palladio already provides adequate means for modeling and simulation of IS designs, this work extends Palladio by modeling and simulation of BP designs. The meta-model extension was already presented in Section 5.3. This chapter presents the approach IntBIIS, by discussing the simulator extension to handle BPs. First, a scheduling policy for human actors is presented in Section 9.1. Then, the impact of time-variant workload on steady-state analysis is discussed in Section 9.2. The simulator extension for integrating BP and IS simulation is described in Section 9.3. Afterwards, Section 9.4 describes how workload burstiness is reflected in the integrated simulation. The chapter concludes with a summary and discussion of future work in Section 9.5.

9.1 Scheduling Policy for Human Actors

As argued in Section 7.4, several aspects of job processing by human actors are comparable to job processing by hardware resources. Consequently, in many cases, human actors can be treated as processing resources like a CPU in simulation. Both resource types offer a certain service to their environment, namely they both process step instances from their waiting queue. Each enqueued step instance carries a demand and lines up one after another in the queue, when the resource is busy. The resource processes the demands induced by the instances in its waiting queue following a certain scheduling policy. However, the scheduling policies commonly applied for simulating hardware resources do not satisfy the requirements for simulating human actors. In particular, first-come, first-served (FCFS) or processor sharing (PS) assume continuous operation without interruptions, which does not take into account suspension of the resource, for example, to reflect lunch breaks or non-working time in simulation. Moreover, in the business context, it is common that some BPs or single actor steps are more important to the organization or their customers than others. Thus, they get preferential treatment before others, or may not be interrupted by a break or non-working time. For example, a BP that provides a service to a customer may get preferential treatment before an intra-organizational management process, due to requirements of the customer on fast service delivery. For these reasons, a new scheduling policy specialized for human actors was developed. It supports suspension of resources and provides preferential treatment of non-interruptible actor steps (having high priority) before interruptible actor steps (having low priority).

The capability of an actor step to delay the suspension of an actor resource is initially independent of its priority. This means that an actor step might receive preferential treatment before other steps, but might not delay the suspension of a resource, or vice versa. In established BP simulators (e.g., [Herbst et al. (1997)]), however, both factors (delay and priority) are considered in conjunction. With regard to the validation of our prediction method IntBIIS in Section 10.5.1, where prediction results are compared to results of an existing simulator, we decided to consider both factors in conjunction in analogy to existing BP simulators. The advantage of an eased validation bears the disadvantage that the factors cannot be investigated independently. For the process analyses conducted in this book, there is no need to consider both factors independent of each other. Considering the factors independent of each other can be easily realized, if required in the future, by adapting the proposed scheduling policy.

The scheduling policy for actor resources processing actor steps is specified by the following rules:

1. Non-interruptible (NI) actor steps have priority over interruptible (I) actors steps, meaning that no instance of an I-step may be processed by an actor resource when there is an instance of a NI-step waiting to be processed.

2. Actor step instances lined-up in the queues are processed in FIFO order, as long as the aforementioned priority condition is not violated.

3. Whenever the actor resource is about to stop processing (e.g., due to an imminent break), the execution of an I-step instance is immediately interrupted while a NI-step instance is still processed completely, even if this means working overtime.

4. If a new NI-step instance is being enqueued while the actor resource is about to stop processing, it is still handled completely before the actor resource is actually suspended. I-step instances, in contrast, do not delay the time until the actor resource stops processing.

Distinguishing NI-steps (high priority) and I-steps (low priority) affects the order of step instances in the waiting queue, since the actor resource processes its waiting queue in FIFO order. A high-priority step instance is always processed before a low priority step instance, even if it joins the waiting queue after the low priority one. This is in contrast to regular PCM processing resources, where all the jobs lined up in their waiting queues have the same priority. Considering different priorities would result in re-arranging the waiting queue at worst each time a new step instance is enqueued, since NI-step instances have to be processed first. Frequent re-arranging of long waiting queues may reduce simulation speed. Therefore, two separate waiting queues were introduced for each actor resource, as depicted in Figure 9.1. One waiting queue lines up NI-step instances and the other waiting queue lines up I-step instances. This allows for separated treatment of both kinds of steps. I-step instances are only processed by the actor resource, if the waiting queue for NI-step instances is empty.

From an external perspective, however, the two waiting queues act as a single waiting queue – they keep pending actor step instances. Thus, in the

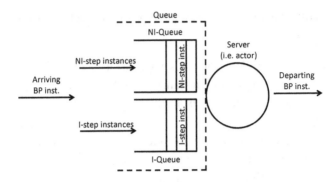

Figure 9.1: Actor Resource

following, the singular form is used by speaking about the waiting queue of an actor resource.

In order to manage the suspension and resuming of an actor resource, it is described as a finite-state automaton [Hopcroft et al. (2006)] by different states and transitions between them. Using a finite-state automaton has several advantages over a strict functional behavior specification. A finite-state automaton allows for a clear distinction of behavior, since each state can be considered in isolation and there is a distinct definition of state transitions. Consequently, mixing the behavior of different states is prevented. Upcoming events can switch the behavior easily by switching the corresponding state. Moreover, a finite-state automaton is easily extensible and adaptable by adding, changing, or removing single states without affecting the entire automaton. At each time point in simulation, the actor resource is in one of the states RunningState, SuspendingState, or SuspendedState. Figure 9.2 depicts the finite-state automaton for actor resources as a state diagram [UML 2.0 (2005)]. The resource initially starts in SuspendedState and resumes to RunningState, as soon as the current simulation time point lies within a working period. In the RunningState, the resource processes the step instances from its waiting queue. If the simulation time exceeds a working period, the resource stops processing (SuspendedState), unless there is an unhandled NI-step instance left or currently enqueued. Since NI-steps delay the suspension of the resource, an additional state (SuspendingState) is required, which represents the resource before an imminent break. This means, the working

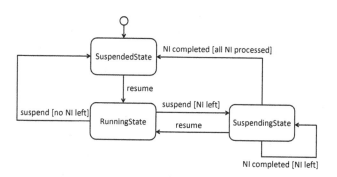

Figure 9.2: States and Transitions for Actor Resources

period is already exceeded, but the resource is still busy by processing an NI-step instance. It will be suspended if all the pending NI-step instances are processed. A resource in SuspendedState or SuspendingState is resumed again (RunningState), at the beginning of the next working period.

The proposed scheduling policy was implemented for actor resources of the integrated simulation described in Section 9.3. Several variants of the proposed scheduling policy are imaginable, such as a separate consideration of delay and priority (as discussed above), or the specification of the priority by an integer value (e.g., from 0 to 3). These variants can be implemented in the future by adapting the actor resource and finite automaton described in this section.

9.2 Business Process Workload

According to [Law & Kelton (2000)], two types of simulation can be distinguished depending on whether there is an obvious way to determine the length of simulation runs – *terminating simulation* and *nonterminating simulation*. For a terminating simulation there is a natural event E that determines the length of each simulation run. E may be specified in several forms depending on the objectives of the corresponding simulation study, such as $E = \{1000\ cars\ have\ been\ created\}$ or $E = \{one\ year\ have\ been\ simulated\}$. For a nonterminating simulation there is no terminating event E. Typically, the simulation is stopped when steady-state with regard to the requested performance measures is reached. A simulation run is said to be in *steady-state* with regard to a certain performance measure, if the performance measure becomes stable in the long run [Law & Kelton (2000)]. This means that the underlying probability distribution does not change any longer when simulation time approaches infinity. Therefore, steady-state analyses are conducted for gathering performance measures with sufficient statistical confidence.

A fundamental property of BPs is workloads varying over time. Consequently, workload has to be considered as a function of time when studying how performance measures evolve as simulation time advances. However, Palladio is oriented towards steady-state analyses, where the focus is on predicting certain performance measures assuming time-invariant workload as simulation time approaches infinity. Therefore, the PCM is extended by time-variant workloads, as described in Section 5.3.3, to reflect changed intensities of BP execution over the course of a day, a month, or even a year and more. Changing workload intensities over simulation time could easily affect the stability of performance measures (i.e., they may no longer follow a stable probability distribution). This is one of the reasons why the original PCM keeps workloads fixed. A side-effect from time-variant workloads is that traditional steady-state analyses of simulated performance measures are often not viable. Analysis techniques known from terminating simulations can be applied, instead, to gather performance measures with sufficient statistical confidence.

If the workload is specified in terms of repeating periods (e.g., when assuming that weeks do not differ in their workload pattern), a special case of steady-state analysis can be conducted, which involves so-called *steady-state cycle parameters* [Law & Kelton (2000)]. A performance measure is said to be a *steady-state parameter* if it is a characteristic of the steady-state distribution of an output stochastic process $Y_1, Y_2, ...,$ where Y is a random variable [Law & Kelton (2000)]. If Y has a steady-state distribution, then the steady-state mean $v = E(Y)$ might be estimated. Given that the time axis is divided into equal-length, continuous time intervals called *cycles*. For example, a cycle is an eight-hour shift. A steady-state cycle parameter is a steady-state parameter of the appropriate stochastic cycle process $Y_1^c, Y_2^c, ...$

The following example is taken from [Law & Kelton (2000)]. Given the customer service process at a call center of an airline. The arrival rate of calls (i.e., BP instances) varies with the time of a day and day of a week, but it is assumed that the pattern of arrival rates is the same from week to week. Let D_i be the delay experienced by the ith arriving call. The stochastic process $D_1, D_2, \ldots$ does not have a steady-state distribution in this example. Let D_i^c be the average delay over the ith week. Then, the steady-state expected average delay over a week, $v^c = E(D^c)$, can be estimated, which is a steady-state cycle parameter.

In the BP context, workload is often described in terms of repeating periods (e.g., per day, per weak, or the like). Process workload is generated by humans, e.g., by placing an order or calling the airline. The daily life of humans often relies on repeating pattern. For example, a working day of a human comprises eight hours from 9 a.m. to 5 p.m. and there is a lunch break from 12 o'clock to 1 p.m. A week comprises five working days and two non-working days. One human might place orders for the next week, every Monday at 10 a.m. Another human may place the next week's order on Tuesday at 3 p.m. All humans that order goods place their order at a certain time on a working day, but no orders will be placed in lunch breaks or on the weekend. The process workload results from aggregating the workload generated by all humans that trigger the BP. Consequently, for many BPs, also workload relies on repeating pattern. In those cases, steady-state cycle parameters are an appropriate means for BP steady-state analysis. If process workload does not rely on repeating periods, terminating simulation with a fixed end event E has to be applied. The confidence of terminating simulation depends on the adequate selection of the end event. The end event has to be selected in a way that a sound basis for statistical comparisons is ensured. This means that a sufficient number of BP instances have been observed before the end event is reached.

9.3 Simulator Extensions

In order to simulate the mutual impact between BPs and ISs, the event-driven PCM simulator EventSim [Merkle & Henss (2011)] was extended[1]. EventSim was specifically developed for extensibility, which is especially

---

[1] The Palladio extension is available online http://sdqweb.ipd.kit.edu/IntBIIS

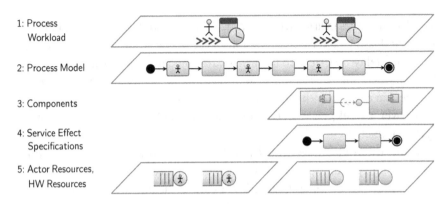

Figure 9.3: Extended Simulation Layers

reflected by the concept of traversal strategies. A traversal strategy encapsulates the simulation behavior for a specific type of action, an ActorStep for example. In this way, the existing simulation semantics for PCM models can be easily modified or extended by registering an adapted or newly created traversal strategy with the simulator. This allows for a better extensibility, compared to Palladio's reference simulator SimuCom. Furthermore, EventSim was shown to be faster and more resource-efficient in several scenarios, compared to SimuCom [Merkle & Henss (2011)]. Simulation speed and resource-efficiency are important in the BP context, since long time-frames are simulated, which often span months, or years, or more.

Inspired by SimuCom, EventSim simulates the operation of an IS at different layers. For simulating BPs, existing layers were extended and new layers were introduced. This is illustrated in Figure 9.3, where a stickman symbol indicates layers and elements introduced in the context of this book. The remaining layers and elements are also part of Palladio's reference simulator. A run of the integrated simulation starts at the topmost layer with simulating time-variant business process workloads. To each BP within a business process model, a workload specification is associated. For each workload specification, the newly developed ProcessWorkloadGenerator spawns a new BP instance, whenever the inter-arrival time specified in the current process trigger period has been passed. If the presumed start time point of the BP instance lies between two process trigger periods, the BP instance is spawned at the beginning of the following period. Each BP instance is then simulated individually by traversing the corresponding action chain specified in the business process model (layer 2). When a BP instance arrives at an action, basically two cases can be distinguished: (i) the simulation encounters an actor step, or (ii) it encounters a system step (i.e., an EntryLevelSystemCall). For the first case, a new traversal strategy was developed, as described hereafter, while the existing traversal strategy is applied in the second case.

In case (i), a suitable human actor is requested (layer 5, left). Suitable means that the actor owns the required organizational role, but also that s/he is able to perform the actor step, as soon as possible. Thus, when multiple actors are available, the actor resource with the shortest waiting queue in terms of pending demand is selected. Thereby, actor resources currently not suspended are preferred. Also, if all actor resources are temporarily suspended (e.g., due to a lunch break), still those with the shortest waiting queue is selected. There are several alternatives to the selection of the actor resource with the shortest waiting queue. The actor resource may be selected randomly. However, work would be distributed randomly. The actor resource with the largest pending working time before suspension could be selected. If all the actor resources are currently suspended, the actor resource who will continue working next may be selected. However, work would accumulate at that resource. Selecting the actor resource with the shortest waiting queue will lead to a balanced dispersion of work, because, after each assignment of work, another actor resource may have the shortest waiting queue. The actor step is instantiated and enqueued. If the selected actor resource is already occupied with another actor step instance, or is temporarily suspended, a certain waiting time is induced. The waiting time not only occurs for the actor step instance, but, in particular, also for the enclosing BP instance. This means that the enclosing BP instance is blocked, until the actor resource is ready to perform.

In case (ii), the system step is instantiated. Resource demands are not issued directly by the system step instance, but emerge as the system request propagates through software components (layer 3), their service effect specifications (layer 4), down to hardware resources (layer 5, right). Like actor resources, hardware resources may block a request by waiting in its waiting queue, leading to a block of the enclosing BP instance.

Moreover, the BP instance may arrive at a sequence of actions for which a particular passive organizational resource is required. The sequence is specified by an AcquireDeviceResource action and a ReleaseDeviceResource action. Using separate actions for acquiring and releasing device resources allows for applying the traversal strategy concept of EventSim. For each action, the corresponding simulation behavior is encapsulated in a traversal strategy. Thus, in contrast to modeling alternatives, e.g., specifying the amount of required device resources as an attribute of ActorStep, this allows for a clear distinction of simulation behavior for processing actor steps and for managing device resources. Device resources are requested via the traversal strategy for AcquireDeviceResource actions that checks whether the requested amount of resources of the corresponding type is available. If available, the requested amount of resources is allocated to the BP instance for processing the sequence of actions. If the amount of requested resources exceeds the available resources, the requesting BP instance is blocked, until the resources are available. After the sequence has been traversed, the passive resources are released again via the traversal strategy for ReleaseDeviceResource actions.

EventSim adheres to the *event scheduling simulation paradigm* [Law & Kelton (2000)]. Events can be fired, deferred, and removed at an arbitrary point in simulation time. This allows for a flexible consideration of changing conditions in simulation. Event scheduling is a useful means for interrupting the processing of I-step instances, due to newly enqueued NI-step instances or suspension of the resources. Thus, it is applied for realizing the scheduling policy for actor resources. An alternative is the representation of each BP instance by a separate thread of simulation, as it is applied in SimuCom. SimuCom adheres to the *process interaction simulation paradigm* [Banks et al. (2009)]. The single threads of simulation are started, stopped, and restarted to reflect changing conditions in simulation. This would also be required for the newly introduced interruption of step instances and suspension of resources. However, the process interaction simulation paradigm, e.g., as described by [Banks et al. (2009)], is known for hampering performance and scalability of the simulation. Moreover, the Java implementation of SimuCom adds another drawback. Each thread of simulation is represented by a preemptive Java thread, which results in an uncontrolled execution order of the threads of simulation. Thus, costly synchronization between Java threads is required to regain control of the execution order of the threads of simulation [Merkle & Henss (2011)]. Event scheduling enables to reduce the need for synchronization. Each thread of simulation is broken down to a number of events and then handled as a sequence of events. Present events schedule other events to occur at a later point in time in simulation. Consequently, the single events can be processed one after another in a single Java thread, which allows for a more efficient simulation.

Two new events were introduced – ProcessingFinishedEvent and SuspendEvent. The ProcessingFinishedEvent indicates that the processing of a particular actor step instance has been finished. Thus, the actor step instance is discarded from the corresponding waiting queue (either NI-queue or I-queue). As specified in the scheduling policy, a newly enqueued NI-step instance interrupts an I-step instance currently processed. This defers the point in time at which the processing of the I-step instance is finished. Consequently, the ProcessFinishedEvent of the I-step instance is removed. Then, the NI-step instance receives service and a new ProcessFinishedEvent is scheduled to occur at the point in time the NI-step instance is expected to be processed. When the processing of the NI-step instance is finished, the pending I-step instance receives service, unless there is another NI-step instance enqueued in the meantime. A new ProcessFinishedEvent is scheduled to occur at the point in time the remaining demand of the I-step instance is expected to be processed. In contrast, if another NI-step instance is enqueued, it receives service and a ProcessFinishedEvent for the NI-step instance is scheduled. The SuspendEvent indicates that a particular actor resource intends to suspend. A NI-step instance delays the suspension if currently processed or enqueued (cf. SuspendingState). Thus, the suspension of the actor resource is deferred by the time required to process the pending NI-step instance. This means that the current SuspendEvent is removed. An updated SuspendEvent is scheduled to occur at the point in time the processing of the NI-step instance is expected to be finished. If there are further NI-step instances enqueued in the meantime, the event is deferred again. In case of an I-step instance currently processed or enqueued when an actor resource intends to suspend, the SuspendEvent is not deferred (cf. SuspendedState). Instead, the ProcessingFinishedEvent of the I-step instance is removed. When the actor resource is resumed again at the beginning of the next working period (cf. RunningState), the next event is scheduled. Thus, the interrupted I-step instance is continued, unless there is a NI-step instance currently enqueued. For continuing the I-step instance, a new ProcessingFinishedEvent is scheduled to occur at the point in time the remaining demand of the I-step instance is expected to be processed.

The existing EventSim sensor framework was extended by sensors to determine BP-related performance measures. The extension comprises sensors for execution time and actor resource utilization. For each actor step instance, the current simulation time is recorded when it is enqueued in the waiting queue of an actor resource. When the actor resource completed the processing of the actor step instance, the current simulation time is recorded again. The difference in time represents the execution time of the corresponding actor step instance. When a BP instance starts traversing an activity, the current simulation time is recorded. When the BP instance has completely traversed the activity, the time is recorded again. The difference in time represents the execution time required by the BP instance for traversing the corresponding activity. The execution time required by a BP instance, to traverse an entire BP, is determined the same way. For actor resources, the waiting queue length is observed whenever the queue state changes. The queue state changes when a new actor step instance is enqueued, or when the resource completed the processing of an actor step instance. Moreover, the time the resource spends in a certain state is recorded. The actor resource utilization (busy/idle ratio) is then calculated from the proportion of the time the waiting queue was empty, to the time at least one pending actor step instance was observed. In addition, the proportion of time the resource was in a certain state is determined in relation to the overall simulation time. The EventSim sensor framework already covers sensors for calculating the response time of system step instances and the utilization of hardware resources. Owing to the extension, the simulation is capable to predict all performance measures introduced in Section 5.4.1. Based on the predicted performance measures, design alternatives can be compared and verified against requirements.

9.4 Representation of Workload Burstiness

The integrated simulation method IntBIIS is capable of reflecting workload burstiness, as described in Section 7.4, due to the scheduling policy and traversal strategies proposed. The simulation considers the BP impact on hardware resource waiting queues, as well as the IS impact on actor resource waiting queues. In dependence upon the individual hardware resource utilization, each system step within the BP design causes the distance between concurrent BP instances to grow or to shrink. This is handled by existing traversal strategies for system steps and their internal actions, as well as by scheduling policies for hardware resources. Likewise, each actor step affects the distance between concurrent BP instances. The proposed traversal strategy for actor steps selects a suitable actor resource for processing a certain actor step instance. An actor resource affects workload burstiness by blocking actor step instances in its waiting queues, if the resource is already occupied. The proposed scheduling policy specifies the order in which an actor resource processes the step instances from its waiting queue. Consequently, the scheduling policy affects the distance between the enclosing BP instances. Similar to system steps, each actor step within the BP design causes the distance between BP instances to grow or to shrink, depending on the individual actor resource utilization. This applies, if all step instances to be processed by a certain actor are of the same type (NI or I). Additionally, priorized processing of NI-step instances before I-step instances affects the distance. For example, a NI-step instance "overtakes" an I-step instance to be processed by the same actor resource, due to its higher priority. "Overtaking" means that the NI-step instance joins the waiting queue after the I-step instance, but is processed at first. Consequently, also the enclosing BP instance "overtakes" the other.

Moreover, the impact of suspended actor resources on the distance between BP instances is considered in simulation. The proposed scheduling policy manages when an actor resource is suspended and when it is resumed again. Consequently, it manages which and when the actor step instances allocated to the actor resource are blocked. Being blocked, the distance of the enclosing BP instances to preceding BP instances that were not blocked, may increase, until the resource is resumed again. Moreover, actor step instances may accumulate in the waiting queue of the resource, while it is suspended, and may then processed shortly after each other, when the resource is resumed. This may decrease the distance between the enclosing BP instances and result in bursts.

Exhausted passive resources have the same effect, since they temporarily block BP instances, until the requested amount of resources becomes available. For device resources, this is controlled by the proposed traversal strategies for AcquireDeviceResource actions and ReleaseDeviceResource actions, respectively. If device resources are exhausted, BP instances arriving at an AcquireDeviceResource action are blocked. Thus, the distance to preceding BP instances that were not blocked increases, until the requested amount of resources is available. Likewise, passive resources within the IS affect the distance between BP instances. Moreover, if passive resources (both, device resources and passive IS resources) are once acquired in bursts, they also may be released in bursts and acquired in bursts again by waiting BP instances. Consequently, the sequence of actions for which the passive resource is required, may exhibit high workload burstiness, caused by acquiring and releasing passive resources in bursts.

In consequence, occasional bursts may arise over simulation time, leading to temporary overload conditions of hardware resources, as well as actor resources. Additionally, occasional bursts may lead to situations in which passive resources are temporarily exhausted, because for a certain period of time, more passive resources are requested than released again. Both, – overloaded processing resources and exhausted passive resources – (a) affect performance measures, since they cause waiting times, due to blocked instances and increased queue lengths, and (b) again affect workload burstiness. This can be reflected by IntBIIS, due to the integrated simulation of BPs and ISs.

The prediction methods BIIS and IntBIIS are demonstrated, based on the order picking process, in the following chapter. The feasibility and practicability of the prediction methods are examined. BIIS prediction results are compared to IntBIIS prediction results, in order to validate which of the proposed methods better resembles measurements from reality.

9.5 Summary and Future Work

In this chapter, the novel approach IntBIIS for the integrated analysis of BPs and ISs using simulation was presented. A holistic simulation was proposed that combines performance prediction on business process level and software architecture level. In contrast to existing approaches, workload burstiness is reflected adequately in simulation, since both, the BP impact as well as the IS impact on workload burstiness, is considered. The approach builds upon the Palladio tool chain to implement the integrated simulation of BPs and ISs. In this way, the alignment of BP designs and IS designs can be supported by comparing the predicted performance measures to requirements. Moreover, design alternatives can be assessed by comparing the predicted performance measures. Further BP-related adaptations of the PCM and the integrated simulation tool support are possible, which is discussed in the following.

Mapping the BP workload to a series of non-overlapping process trigger periods, as described in Section 5.3.3, is one established way to reflect time-variant workloads in BP simulation (e.g., [Herbst et al. (1997)]). This is feasible for a variety of application scenarios, as described in this book, for example, the decomposition of a day in several shifts and breaks. However, in scenarios with high workload burstiness at the process starting position, this approach results in a large number of small process trigger periods. Although high workload burstiness at the process starting position could be handled by the proposed approach, as demonstrated on the order picking process in Section 10.3, other approaches could reduce modeling effort. Another way is to represent workload as a time series of BP instance arrival rates. As discussed in Section 5.3.3, time series are not suitable for initial design analysis, since they reflect measurements in reality, which are often not available, and are hard for humans to read, to specify, and to adapt. However, in cases of high workload burstiness at the process starting position, they may reduce effort for workload specification. Moreover, time series can be decomposed, which may allow for further analysis of BP workloads. In the future, time series may be introduced, in addition to process trigger periods, as further type of workload specification for application scenarios, where workload could be exactly measures, in advance.

BP instances may be blocked in the waiting queues of processing resources before receiving service and due to limited capacity of passive resources, which is described in this thesis. Furthermore, BP instances may also be blocked due to missing information objects required for processing an actor step, which may affect the BP performance. For example, for taking items out of the store, one has to know which items are required. This may be described in an information object called order list. The items cannot be taken out of the store, until the order list is available. Consequently, the corresponding BP instances are blocked. Information object availability was not addressed in this thesis, because this thesis is focused on performance prediction, building upon concepts from queuing network theory. Thus, it is investigated how a certain workload specification affects the performance measures of a given BP and IS design. Information object availability, however, is not dependent on the workload specification. A missing object may block a BP instance, even if there are no concurrent BP instances at the resources. Mostly, information dependency is represented in the control flow between steps, meaning that the input objects of an actor step is the output of a predecessor actor step. If the information object is provided from an external organization unit, e.g., the order list comes from another department that had checked the list for item availability before, it may not be available when required. In this case, it might be interesting to include information availability in design evaluation in the future. In order to address this open topic, the business process model has to be extended by elements representing information objects, as well as by input and output relations between steps and activities and even BPs.

The BP model elements proposed in this thesis extend a monolithic meta-model. Likewise, the BP-specific simulation behavior is an extension to a monolithic simulator. A better modularization of the PCM and related simulators is a topic of future work. This is especially required when including further quality aspects in the future, which is discussed in more detail in Section 11.4.1.

In Section 10.5.2, this thesis argues that indicators for the practicability of the integrated tool support from third-party users' view can be transfered from prior validations of the original Palladio tooling. Third party users are those who were not involved in the development of the tooling and the underlying concepts, and are not dependent on the developers. In the future, further investigation on the practicability of the BP-specific parts of the tool support are necessary. Controlled experiments involving third-party users (e.g., students) seem to be appropriate means for further investigations. Moreover, extensions to the usability and functionality of the integrated tooling are topics of future work. This may include the extension to existing graphical model editors for the new model elements. Usage-specific views may be specified to keep track of large models. For example, model elements for acquiring and releasing device resources may be hidden, when focusing on actor steps and system steps. A simulation suite that allows for specifying a series of experiments while single properties of the model are changed from experiment to experiment, is another possible extension.

The PerOpteryx approach [Koziolek et al. (2011)] supports the optimization of component-based software architectures for several quality aspects in relation to costs. It automatically improves PCM instances for performance by using a multi-objective evolutionary algorithm. By exploring the design space of an IS design it generates Pareto-optimal design candidates. The design space determines which parts of a design are allowed to be adapted. PerOpteryx may be extended for BP design space exploration building upon the integrated simulation approach proposed in this thesis. On the one hand, this may support the optimization of a BP design without taking into account the IS. On the other hand, this may support alignment, by including the mutual impact between BP and IS in design optimization. Based on a manually created overall design of BP and IS, the automatic variation of the design components, with respect to quality aspects and costs for realization, would be enabled. By automatic exploration of diverse variants, it can be investigated which quality can be achieved under which effort. Moreover, automatic variations of workloads or resource allocation (human resources as well as hardware resources) supports scalability exploration.

With increasing number of possible design variations, the exploration of the entire design space is no longer feasible. The development of suitable meta-heuristics for reducing the number of design alternatives, without loss of expressibility, is another topic of future work.

The PCM tool chain provides transformations of PCM instances to the LQN and QPN formalism, which enable a faster analysis of the models, compared to corresponding PCM simulators. Currently, a compatible transformation for BPs covering the model elements introduced in this thesis is not available. Moreover, related simulators currently do not support time-variant workloads. The PCM transformations and dedicated simulators may be extended by the new model elements in the future. This would allow to benefit from the efficiency of the formalisms in at least certain scenarios, even if LQNs and QPNs do not have support for complex scheduling strategies (e.g., for suspendable resources), as discussed in Section 8.5.2.

10 Validation

> In questions of science, the authority of a thousand is
> not worth the humble reasoning of a single individual.
>
> — *Galileo Galilei, 1564–1642* —

Frequently, prediction methods are only applied to fictitious examples, because their application to a real-life example, in practice, is a challenging task. Thus, there is little documented experience in applying BP simulation or IS simulation methods in practice. [Melao & Pidd (2003)] analyzed several case studies concerned with BP simulation. They concluded, "little is known about the actual practice of business process simulation". [Koziolek et al. (2013)] provided an overview of recent performance prediction case studies and experience reports related to software architecture. They concluded that most studies reported on prediction accuracy, but not on the effort required to achieve this accuracy. None of the case studies and experience reports found report on the acceptance of prediction methods from the practitioner's point of view. Moreover, decisions required for applying the methods in practice, as well as experiences made, are rarely included in the publications. Limited experience in applying prediction methods results in uncertainties related to:

- whether the required input information can be gathered in sufficient quantities and quality in practice.
- how much effort is required to gather the information in practice.
- how much effort is required to apply the approaches in practice.
- whether the approaches can be applied in practice as described.
- whether the approach provides the promised results with the promised prediction accuracy in practice.

These uncertainties result in limited willingness, or even reluctance, of practitioners, to apply prediction methods in the design phase, even though they could benefit significantly, e.g., by saving time and costs caused by rework in subsequent development phases. This chapter presents the results of a real-life case study to address the uncertainties. It describes the validation of the prediction methods BIIS and IntBIIS presented in Chapter 8 and Chapter 9. The validation is based on the order picking process – a real-life example introduced in Chapter 6. Section 10.1 specifies different types of validation for prediction methods. The research questions and hypothesis used in the validation are listen in Section 10.2. Decisions and workarounds required to apply BIIS and IntBIIS in practice are discussed in Section 10.3. The validation of the feasibility of BIIS and its acceptance from practitioners' point of view is described in Section 10.4. The validation of the feasibility of IntBIIS and the practicability of the integrated tool support is presented in Section 10.5. The chapter concludes with a discussion of threats to validity in Section 10.6 and a summary of the validation results in Section 10.7.

10.1 Types of Validation

[Böhme & Reussner (2008)] introduce three types of validation for prediction methods – metric validation (Type I), applicability validation (Type II), and benefit validation (Type III). [Martens (2007)], [Becker (2008)], and [Koziolek (2008)] distinguish the three types while validating Palladio. [Koziolek (2008)] adapted the specifications of the types as addressed below. In the context of this book, we extend the specifications by [Böhme & Reussner (2008)], which is described in the following.

10.1.1 Type I: Feasibility

Type I (Feasibility) studies validate the prediction accuracy of a method by comparing the prediction results to reference values (e.g., measurements). Therefore, an implementation of the prediction method is required for Type I studies. In this book, Type I studies also include the validation of the feasibility of the method application. This means whether preconditions for the application of the method can be met, and whether the method provides the intended output.

This type of study is conducted to validate whether BIIS and IntBIIS yield accurate results, under the assumption that their inputs were accurate (cf. [Koziolek (2008)]). The prediction results of the two prediction methods are compared to values measured in reality, as well as to results of the other method. Prior to this, it is investigated whether all the input entities required to apply BIIS and IntBIIS can be gathered. Input entities are elements of the PCM (inclusive extension), as introduced in Section 5.2 and 5.3, or elements of similar meta-models (cf. [Herbst et al. (1997)]). In addition to impact prediction, it is also examined whether the methods are able to support the activities decision support and requirements verification introduced in Section 8.2.

10.1.2 Type II: Practicability

Type II (Practicability) studies validate the practicability of a method, when it is applied by the target users, instead of the method developers. Type II studies investigate the maturity of the tool support and the interpretability of the results delivered by the tool support [Koziolek (2008)]. If humans are involved in data gathering, Type II studies can be conducted as an experiment or case study including human participants [Böhme & Reussner (2008)].

In this book, three aspects regarding practicability are observed.

- Acceptance from the viewpoint of potential method users and method participants is examined in a real-life case study. Humans involved in the case study are called subjects in the following. Method users comprise the subjects that perform the approach, as well as the subjects that use or benefit from the results of the approach. Method participants comprise the subjects that were consulted to gather input entities required to perform the approach.

- The effort for eliciting input entities as well as the effort for applying the prediction methods is investigated in the case study as an aspect of acceptance.

- The practicability of the tool support is discussed. Therefore, we build upon prior empirical validations [Martens (2007)].

10.1.3 Type III: Effort-Benefit

Type III (Effort-Benefit) studies analyze the effort-benefit ratio. A model-based prediction method usually leads to higher up-front effort in early stages of development. The higher effort is expected to be compensated by the reduction of rework in subsequent phases [Koziolek (2008)]. A Type III study compares the effort for conducting the same project at least twice [Böhme & Reussner (2008)]. Once, without using the prediction method, which may cause higher effort for rework, and once, using the prediction method, which may cause higher up-front effort. The benefit of the prediction method is assessed by comparing the effort of both projects. Type III validations are very seldom conducted, due to (a) high effort is required and (b) it is unlike to convince an organization to conduct a project many times [Böhme & Reussner (2008)]. For these reasons, a Type III validation is not conducted in this book.

Although the requirements of a Type III study could not be fulfilled, potential users of the proposed methods were asked whether the benefits achieved in the case study compensate for the effort required from their perspective, to assess the effort-benefit ratio. This is analyzed as an aspect of acceptance (Type II).

10.2 Research Questions and Hypotheses

This section first presents the goals regarding the validation of BIIS and IntBIIS. Then, related research questions and hypotheses are listed.

BIIS is not focused on a specific simulation tool support. In order to realize BIIS in the case study, we build upon the existing tooling of the simulation approach ADONIS [Herbst et al. (1997)] and the original Palladio tool chain. ADONIS enables the simulation of BPs and organizational resources for business evaluation and process optimization. Palladio was introduced in Section 5.2. These tools were chosen, because they cover best the requested modeling concepts for their specific domain. IntBIIS was realized by the

Palladio extension, as described in Chapter 9. In the case study, the order picking process was modeled both with ADONIS and the Palladio extension. For both methods – BIIS and IntBIIS – the IS was modeled with Palladio. The models are parametrized with measurements and observations from reality.

The goals regarding the validation of BIIS are to get an understanding of the feasibility and practicability of BIIS. Since BIIS builds upon established tools, which are considered matured, the validation of the practicability of BIIS is focused on the acceptance from the practitioners' perspective. According to the Goal Question Metric (GQM) template [Basili et al. (1994)], these goals can be reformulated as:

- **Goal 1**: Analyze BIIS for the purpose of understanding with respect to feasibility from the viewpoint of method developers.

- **Goal 2**: Analyze BIIS for the purpose of understanding with respect to acceptance from the viewpoint of (potential) method users and method participants.

The goals regarding the validation of IntBIIS are to get an understanding of the feasibility of the method and the practicability of the tool support. Regarding the practicability of IntBIIS the validation focuses on the tool support, because there is no significant difference between the application of BIIS and IntBIIS from the users' point of view, as described in Section 10.2.3 and Section 10.2.4. According to the GQM template, these goals can be reformulated as:

- **Goal 3**: Analyze IntBIIS for the purpose of understanding with respect to feasibility from the viewpoint of method developers.

- **Goal 4**: Analyze the integrated tool support for the purpose of understanding with respect to practicability from the viewpoint of (potential) tool users.

10.2.1 Feasibility of BIIS

In order to investigate goal attainment regarding the feasibility of BIIS, first the elicitation of entities required as input to BIIS is examined. Then, the activities impact prediction, decision support, and requirements verification are demonstrated, and the prediction accuracy of BIIS is analyzed. Thus, the following research questions (RQ) and hypotheses (H) are used.

RQ1: Can all the required entities be elicited in the case?

The hypothesis **H1** is that all the required entities can be elicited in the case. This means that, for each entity, at least one elicitation technique is available in the case.

RQ2: Can BIIS be used in the case to predict the impact of a BP design on the performance of an IS, and vice versa?

The hypothesis **H2** is that BIIS can be used for design impact prediction in the case.

RQ3: What is the performance prediction accuracy of BIIS in the case?

The prediction accuracy refers to the deviation between predicted performance measures and performance measures recorded in reality, under the assumption that the input to BIIS is accurate. The hypothesis **H3** is that BIIS yields adequate prediction accuracy. This means that the predicted and measured probability distributions follow a similar trend and the deviation between the time mean values is below 30 percent. A common precept in model-based performance prediction is that, for practice-oriented models, deviations in time mean values less than 10 percent are considered as good results and deviations up to 30 percent in time mean values are considered as acceptable results. The interpretation of prediction accuracy, however, is strongly dependent on the BP or IS to be predicted and the context in which the prediction is conducted. Prediction errors up to 30 percent for various performance measures is commonly used as a hypothesis for industrial applications of performance prediction approaches (cf. [Koziolek et al. (2013)]).

RQ4: Can BIIS be used in the case to compare design alternatives by comparing the predicted performance measures?

The hypothesis **H4** is that BIIS can be used to support the decision for a design alternative by comparing predicted performance measures in the case.

RQ5: Can BIIS be used in the case to verify a proposed BP and/or IS design against a requirement?

The hypothesis **H5** is that BIIS can be used to verify whether a BP or IS design will violate a requirement in the case.

The RQs related to feasibility were answered by applying BIIS in the case study. An application of BIIS by us may not have been objective, since we developed the method. Therefore, BIIS was applied to the case by Herbert Lenz, as a part of his Master's thesis [Lenz (2012)], to exclude influence factors of the method developers. The BP, as well as the IS, were unknown to the student, before the case study.

10.2.2 Practicability of BIIS

Goal attainment regarding the acceptance of BIIS is investigated from different viewpoints in the case study. On the one hand, acceptance is analyzed from the viewpoint of potential method users. On the other hand, acceptance is analyzed from the viewpoint of the subjects who provide input entities of the method (i.e., the method participants).

Acceptance from the viewpoint of potential method users is determined by building upon the Technology Acceptance Model (TAM) [Davis et al. (1989)] and the Theory of Reasoned Action (TRA) [Fishbein & Ajzen (1975)]. TRA is a theory for predicting a person's intention to behave in a certain manner. A person's behavioral intention results from her/his attitude towards behavior and her/his subjective norms [Fishbein & Ajzen (1975)]. TAM is an adaptation of TRA tailored for modeling user acceptance of information technology [Davis et al. (1989), Al-Gahtani (2001)]. In TAM, the strength of a person's intention to use a technology determines its actual use. Intention to use a technology is determined by its perceived usefulness and its perceived ease of use [Venkatesh & Davis (2000)]. The variables of TAM and TRA are defined as follows:

- Usefulness is defined as a person's "subjective probability that using a specific application system will increase her/his job performance within an organizational context" [Davis et al. (1989)] (TAM).
- Ease of use refers to the degree to which a person expects the target system or technology to be free of effort [Davis et al. (1989)] (TAM).

- A person's intention to use, reflects whether s/he can imagine using the technology in the future or not (TAM, TRA).
- Subjective norm refers to "the person's perception that most people who are important to him think he should or should not perform the behavior in question" [Fishbein & Ajzen (1975)] (TRA).
- A person's attitude towards a behavior results from her/his salient beliefs about the consequences of performing the behavior, multiplied by the evaluation of those consequences [Fishbein & Ajzen (1975)] (TRA).

Since TAM is an adaptation of TRA, there are some overlaps between the variables of TAM and TRA. Intention to use/behave occurs in both theories. Attitude towards behavior overlaps with usefulness. However, according to the definitions, attitude towards behavior addresses consequences in general, whereas, usefulness focuses on consequences related to the job performance. Thus, both variables are included in the case study. Moreover, it is investigated whether the activities supported by BIIS (impact prediction, decision support, and requirements verification) are important to the subjects at all. It is required to know how important the activities are to the subjects, in order to interpret the subjects' answers related to usefulness. The resulting research questions and hypotheses are:

RQ6: Are the activities supported by BIIS important to the subjects?

Hypothesis **H6** is that the activities supported by BIIS are important to the subjects.

RQ7: Does BIIS make it easier to perform the activities?

Hypothesis **H7** is that BIIS makes it easier to perform the activities (usefulness).

RQ8: Is BIIS easy to use in practice?

Hypothesis **H8** is that BIIS is easy to use (ease of use).

RQ9: Do the subjects have a specific intention to use BIIS?

Hypothesis **H9** is that the subjects have a concrete intention to use BIIS (intention to use).

RQ10: Do the subjects expect that other people think they should use BIIS?

Hypothesis **H10** is that the subjects expect other people to think they should use BIIS (subjective norms).

RQ11: Do the subjects expect concrete consequences by using BIIS?

Hypothesis **H11** is that the subjects expect concrete consequences by using BIIS (attitude towards use).

Moreover, the effort required for entity elicitation and for performing each step of BIIS in the case are observed. It is investigated whether the benefits of BIIS compensate for the effort required from the subject's point of view. The resulting research questions and hypothesis are:

RQ12: How high is the effort for entity elicitation?

RQ13: How high is the effort for executing BIIS?

RQ14: Do the benefits of BIIS compensate for the required effort?

Hypothesis **H14** is that the benefits of BIIS compensate for the effort required in the case from the subjects' point of view.

Acceptance from the viewpoint of the subjects who provided input entities of BIIS is determined using the following research question and hypothesis.

RQ15: What is the subjects' impression of the entity elicitation phase?

Hypothesis **H15** is that the subjects had a good impression of the entity elicitation phase. In order to assess the subjects' impression, we asked whether they could provide the requested information quickly, whether they were annoyed by entity elicitation, whether they find the entity elicitation useful, and whether they would help to provide the entities again.

Answers to the RQs related to acceptance were obtained through questionnaires (see the *OnlinePLUS* material of this book on www.springer.com) filled in by the experts of the organization and the master student. Experts of the organization who represent potential users of BIIS filled in the corresponding questionnaire after a presentation. The presentation comprised an introduction to BIIS, a description of the application of BIIS to the case, and a summary of the case study results. Experts of the organization who provided input entities of BIIS filled in the corresponding questionnaire after the entity elicitation phase. The master student who applied BIIS filled in the corresponding questionnaire after the application was finished. The questionnaires contain predefined statements that the subjects had to assess. It is important to use predefined statements to ensure that the subjects' responses are comparable to one another. Additionally, individual feedback is gathered by asking for free text responses. As the number of subjects available for the survey was quite small, the survey aims to collect as much individual feedback as time permitted. Therefore, the questionnaires ask for rationales related to the assessment of each predefined statement and also contain free text questions. The subjects scored each statement on a six-point Likert scale [Likert (1932)], i.e., the scale spans from one to six. A Likert scale was chosen as it is an established approach to scale subjects' responses in survey research. If the majority of the subjects tick four or a higher value on the Likert scale, the statement is considered confirmed. If less than the majority of the subjects tick four or a higher value on the Likert scale, the statement is considered rejected.

10.2.3 Feasibility of IntBIIS

Applying the integrated simulation method IntBIIS, instead of BIIS, the same input entities have to be elicited and the same models have to be created. Moreover, also the activities supported by IntBIIS are the same. Consequently, the results of RQ1, RQ2, RQ4 and RQ5 can be applied to IntBIIS as well. Regarding the feasibility of IntBIIS, we focus on prediction accuracy, which results in the following research questions and hypotheses.

RQ16: Does IntBIIS correctly reflect workload burstiness in simulation?

In the real-life example, too much influence factors are involved that may hamper the observation of workload burstiness. Thus, the minimum example introduced in Section 7.4 is used to examine how workload burstiness is reflected by BIIS and IntBIIS.

The hypothesis **H16** is that IntBIIS correctly reflects workload burstiness in the minimum example, where it is not correctly reflected by BIIS.

RQ17: What is the performance prediction accuracy of IntBIIS in the real-life case study?

The hypothesis **H17** is that IntBIIS yields adequate prediction accuracy. This means that the predicted and measured probability distributions follow a similar trend, and the deviation between the time mean values is below 30 percent.

10.2.4 Practicability of IntBIIS

From the users' point of view, the application of IntBIIS does not significantly differ from the application of BIIS, as described above. There are merely some minor differences, which are described in the following. The notations of the business process model and the organization environment model in Palladio slightly differ from those in ADONIS. All the models are integrated in a single tooling, instead of two different tools. There is a unique way of simulation setting and execution applying IntBIIS, where it is specific to the corresponding toolings applying BIIS. Simulation results are presented in a unique manner. Deriving an IS usage profile and extending the business process model are not required any longer, which will reduce the effort required to apply the approach. Considering this, the results of the RQs related to the acceptance of BIIS can be applied to IntBIIS, if the integrated tool support is matured enough to handle real-life BPs.

RQ18: Is the integrated tool support practicable for a real-life example?

The hypothesis **H18** is that the integrated tooling is practicable. This mean (a) it is matured enough to be applied to a real-life example and (b) it is matured enough to be applied by third-party users.

10.3 Applying BIIS and IntBIIS in Practice

This section describes how BIIS and IntBIIS were applied to the case. Moreover, important decisions and workarounds required to map reality to models, as well as the model fitting, are described.

First, the input entities were elicited, as described in Section 10.4.1. Based on the elicited entities, the business process model, the organization environment model, the software architecture model, and the hardware environment model were constructed.

The first challenge was to model the workload burstiness at the process start position. The BP instances start traversing the BP design in several bursts. Between the bursts, there are long time-frames in which no BP instances start traversing. Owing to the long time-frames between the bursts, a mean distance between all the BP instance start time points over the whole day (i.e., a time-invariant inter-arrival time) would not adequately reflect the workload burstiness at the process start position. Therefore, an exemplary day was recorded. The day was decomposed into several process trigger periods. In each period, the distance between the BP instance start time points is about the same. Each period represents a burst. The periods' inter-arrival times are initially specified as the mean distance between the BP instance start time points in the corresponding period. Per period, the start time point of the period, the end time point of the period, and the inter-arrival time were specified in the business process model. Then, the period specifications were adapted, in order to approach the workload in simulation to the workload observed in reality. An alternative to workload specification in the form of process trigger periods is the usage of time series. However, time series are neither supported by ADONIS, nor by the Palladio extension, due to the reasons described in Section 5.3.3.

Applying BIIS, another challenge was to represent system steps in the ADONIS process model. ADONIS (like most BP modeling tools) does not support the modeling of system steps, but only allows for specifying general (human) activities. Each activity is allocated to a role (abstraction of a human actor) which is responsible to perform the activity. ADONIS also does not allow for modeling hardware resources, but for modeling human actors. Thus, a new actor was created who represents the IS. The actor is available 24 hours a day to process system steps. We assigned the system steps (modeled as activities in ADONIS) to the actor that represents the IS. For each system step, the mean response time is predicted using Palladio. The predicted response time is modeled as a delay (cf. resting time) annotated to the corresponding activity in the ADONIS process model. This way, the response time of the system step is included in simulation, without demanding the actor, which would result in inappropriate waiting times. Moreover, in order to approximate the distribution of a delay measured in reality, we had to use a workaround by modeling a path branch, as probability distributions cannot be specified for delays in ADONIS. The probability distribution was approximated by modeling a certain probability and a constant delay per path. In contrast, applying IntBIIS, the system steps and the IS could be modeled easily, using the corresponding PCM model elements. The distribution of the delay was approximated in a similar way to avoid influence factors caused by modeling.

Human actors, as well as hardware resources, execute several BPs, such as loading and shipping, concurrent to the order picking process. The resources are demanded by the concurrent BPs, which causes waiting times in the order picking process, due to increasing waiting queue lengths. However, it was not possible to model all concurrent BPs and include them in simulation, because there would be high additional effort required to include the concurrent BPs in the study. Thus, we decided to estimate the default resource utilizations that reflect the load induced by concurrent BPs. Estimation of concurrent load is a common procedure in performance prediction. For human actors, several actor steps were added to a concurrent BP within the business process model. Actor steps were added until the minimum and maximum value of the execution time distribution of the order picking process in simulation approached the minimum and maximum value of the distribution measured in reality. This was applied because we could not measure the default actor resource utilization. For hardware resources used in the order picking process, the default utilization was measured in reality. Then, hardware resource demands were added to a concurrent IS usage profile until the simulated resource utilization approached the measured resource utilization.

Then, step 1 of BIIS was applied by deriving the IS usage profile from the business process model. Each system step in the business process model was identified and represented by a usage scenario within the Palladio usage model. Afterwards, for each system step (i.e., usage scenario in Palladio), a workload has to be specified. The challenge was to determine the workload per system step. The original PCM does not allow specifying workloads that vary over time. Consequently, a sequence of periods, as we did for process modeling, could not be specified. A BP workload varying over time cannot be mapped to a time-invariant workload specification, without approximations. The approximations used for modeling the system step workloads are described in the following. The time points when the BP instances arrive at the system steps could be taken out of the database. Since BP instances start traversing the BP design in bursts, a mean value approximation of the distances between their arrival at the system steps could not adequately reflect workload burstiness. We decided to use the minimum distance between two BP instances arriving at the first two system steps (cf. release-order.pdf in the *OnlinePLUS* material of this book on www.springer.com) as a worst-case workload approximation for these system steps. The worst-case approximation was chosen to reflect high burstiness. For each BP instance, the individual response time of the system step sendToWHM may differ significantly. After the system step sendToWHM, BP instances line up in the waiting queue of the fork-lift driver and the fork-lift driver processes each BP instance one by one. Owing to the difference in response time and duration of processing the single BP instances, bursts are "sleeked". This means that for the following steps within the BP design, BP instances are distributed more equally than for the first two steps. Even though, occasional bursts can still occur. Thus, the workloads of the following system steps in the BP are modeled as probability mass functions [Stewart (2011)]. A probability mass function enables to specify the probability that a discrete random variable is exactly equal to a certain value. This information could be obtained from the database measurements. In contrast, applying IntBIIS, the derivation of an IS usage profile is not required at all, since the business process model is directly included in the integrated simulation.

Based on the IS usage profile derived from the business process model, as well as the software architecture model and the hardware environment model, step 2 of BIIS was performed. The IS simulation predicted the mean response time of all the system steps in the BP, as well as the utilization of the hardware resources. Then, the business process model was extended by the IS simulation results (step 4). The decision about which system steps affect the BP performance and, therefore, must be represented in the business process model, was straightforward, as described in Section 10.4.1. The workaround applied for extending the ADONIS process model was already described earlier in this section. Then, the BP performance prediction was conducted (step 5). In contrast, applying IntBIIS, it is not required to extend the business process model. Moreover, BP analysis and IS analysis are covered by a single simulation.

Finally, step 3 and step 6 of BIIS were executed in order to verify the designs against requirements and to compare several design alternatives. This was performed in a similar way while applying IntBIIS.

10.4 Validation of BIIS

This section answers the research questions related to the feasibility of BIIS and its acceptance from the practitioners' point of view.

10.4.1 Feasibility

The feasibility of BIIS is validated by demonstrating the entity elicitation and the activities impact prediction, decision support, and requirements verification supported by BIIS. Moreover, the prediction accuracy of BIIS in the case is discussed. The entity elicitation and the activities supported by BIIS were conducted as a part of the Master's thesis by Herbert Lenz (cf. [Lenz (2012)]).

Entity Elicitation: In order to elicit the input entities, four experts of the organization's IT department and one process-responsible expert were interviewed. Moreover, several database analyses, measurements, IS reverse engineering, and observations of the process in reality were conducted. The elicitation started with the BP entities, since, based on the actor steps and systems steps within the BP, it was easy to identify the required roles and actors, as well as the software components invoked within the BP. The process model depicted in a simplified form in Figure 6.1 and in complete form in the *OnlinePLUS* material of this book resulted from several interview sessions with the experts of the organization. Moreover, database analysis and observations in reality were conducted to elicit entities required for model construction, for example, path probabilities or number of loop iterations. In order to construct the IS model, reverse engineering of software components and interviews with IS experts were conducted. Performance-relevant data from reality, such as resource demands, frequencies, and workloads, were measured using database analysis and time stamps within the IS. In order to check the measurements, the execution of several BP instances were observed and further interviews with BP and IS experts were conducted. From the interviews and observations further performance-relevant data, not available in the databases or via time stamps in the IS, were gathered, for example, the processing time of actor steps. The execution time distribution depicted in Figure 10.1 was measured over a period of more than six weeks. It represents per BP instance the time required from the process start position to the process end position. The response time distribution depicted in Figure 10.2 also was measured over the six-week period. Further details on the entity elicitation can be found in [Lenz (2012)]. Most of the entities could be elicited reliably. For two of the entities workarounds were required, which are discussed in the following.

(1) As described in Section 10.3, several BPs are performed concurrently by the actors of the organization. The elicitation of all BPs performed concurrently to the order picking process would exceed the scope of the Master's thesis. Thus, the student only include approximations of them in simulation.

(2) After the order data is inserted into the Oracle database , there is a delay before the data becomes visible to the fork-lift driver. The delay occurs in the WHM component. The source code of the WHM component is not available to the experts of the organization, because a maintenance contract has expired. Hence, it was a black box to the student. The student could not add time stamps to exactly measure the delay. He roughly estimated the delay based on issue tracker entries, discussion with experts, and by observing several BP instances. The delay is about 17 minutes on average. The probability distribution of the delay is estimated based on the probability distribution of the overall execution time of the BP.

The student could elicit all the required input entities of the order picking process and the involved IS in the case, even though using workarounds for two of the entities. Hence, hypothesis H1 (all the required entities can be elicited) is confirmed.

Impact Prediction: The activity impact prediction was demonstrated by predicting performance measures of the IS and the BP. First, the response time of all the system steps within the BP, as well as the utilization of the hardware resources, were predicted. The predicted mean response time of the system step sendToWHM is 433 seconds (7 minutes and 13 seconds). The predicted mean response time of the other system steps is in a millisecond range. Thus, other system steps are neglected in the following as they do not significantly impact the BP performance. The predicted CPU utilization of the server Prometheus is 21.9 percent and the predicted CPU utilization of the server Windos is 27.5 percent. Hard disk utilization is negligible in the case study, as almost all the requested data is contained in caches. Second, the execution time of the BP was predicted while considering the mean response time of the system step sendToWHM as a factor of BP performance. The predicted mean execution time of the BP is 4 954 seconds, about 1 hour and 23 minutes. As we were able to demonstrate the prediction of the BP impact on the IS performance, as well as the prediction of the IS impact on the BP performance, hypothesis H2 (BIIS can be used for design impact prediction) is confirmed.

Note, we do not report on the utilization of human resources since (a) we were not allowed to measure the individual utilization of an actor and (b) actor utilization is not contained in the ADONIS simulation results. The server Thor4 is not included in the comparison, because the server was destroyed in a thunderstorm before we could measure the utilization of its hardware resources. The corresponding software components were then migrated to a virtual machine, which resulted in different resource utilizations.

In order to answer RQ3, predicted performance measures were compared to performance measures recorded in reality. Table 10.1 gives an overview of the simulation results and shows the deviations in percent.

Each working day is divided into three shifts (early shift, late shift, and night shift), but only one shift – the late shift – was recorded. The late shift was chosen, because mainly the orders are packed in this shift. This was the result of a six-week observation of the process in reality and was also stated by the process-responsible expert. Consequently, the models and corresponding simulation runs also consider only the late shift. BP instances that cannot completely traverse the BP in a single shift are carried over to the next shift, where they continue traversing. Since the early shift was not modeled, there is no way for the simulation to know the amount of work carried over to the late shift. To mitigate this problem, the carryover to the late shift is approximated with the carryover from late shift to night shift of the previous day. This

Table 10.1: Performance Measures and Simulation Results (as-is Design)

measure	measured [s]	predicted [s]	deviation [%]
Mean process execution time	5 326	4 954	7.0
Minimum process execution time	754	754	0.0
Quartile 1	2 862	2 630	9.2
Quartile 2	4 688	3 814	18.6
Quartile 3	6 964	5 798	16.7
Maximum process execution time	24 610	27 010	9.8
Mean response time sendToWHM	437	433	0.9
measure	**measured [%]**	**predicted [%]**	**deviation [%]**
CPU utilization Prometeus	23.05	22.3	3.25
CPU utilization Windos	27.16	27.5	1.25

represents a worst case approximation of the carryover, since most orders are packed in the late shift. The carryover from one shift to another is quite small. Even in the late shift, the carryover is about one BP instance on average. Thus, the carryover does not significantly affect the simulation results.

In reality, no significant differences in execution time among recorded working days were observed. The simulation results reflect this observation, which is why simulation of longer periods can be considered as a sequence of replicated simulation runs. With each further simulated day, an additional replication is received leading to an improved confidence in the simulation results. Thus, a terminating simulation over one year was conducted to gather a sufficient large amount of replications. With this technique, a sound basis for statistical comparisons is ensured.

Figure 10.1 shows a comparison of the distributions of the predicted BP execution time and the BP execution time measured in reality. The left side depicts the estimated probability density, where the right side shows the corresponding cumulative density. It is seen that the curve of ADONIS results and the curve of measurements follow a similar trend. Compared to the measured curve, the simulated curve shows higher peaks, but less variance in execution time, which is reflected by the width of the curves. The deviations between both probability distributions may be explained by the following reasons:

- It is hard to map the behavior of human actors in reality to simulation. Actors do not always behave in exactly the same way. For example, actors do not always start processing the next step directly after the former has been finished. Sometimes, they have to take a break within a working period (e.g., to go to the toilet) or have a short conversation.

- The processing rate of actors may differ from one actor to the other in reality. Even the processing rate of a certain actor may vary, for example, if the actor is tired or ill. In simulation, a constant processing rate is assumed, which is discussed in detail in Section 11.3.

- Simulation methods rely on the assumption that the input is accurate. The order picking process is a real-life example. Thus, it is hard to gather accurate data. For example, data gathered in an interview or an observation typically has a certain deviation to reality. Therefore, we used measurements, such as database entries or time stamps, wherever possible.

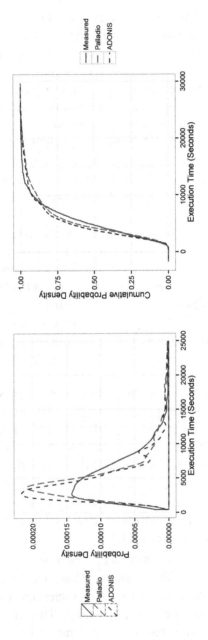

Figure 10.1: Probability Distributions Process Execution Time

However, for some entities, interviews, observations, or even estimates had to be used. Moreover, also the model construction, as described in Section 10.3, may affect prediction accuracy. Considering this, simulation inputs might have limited accuracy.

Figure 10.2 shows a comparison of the distributions of the predicted response time of the system step sendToWHM and the response time measured in reality. It is seen that the probability distributions are almost identical. The mean values are also very close. This is because the response time mainly results from a delay caused by a design flaw (whose probability distribution was measured and modeled as simulation input), and less from the utilization of hardware resources (which is evaluated during simulation).

Compared to related performance prediction studies (as described in [Koziolek et al. (2013)]), adequate prediction accuracy in mean process execution time and mean response time could be achieved in the case. However, response time was determined mainly by the delay, as mentioned above. As the probability distributions follow a similar trend and the deviations in mean values are far below 30 percent, hypothesis H3 (BIIS yields adequate prediction accuracy) is confirmed.

Decision Support: The ability of BIIS to support design decisions is demonstrated in the case study by modeling several design alternatives of the BP and the IS currently discussed in the IT department of the organization. As shown in Table 10.1, the system step sendToWHM significantly affects the BP performance. Moreover, after the system step, there is another delay of about 17 minutes on average, before the order data is available to the fork-lift driver (as mentioned at the beginning of this section). Currently, a redesign of the IS is being discussed in the organization. The STLS and the Oracle database should be removed, and the WHM should be replaced by the WMS component. The WMS component should be deployed on a server called Logistikos. The proposed deployment model is visualized in Figure 10.3. Data no longer has to be transferred between several databases. All the data will already be contained in the ADS database and will be released by setting a flag. This is handled by the new system step releaseOrder that replaces the system step sendToWHM. However, the impact of design changes on the

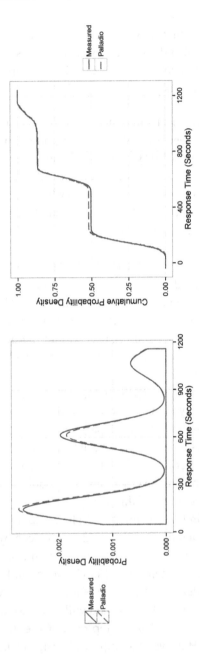

Figure 10.2: Probability Distributions Response Time

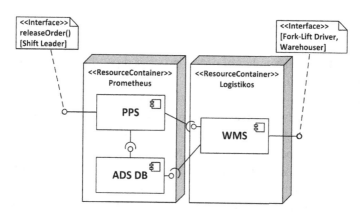

Figure 10.3: Software Component Deployment Model (IS design alternative)

performance of the IS and the BP is unclear. Hence, BIIS was applied to predict the impact of design changes.

Table 10.2 compares predicted performance measures of the as-is system (STLS + WHM) to predicted performance measures of the proposed design alternative (WMS). The time for releasing an order is significantly reduced to about 39 milliseconds. Moreover, the delay after sendToWHM is eliminated, since the legacy component WHM is replaced. Both contributes to a reduction of the BP execution time.

There are often large waiting times in the BP before the fork-lift takes goods out of the stock and before the warehouser transports the goods on a location where they are packed. BIIS was applied to analyze how the waiting times change, if more actors are available in the BP. Two alternative designs

Table 10.2: Simulation Results for Alternative IS Design

Process with ...	$STLS + WHM$ [s]	WMS [s]
Mean process execution time	4954	2560
Mean response time sendToWHM/releaseOrder	437	0.039

were analyzed – adding an additional warehouser and adding an additional fork-lift inclusive driver. For each design alternative, the mean BP execution time and the mean number of orders processed per day were predicted, as shown in Table 10.3.

The table clearly shows that the greatest savings in waiting time within the BP can be achieved using the WMS component and an additional fork-lift inclusive driver. As the comparison of several design alternatives based on the predicted performance measures could be demonstrated in the case study, hypothesis H4 (BIIS can be used to support the decision for a design alternative) is confirmed.

Requirements Verification: The ability of BIIS to verify a design against requirements is demonstrated by comparing the prediction results to the requirements listed in Chapter 6. As shown in Table 10.2, R1 is not satisfied by the as-is IS design (WHM + STLS) as the system step sendToWHM already lasts more than 7 minutes on average, whereas, the requirement is fulfilled by the proposed IS design (WMS), since the new system step releaseOrder only lasts 39 milliseconds on average. R2 is satisfied by all the design alternatives, as shown in Table 10.3. R3 is best fulfilled in case of WMS and an additional fork-lift driver, since waiting time was reduced most significantly for this design alternative. Combinations of the designs shown in Table 10.3 may lead to even higher reductions of waiting time. This can be explored using BIIS. As the ability of BIIS to verify design alternatives against requirements could be demonstrated, hypothesis H5 (BIIS can be used for requirements verification) is confirmed.

In the case study, all the required simulation inputs could be elicited and the ability of BIIS to perform the activities impact prediction, decisions support, and requirements verification could be demonstrated. Moreover, BIIS yields accurate prediction results in the case. Thus, the feasibility of BIIS is confirmed in the case.

10.4.2 Practicability

The acceptance of BIIS from the practitioners' point of view is validated based on the questionnaires introduced in Section 10.2.2. Note, the ques-

Table 10.3: Simulation Results for Alternative BP Designs

Process with ...	$STLS+$ WHM $[s]$	WMS $[s]$	$WMS+$ *additional* *warehouser* $[s]$	$WMS+$ *additional* $fork-lift$ $[s]$
Mean process execution time	4 954	2 560	2 401	1 651
Mean number of orders processed (decimal places truncated)	30	31	31	32

tionnaires are in German and the subjects also answered in German. For this book, the subjects' answers were translated into English. The subjects' individual feedback is given in quotes in the following.

The group of potential users of BIIS comprised five experts of the organization. In the survey, the subjects were asked for their responsibilities, which are shown in Table 10.4. They were not asked for their roles, since roles were not clearly defined in the organization. The responsibility of a subject easily allows drawing inferences on his or her organizational role(s). As shown in the table, the subjects' responsibilities match the roles supported by BIIS in the joint development of BPs and ISs.

The master student was also included as a subject in the survey. The student does not have any responsibilities in the organization. Responses of the student are marked by an "S" in the following to clearly separate them from practitioners' responses. Moreover, also subjects from the organization involved in the entity elicitation were asked about their impression of the entity elicitation phase.

Activity Importance: First, the subjects were asked whether the three activities supported by BIIS are important to them at all. This question was put to the subjects from the organization as well as to the subject who applied the method. Table 10.5 shows the subjects' responses. Rows represent the

Table 10.4: Responsibilities of Subjects

Subject#	Responsibility
1	Order picking process, process requirements
2	Hardware administration
3	Project costs and goals
4	IT requirements, software components, software administration
5	IT requirements, software components, software administration, hardware administration, project costs and goals

statements and columns represent the possible responses. Per cell, the number of subjects who gave the corresponding response is annotated. Owing to the small number of subjects, we do not apply means, such as a box plot diagram, commonly used in empirical studies, but use tables instead.

As shown in the table, the activities supported by BIIS are highly important to the subjects as they mostly ticked 5 or 6 on the Likert scale. Thus, hypothesis H6 (activities supported by BIIS are important to the subjects) is confirmed. One subject justified his assessment by stating, "in the present dissatisfaction with the existing IS, the comparisons are enormously important". Other subjects consider the activities as important for "decision making", to "select the best alternative", or important in "case of dispute, if the performance does not seem to be sufficient". Moreover, the subjects consider the activities as relevant to "identify bottlenecks", or to determine the "dimensioning of hardware acquisition", or to "control requirements", and "avoid implementing the wrong thing".

Usefulness: The usefulness of BIIS is investigated by asking the subjects whether BIIS makes it easier to perform the activities. This question was

Table 10.5: Activity Importance

How important are the following activities to you?	1: Strongly disagree	2: Disagree	3: Rather disagree	4: Rather agree	5: Agree	6: Strongly agree
Impact pred. IS on BP is important	0	0	0	1	2	2 (+S)
Impact pred. BP on IS is important	0	0	0	0	2	3 (+S)
Mutual impact pred. is important	0	0	0	0	2	3 (+S)
Decision support is important	0	0	0	0	1	4 (+S)
Requirements verification is important	0	0	0	0	1	4 (+S)

put to all subjects. Table 10.6 shows the subjects' assessment on the Likert scale. All subjects ticked 5 or 6 on the Likert scale. The subjects strongly confirm the usefulness of BIIS. Thus, hypothesis H7 (BIIS makes it easier to perform the activities) is confirmed. One subject stated, "only on the basis of data collection followed by simulation a comparison respectively impact prediction is possible at all". Another subject justified his decision by stating, "through modeling it is possible to simulate arbitrary models with little effort and without expert knowledge". Another subject mentioned, "by breaking down complex BPs into small entities that can be simulated, impact can be identified which possibly cannot be identified by expert estimations. By using simulation this can be predicted very easily" and "by using simulation we have facts that can be compared objectively". The student who applied the method stated, "since I am not an expert, the prediction and comparison was only possible by using BIIS".

Ease of Use: We asked the student who applied the method, whether BIIS was easy to use. Table 10.7 depicts the subject's responses with an "X".

Table 10.6: Usefulness of BIIS

Please characterize the usefulness of BIIS in relation
to the following activities

BIIS makes it easier to …	1: Strongly disagree	2: Disagree	3: Rather disagree	4: Rather agree	5: Agree	6: Strongly agree
… predict the impact of IS on BP	0	0	0	0	3	2 (+S)
… predict the impact of BP on IS	0	0	0	0	3	2 (+S)
… predict the mutual impact of BP and IS	0	0	0	0	5	S
… compare design alternatives	0	0	0	0	4	1 (+S)
… verify a design against requirements	0	0	0	0	4	1 (+S)

As the subject always ticked 5 or 6 on the Likert scale, H8 (BIIS is easy to use) is confirmed. The subject justified his assessment as follows. While deriving the IS usage profile "system steps could be identified easily in the process model" and "workload could be taken from the database". For IS simulation he stated "simulation time has to be defined". An inquiry revealed that he was referring to the configuration of the simulation. The execution of the simulation was perceived as easy by the subject. Regarding the comparison of the simulation results to the results of design alternatives or to requirements the subject mentioned "only numbers had to be compared". The subject assessed the extension of the process model as easy, "since only one system step has to be added" to the model. For BP simulation also, the student stated "simulation has to be configured". The assessment of the BP simulation results was again perceived as easy, since "only numbers had to be compared".

Table 10.7: Ese of Use of BIIS

Please characterize BIIS						
It was easy to ...	1: Strongly disagree	2: Disagree	3: Rather disagree	4: Rather agree	5: Agree	6: Strongly agree
... derive the IS usage profile from the process model						X
... perform the IS simulation					X	
... compare IS simulation results to results of other IS simulations/ to requirements						X
... extend the process model by IS simulation results						X
... perform the BP simulation					X	
... compare BP simulation results to results of other BP simulations/ to requirements						X

Intention to Use: In order to determine the subjects' intention to use BIIS, they were asked whether they are motivated to use BIIS in the future. This question was put to all subjects. The subject's assessments are shown in Table 10.8. The subjects mostly ticked 4 or 5 on the Likert scale. Thus, hypothesis H9 (the subjects have a concrete intention to use BIIS) is confirmed. Only one subject ticked 3 for the statement related to requirements verification. However, he does not add a justification. One subject justified his assessment by stating that he considers BIIS as an "efficient way to estimate BPs and ISs that are planed, but do not exist yet". Another subject expects that "in future projects, BIIS can lead to a prediction free of

Table 10.8: Intention to Use BIIS

Would you use BIIS in the future?						
I am motivated to use BIIS ...	1: Strongly disagree	2: Disagree	3: Rather disagree	4: Rather agree	5: Agree	6: Strongly agree
... for future impact predictions	0	0	0	2	3 (+S)	0
... as support for future decisions	0	0	0	2	3 (+S)	0
... for future verifications of design against requirements	0	0	1	1	3 (+S)	0

surprises". Another subject mentioned, "as soon as the models are created, impact can be predicted very well. This of course only makes sense for a certain complexity". BIIS is rated as an "interesting approach with potential" by another subject.

Subjective Norms: In order to address the attribute subjective norms, we asked the subjects whether they expect other people to think they should use BIIS. This question was only put to subjects from the organization. The subjects' assessment is shown in Table 10.9. Most subjects ticked 4 or 5. Only one subject ticked 3. He justified his assessment by stating that "others do not know" BIIS. One subject was unable to assess this statement. One subject (ticked 4) stated that it depends on the concrete project or task whether others would want him to use BIIS. For the comparison of the two ISs he does not think that others want him to use BIIS. Another subject (ticked 5) justified his decision by stating that BIIS provides "a better way of prediction". Thus, he expects that others want him to use BIIS. Since the majority of the subjects ticked a value higher or equal to 4, the hypothesis H10 (the subjects expect other people to think they should use BIIS) is confirmed.

Attitude towards Use: It is also investigated which concrete consequences the subjects expect of using BIIS. Therefore, the subjects were

Table 10.9: Subjective Norms

What would other people think of BIIS?						
	1: Strongly disagree	2: Disagree	3: Rather disagree	4: Rather agree	5: Agree	6: Strongly agree
Others would want me to use BIIS	0	0	1	1	2	0

asked for advantages and disadvantages that they expect from the method. This question was put to all subjects. If an advantage or disadvantage was mentioned by more than one subject, the number of subjects is shown in brackets. The subjects expected the following advantages of BIIS.

- "Reliable predictions of performance impacts and benefits of changes on process and IT". (5)
- "Early alignment of IT and process" (3)
- "Decisions are better to justify" (2)
- "Simplified representation of complex processes" (2)
- "Basis for decision making"/ "Good basis for decisions on changes"
- "Objective estimation of alternative designs" / "Objective comparison of several IT and process designs"
- "Reliability for future decisions"
- "Identification of violating processes/resources"
- "Easy estimation of certain design changes"
- "Owing to the detailed specification, processes become much clearer"
- "Good for predictions that are hard to estimate by experts, e.g., utilization of the system"
- "Selection of the 'right' IT design or process design possible"

The subjects expected the following disadvantages of BIIS.

- "Strong dependency on the quality of input entities" (3)
- "Additional effort required for entity elicitation" (2)
- "Difficulty of collecting realistic data"
- "Approach requires certain tools"

Since all subjects expected concrete consequences by using BIIS, hypothesis H11 (the subjects expect concrete consequences by using BIIS) is confirmed. The listing clearly shows that there are far more positive consequences expected from BIIS than negative ones.

Effort-Benefit-Ratio: In order to answer RQ12, the student recorded the effort required for eliciting each kind of entity in the case study. The overall effort required for eliciting the initial set of entities was about 33.5 person hours. The elicitation of additional entities of the design alternatives discussed in Section 10.4.1 lasted about 80 person minutes (pmin). A detailed description of the effort per kind of entity can be found in [Lenz (2012)].

In order to answer RQ13, the student recorded the effort required to perform the single steps of BIIS in the case study. The initial creation of the business process model, the organization environment model, the software architecture model, and the hardware environment model took about 9 person hours. The adaption of the simulation models for the different design alternatives discussed in Section 10.4.1 took about 40 pmin. The effort required to perform the steps of BIIS is shown in Table 10.10. Conducting the steps of BIIS took about 1.5 person hours in total. The overall effort required in the case study was about 46 person hours.

Next, the subjects were asked which benefits of BIIS they identified in the presented case. We expected that the subjects considered this question from the viewpoint of the particular case. However, some subjects seemed not to clearly distinguish this question from the question about general advantages and disadvantages, since they answered in a general way. The subjects' responses are listed in the following.

- "Changes in the existing system can be simulated reliably, impact on the process can be identified"

- "Confirmation of the decision to replace WHM"
- "Decision support on the extent of acquisition of hardware"
- "Cost savings as decisions are profound"
- "Better alignment of process and IT" (2)
- "Possibility of prediction on the required hardware utilization" (2)
- "Mutual negative impacts of system components and process can already be identified during the design phase" (2)
- "Selection of the best IS design possible"/ "Selection of an adequate design (BP and IS) from a set of proposed designs"
- "Easy to understand, even for 'non-experts' "
- "One can be sure how certain changes will affect and which adaptation/changes are worthwhile"
- "Estimation of adaptations of process and IT and mutual impacts between them"
- "Changes on the process can be simulated"
- "As-is/to-be comparison possible"

Then, the subjects were asked what would be an adequate effort, in their opinion, to reach the benefits of BIIS that they mentioned before. The responses are listed in Table 10.11.

As shown in the table, only the effort mentioned by Subject 5 widely differs from the effort the student needed in the case study. For Subject 1

Table 10.10: Overall Effort BIIS

Step of BIIS	Effort
Derive/adapt IS usage profile	45 pmin
IS performance simulations	15 pmin
Extend process model	< 5 pmin
BP performance simulations	25 pmin
Assess simulation results	5 pmin

Table 10.11: Effort Stated by Subjects

Subject#	Effort
1	5 to 10 person days.
2	15–30 person hours. Note: the subject stated that he only mentioned the effort for hardware purchases. He does not feel able to make a statement for other areas.
3	About 40 person hours
4	70 to 80 person hours
5	20 person hours

and Subject 4, even a much higher effort would be acceptable to reach the benefits. Subject 2 was only able to make a statement for the effort related to hardware purchases.

Finally, the subjects were asked whether the benefits of BIIS compensate for the effort required from their point of view. This question was put to all subjects. Table 10.12 shows the subjects' assessments. All subjects score that the benefits of BIIS compensate for the effort required in the entity elicitation phase as well as for the effort required for performing the simulations. As all subjects ticked a value higher or equals 4, hypothesis H14 (the benefits of BIIS compensate for the effort required from the subjects' point of view) is confirmed. One subject stated that the entity elicitation required "too much effort for small and medium sized projects". "For large projects the effort is justified" from the subject's point of view. Another subject mentioned that he considered the effort as "justified, since the elicited entities are the basis of a variety of simulations". All subjects confirmed that the benefits of BIIS compensate highly for the effort of performing the simulations. The subjects considered this effort as minor, compared to the effort required for entity elicitation. One subject explicitly stated "little effort for creating the simulation models and for deriving the usage profiles".

Table 10.12: Ratio Benefit and Effort

Please characterize the ratio of benefit to effort
for the application of BIIS in the present case

The benefits of BIIS compensate for ...	1: Strongly disagree	2: Disagree	3: Rather disagree	4: Rather agree	5: Agree	6: Strongly agree
... the effort required for entity elicitation	0	0	0	2	2 (+S)	1
... the effort required for performing the simulation	0	0	0	1	(S)	4

Entity Elicitation: The subjects involved in the entity elicitation phase were asked about their impression of the entity elicitation. The subjects assessed predefined statements as presented in Table 10.13. All subjects perceived that they could provide the requested entities quickly. Except for one subject, entity elicitation was not annoying to them. Mainly, the subjects found the entity elicitation useful. One subject (ticked 2) stated that the process specification was already available in a similar form. However, this process specification was much too high level for simulation purposes and incomplete, since it does not comprise relevant parts of the process. Thus, the process entities had to be elicited again. Another subject (ticked 4) justified his assessment by stating that the IS would be replaced by another soon. All subjects involved in the entity elicitation would again help to provide the entities. Considering this, hypothesis H15 (the subjects had a good impression of the entity elicitation phase) is confirmed.

In conclusion, all hypotheses were confirmed in the case study. Consequently, BIIS is accepted from the practitioners' point of view in the case.

Table 10.13: Impression of Entity Elicitation

Please share your impression of the entity elicitation.	1: Strongly disagree	2: Disagree	3: Rather disagree	4: Rather agree	5: Agree	6: Strongly agree
I could provide the requested information quickly	0	0	0	0	1	4
It was annoying to provide the information	1	3	0	1	0	0
It is useful to elicit the information	0	1	0	2	0	2
I would again help providing the information	0	0	0	0	0	5

10.5 Validation of IntBIIS

This section answers the research questions related to the feasibility of IntBIIS and the practicability of the integrated tool support.

10.5.1 Feasibility

Workload burstiness within the BP is influenced by hardware resources as well as actor resources. It is assumed that Palladio correctly simulates the behavior of hardware resources, as demonstrated in several case studies (e.g., [Becker et al. (2009), Martens et al. (2011)]). Workload burstiness within the process is correctly represented by IntBIIS, if also the actor resources' behavior is correctly simulated.

First, the minimum example introduced in Section 7.4 is investigated to answer RQ16. If the prediction results match the expected results shown in Table 7.1, the feasibility (Type I) of the integrated simulation is confirmed for the minimum example. BIIS, as well as IntBIIS, were applied to the minimum example, in order to analyze how workload burstiness is reflected. Using BIIS, the actor step AS1 was modeled with ADONIS and the system step ISS1 was modeled with the original Palladio tooling. IS simulation and BP simulation were conducted in isolation. Using IntBIIS, both AS1 and ISS1 were modeled with the Palladio extension. The integrated simulation comprises the IS and the BP. The mean response time of ISS1 predicted by BIIS is 1.0 time units, since the BP instances arrive at ISS1 in a distance of two time units. The distance between the BP instances does not shrink at AS1, due to isolated simulations. Consequently, workload burstiness is not correctly represented by using BIIS. The mean response time of ISS1 predicted by IntBIIS is 1.5 time units. Both BP instances arrive at ISS1 at the same time. The shrinking distance between the BP instances at AS1 is correctly reflected by the integrated simulation.

The minimum example shows the impact of workload burstiness on performance prediction. IntBIIS correctly reflects workload burstiness in simulation. Therefore, the IntBIIS result matches the expected mean response time of ISS1. Thus, hypothesis H16 (IntBIIS correctly reflects workload burstiness in the minimum example) is confirmed. In contrast, BIIS exhibits a high deviation of about 33 percent, as workload burstiness is not correctly represented.

In order to answer RQ17, the real-life example is used again. The results of IntBIIS were compared to values measured in reality. Mapping a BP from practice to a model is a challenging task as discussed in Section 10.4.1. Thus, the results of IntBIIS were compared additionally to the results of BIIS to exclude influencing factors caused by modeling. If the results match, the feasibility (Type I) of IntBIIS is confirmed for the real-life example.

In the following, Palladio denotes the realization of IntBIIS and ADONIS denotes the realization of BIIS.

While the Palladio model explicitly reflects the mutual impact between the BP and the IS, the ADONIS model takes into account only how the IS affects the BP performance, but not vice versa. Palladio predicted a mean process execution time of 5 409 seconds (about 1 hour and 30 minutes). ADONIS predicted a mean value of 4 954 seconds (about 1 hour and 23 minutes). In reality, a mean process execution time of 5 326 seconds (about 1 hour and

Table 10.14: Earth Mover's Distance between Predictions and Measurements

Palladio vs. Measured:	559.43
ADONIS vs. Measured:	696.66
Palladio vs. ADONIS:	460.05

29 minutes) was measured. The deviation between the Palladio result and the measurements is about 1.5 percent which is far below the threshold of 30 percent.

The distributions of the predicted and measured process execution time can be seen in Figure 10.1 on page 170. The figure shows, the Palladio curve follows a similar trend than the measured curve and the ADONIS curve. Compared to the measured curve, also the Palladio curve shows higher peaks, but less variance in execution time.

Figure 10.1 also indicates some deviations between the ADONIS curve and the Palladio curve. Deviations may be caused by different simulation strategies of both methods and the mutual impact on workload burstiness, which is considered in Palladio but not in ADONIS. It is hard to judge visually which of the simulation methods performs better in our scenario – BIIS or IntBIIS. This is why a distance measure was applied to make the mutual differences tangible. The earth mover's distance (EMD) [Rubner et al. (1998)] was chosen, because it operates in an intuitive manner and takes into account differences both in shape and location of probability distributions. Given two probability distributions, the EMD algorithm calculates their distance in terms of the effort which must be undertaken to transform one distribution into the other. Figuratively speaking, a distribution's probability mass is moved to the distribution under comparison, until they are aligned [Rubner et al. (1998)]. The amount and distance of mass transported yields the EMD metric. The results are shown in Table 10.14.

Although the reported values are dimensionless, they meet the definition of a metric and, thus, are suited to give an impression on relative distances. With a distance of 559 and 697 for Palladio and ADONIS, respectively, Palladio resembles the measured distribution better than ADONIS. The distance of 460 between Palladio and ADONIS is comparatively

Table 10.15: Execution Time (Probabilities Rounded)

Execution Time (Seconds)	Probability (Palladio)	Probability (ADONIS)	Probability (Measured)
0–5 000	0.63	0.67	0.54
5 000–10 000	0.26	0.25	0.38
10 000–15 000	0.07	0.04	0.07
15 000–20 000	0.03	0.02	0.01
20 000–25 000	0.01	0.01	0.00
25 000–30 000	0.00	0.00	0.00

small, which reflects the aforementioned observation that both curves follow a similar trend. Comparing the probabilities for various ranges of execution time (cf. Table 10.15) leads to a similar conclusion. Except for the range 15 000 to 20 000, compared to ADONIS, Palladio yields for each range a probability closer or equal to the probability calculated from real-world measurements. This observation is also supported by the three quartiles Q1, Q2 and Q3 shown in Table 10.16. For all quartiles, the predictions with Palladio are closer to the measurements than ADONIS.

In summary, these findings confirm the feasibility of the integrated simulation method IntBIIS. Hypothesis H17 (IntBIIS yields adequate prediction accuracy) is confirmed. Compared to BIIS, IntBIIS seems to have a higher prediction accuracy as the mean values, distances, probabilities, and quartiles consistently indicate.

10.5.2 Practicability

Since there are several analogies between BP simulation and IS simulation, there are also several analogies in the application of the corresponding tool supports. Similar models have to be created. As described in Section 5.3, the business process model is constructed based on the usage model and the

Table 10.16: Quartiles for the Probability Distribution from Figure 10.1
(Decimal Places Truncated)

Simulator	Min	Q1	Q2	Q3	Max
Measured	754	2 862	4 688	6 964	24 610
Palladio	400	2 988	4 208	6 184	27 560
ADONIS	754	2 630	3 814	5 798	27 010

organization environment model is the counterpart of the hardware environment model. The simulations are configured and executed in a similar way. Performance measures, such as mean response/execution time or resource utilization, predicted by the tool support and presented to the user are closely related.

The practicability of the original Palladio approach and the related tool support was validated in [Martens (2007)]. The results confirm the practicability of Palladio for third-party users. In the following, the maturity and practicability of the integrated tool support is discussed. In this book, the original Palladio tool chain was extended by model elements (cf. Section 5.3) and simulation behavior (cf. Section 9.3). Thus, the practicability of the integrated tool support is largely determined by the practicability of the original Palladio tool chain. From the users' perspective, the Palladio tool chain comprises the graphical editors for modeling PCM instances, the execution of the simulation and the presentation of the simulation results [Becker et al. (2009)]. These features were validated by [Martens (2007)] as an influence factor of practicability. In the following, the extensions to these features are discussed.

Editors: Currently, we are extending the Palladio tool chain by a new graphical editor for organization environment models. Moreover, we are extending the usage model editor by the new meta–model elements introduced in Section 5.3.2.

Simulation Execution: The Palladio tool chain provides automated model checking for violations of constraints and automated execution of the simulation. Simulation settings can be edited in a configuration dialog. The simulation execution functionality was reused for BPs without making changes.

Presentation of simulation results: The Palladio tool chain provides a sensor framework to record events in simulation and calculate performance measures. Moreover, the Palladio tool chain provides a charting framework to visualize performance measures in several forms, such as histograms or cumulative distribution functions. Sensors related to the new model elements and corresponding performance measures, such as execution time distributions of actor steps or utilization of actor resources, were added, as described in Section 9.3. Thus, BP-related performance measures can be calculated and visualized using the extended tool support.

None of the functionality, basic behavior, or visualization related to the features were changed, but applied to the integrated tooling. Thus, indicators for the practicability from the third-party users' view can be transferred from the results by Martens, assuming that business analysts and process designers have similar requirements on the practicability of a modeling and simulation tool than the roles in the Palladio development process. For business analysts, this impression may be supported by the partial overlap of roles, as discussed in Section 5.2. We are confident that the integrated tool support is practicable for third-party users, however, this needs to be further investigated in the future.

In the case study, the integrated tool support could be used to (a) model a BP and an IS from practice, (b) execute the simulation of the BP and the involved IS, and (c) receive interpretable simulation results (as shown in Figure 10.1). Thus, the integrated tool support is considered matured and practicable enough to handle real-life BPs. Hypothesis H18 (the integrated tooling is practicable) is confirmed.

10.6 Threats to Validity

In case study research, four aspects of validity have to be distinguished [Runeson et al. (2012)] – internal validity, external validity, construct validity, and conclusion validity (i.e., reliability).

10.6.1 Internal Validity

Internal validity is concerned with the causal relations of the investigated factors to other factors. A potential threat to internal validity of the survey on the acceptance of BIIS is that the master student knew that the author was the developer of BIIS. The student might thus have been biased towards BIIS. That is why we explicitly adverted to the student that he should assess the approach objectively and stated that both, positive and negative feedback, is desired. When comparing the assessments, the student's response does not differ significantly from the practitioners' responses. Thus, there is nothing that indicates that the student have been biased.

In the case study, simulation results were compared to measurements from reality. Reality was mapped to a model that was input to the simulation. Consequently, the mapping from reality to the model may influence the simulation results, as described in Section 10.4.1. Therefore, the results of BIIS were compared to the results of IntBIIS to exclude influence factors caused by modeling. However, both simulation methods use different simulation strategies, which again may influence the simulation results although the models used in the simulations are very similar, except for some minor tool-specific adaptations (such as described in Section 10.3).

10.6.2 External Validity

External validity is concerned with the generalization of the findings of a specific study stetting for others. According to [Runeson et al. (2012)], in case study research, the representativeness of a sample case may be sacrificed to achieve a deeper understanding and better realism of the phenomena under study. Consequently, the results achieved in this case might not be transferable to an arbitrary other case, due to the individual properties of each case. However, the case study gives an important insight into the application of BIIS and IntBIIS in practice, which provides indicators for cases having similar properties.

10.6.3 Construct Validity

Construct validity is concerned with the relation of the actual observation and the researcher's intended observation. In the particular case of the order picking process, BP workload did not suffice to drive the IS into an overload situation. The joint impact of BP resources and IS resources on workload burstiness also does not significantly affect the simulation results, as shown in Figure 10.1. The order picking process was not selected with the focus on these criteria, but, rather as it represents a real-life example. Nevertheless, the minimum example demonstrated the mutual impact on workload burstiness, which significantly affected performance. IntBIIS was able to adequately reflect both cases in simulation as described in Section 9.4 and demonstrated in Section 10.5.1.

Another issue related to construct validity is an insufficient operationalization of the variables of TAM and TRA in the questionnaires on the acceptance of BIIS. The questionnaires were not evaluated under realistic conditions prior to the study and could have measured something different from the TAM and TRA concepts. However, similar measurement instruments were applied in several previous studies (cf. [Heidrich (2009), Menzel (2012), Armbrust (2010)]). In Software Engineering, it is not uncommon to work with non-validated measurement instruments derived from TAM and TRA, as the studies mentioned above demonstrate. Nevertheless, prior to the study, we conducted several reviews and test-surveys within the Software Engineering research group at University of Heidelberg to test and improve the measurement instrument, and the material used.

10.6.4 Conclusion Validity

Conclusion validity (reliability in [Runeson et al. (2012)]) is concerned with the relation of output and the specific researcher (i.e., whether another research came to the same results). In the survey, mostly an overwhelming majority of the subjects decided in favor of BIIS. Thus, there is no interpretation required that may lead other researchers to other conclusions. In the minimum example, IntBIIS matched the expected mean value for adequate workload burstiness, whereas, BIIS exhibits a high deviation. Consequently, no interpretation may lead a research to another conclusion. In order to analyze the probability distributions of the simulation results related to the order picking process, statistical tests were applied which give a reasonable evidence and reduces the need for interpretation.

10.7 Summary

This chapter presented a validation of the prediction methods BIIS and IntBIIS based on a real-life example. First, a Type I study was conducted, where the elicitation of input entities to the prediction methods, as well as the activities impact prediction, decision support, and requirements verification were demonstrated. The prediction accuracy of the methods were determined by comparing prediction results to measurements from reality and results of the other method. The comparison showed that the curves of the probability distributions follow a similar trend and the deviations in mean value are far below the common precept of 30 percent. The prediction of BIIS shows a deviation in mean value of 7 percent, where IntBIIS exhibits a deviation of 1.5 percent. While analyzing the probability distributions it is shown that the curve of IntBIIS results is closer to the measured distribution than the curve of BIIS results. Moreover, it was demonstrated that IntBIIS correctly reflects workload burstiness, where it was not correctly represented by BIIS. Since all the hypotheses regarding feasibility were confirmed, the prediction methods BIIS and IntBIIS are considered feasible.

Then, a Type II study was conducted, where the acceptance of BIIS from the practitioners' view was examined in a survey. The survey results confirmed that BIIS is accepted by the practitioners. Since the application of IntBIIS does not significantly differ from the application of BIIS, we conclude that also IntBIIS would be accepted by the practitioners. Moreover, the practicability of the integrated tool support was discussed based on the real-life example and the practicability of the original Palladio tool chain. Since all the hypotheses regarding acceptance from the practitioners' view and practicability were confirmed, the prediction methods BIIS and IntBIIS are considered practicable.

Part III

Conclusion

11 Summary and Future Work

Science knows only one commandment

–

contribute to science.

— Bertolt Brecht, 1898–1956 —

This chapter concludes the book. First, the contributions presented in this book are summarized in Section 11.1. The benefits are pointed out in Section 11.2 by describing how the contributions support the roles in the joint development of BPs and ISs. Then, a description of the assumptions and limitations is given in Section 11.3. Finally, future work is discussed in Section 11.4.

11.1 Summary

For the alignment of BP quality and IS quality, several problems, as described in Section 1.2, have to be addressed. First, BP quality and IS quality must be characterized. While there are several quality models regarding IS quality, there is no comprehensive understanding of BP quality (**P1**). This book proposed the BPQRM, a holistic quality model for BPs. Second, quality aspects have to be represented in conceptual models, together with functional aspects, to allow for a complete representation of BPs and ISs. While there are notations considering quality aspects of ISs, current BP modeling notations do not aim to express quality aspects (**P2**). Based on the BPQRM, this book proposed a modeling approach to represent a comprehensive set of quality aspects in a BP model. Third, BP designs and IS designs have to be aligned with respect to quality. However, the mutual impact between BPs and ISs is unknown at design-time (**P3**). This book proposed the prediction methods BIIS and IntBIIS, for the alignment of BPs designs and IS designs with respect to performance. In the following, a detailed summary of the main contributions is given.

The BPQRM establishes a comprehensive understanding of BP quality, by allocating quality characteristics to the BP components activity, resource, information object, and actor. A multi-level hierarchy of quality aspects was introduced to decompose characteristics to measures relevant in a specific BP. Since the BPQRM serves as a checklist for selecting relevant quality aspects, it supports a comprehensive quality assessment and requirements elicitation. Moreover, it is a foundation for investigating quality-relevant dependencies between the BP components. The BPQRM was compared to related quality models from literature to argue for its comprehensiveness. One possible application of the BPQRM was demonstrated by developing an approach to create a questionnaire for process improvement. For questionnaire construction, characteristics relevant to the process of writing discharge letters, a real-life process at the University Hospital Heidelberg, were selected from the BPQRM. Then, related attributes and corresponding measures were identified. This demonstrates the ability of the BPQRM to be tailored to a specific BP. Based on the measures, questions were created and put to subjects in an interview study. Potentials for process improvement were identified from the interviewees' responses. Experts at the hospital consider the effort for constructing the questionnaire as adequate, and confirm the usefulness of the interview findings for process improvement. Thus, the practicability of the BPQRM could be demonstrated for one application.

The proposed quality modeling approach allows for a holistic representation of the quality characteristics of the BPQRM within a BP model. To each quality characteristic, a graphical symbol is assigned, which can be annotated to the corresponding elements within the model. Quality attributes and related measures are associated to the quality characteristics, but are not visible in the model. Thus, a comprehensive set of quality aspects can be represented without a major increase of the complexity of the process model. This way, quality is put in the focus of the modeler, because s/he can capture quality aspects together with functional aspects within the model. The modeling approach was compared to related approaches from literature and tools from practice, which confirms its comprehensiveness. Prototypical tool support for the approach was applied to document quality aspects captured for the process of writing discharge letters. This demonstrates the applicability of the modeling approach and tooling to a real-life example.

Three types of mutual impact between BPs and ISs were distinguished in this book. These are the BP impact on IS performance, the IS impact on BP performance, and the joint impact on workload burstiness. The prediction method BIIS defines interfaces between existing BP simulations and IS simulations. Simulation is conducted in isolation and performance-relevant information is exchanged ex-post, via the interfaces. The derivation of the IS usage profile for IS simulation from a BP model was described. An analysis of BIIS showed that workload burstiness is not adequately reflected using isolated simulation. It was demonstrated that workload burstiness can significantly affect performance, which results in limited prediction accuracy of approaches built upon isolated simulations.

The integrated prediction method IntBIIS extends the Palladio approach by meta-model elements and simulation behavior to reflect BPs and their organizational environment. IntBIIS adequately represents workload burstiness, due to the integrated simulation of BPs and ISs. The business process model constructed based on the PCM usage model enables the specification of BPs. The organization environment model allows for modeling human actors, their organizational role(s), and their equipment, such as devices or machines. A novel type of time-variant workload specification was introduced to allow for analyzing how performance measures evolve, when workloads vary over simulation time. A novel scheduling policy reflecting the behavior of human actors was specified. Novel traversal strategies were specified to define the behavior when simulation encounters an actor step, an activity, or a sequence of actions for that a certain equipment is required. The Palladio simulator EventSim was extended by BP simulation behavior, including the time-variant workload, the scheduling policy for human actors, and traversal strategies, in order to realize IntBIIS.

An empirical study, based on a real-life example, was conducted in order to validate the proposed prediction methods and modeling extensions. The example comprises the order picking process and the involved IS at Thor GmbH. First, input entities to the prediction methods were captured and the effort required was recorded. BIIS was applied to the case to predict the performance of the as-is design of the BP and the IS, to compare the as-is design to alternative designs, and to verify the designs against requirements. Moreover, as-is prediction results were compared to measurements from reality. Namely, predicted and measured execution time of the order picking process was compared. The comparison showed that BIIS yields adequate prediction accuracy. The probability distributions of the performance measures follow a similar trend and the deviation in mean value is 7 percent. Compared to a common precept in model-based performance prediction, where, for practice-oriented models, deviations in mean value up to 30 percent are considered as acceptable, this is adequate accuracy. The prediction accuracy yielded is often sufficient to assess different design alternatives. Thus, the feasibility of BIIS was confirmed in the case study. Practitioners involved in the application of BIIS were surveyed. The acceptance of BIIS from practitioners' point of view was investigated in the survey using a questionnaire constructed based on TAM and TRA. The survey confirmed the acceptance of BIIS from the practitioners' perspective. It was argued that the application of IntBIIS is close to the application of BIIS and, consequently, IntBIIS would also be accepted by the practitioners. The validation of IntBIIS regarding feasibility focused on prediction accuracy. Again, predicted and measured execution time distributions of the order picking process were compared. The comparison showed a deviation in the mean value of about 1.5 percent for IntBIIS. The IntBIIS results also resemble the measured distribution better than the BIIS results, as a statistical analysis proved. The integrated tooling could be applied to map the real-life example to a model and to predict performance measures based on the model. This demonstrates the practicability of the tool support in the case study. Moreover, indicators for the practicability from third-party users' view were discussed based on the original Palladio tool chain. Both gives confidence regarding the practicability of the integrated tooling. However, further investigation in this direction is required in the future.

In the real-life example, too many influence factors are involved that may hamper the observation of workload burstiness. Thus, the representation of workload burstiness in simulation and its impact on performance prediction was investigated in a minimum example. Expected and predicted performance measures were compared. The example demonstrated that workload burstiness is not adequately reflected by isolated simulations, which resulted in a deviation between expected and predicted mean value of about 33 percent using BIIS. In contrast, IntBIIS correctly reflected workload burstiness, which resulted in a match of expected and predicted mean value in the example.

11.2 Benefits

The formerly summarized contributions shall improve the alignment of BP quality and IS quality. They target requirements engineers, system designers, hardware administrators, process designers, and business analysts in the joint development of BPs and ISs, as introduced in Section 1.1. This section describes how the various roles can benefit from the contributions, while performing their activities.

The comprehensive understanding of BP quality established by the BPQRM supports business analysts in specifying relevant and verifiable quality requirements. Using the BPQRM as a checklist avoids neglecting quality requirements important for a specific BP. For requirements verification (cf. iv. on page 3), the business analyst must determine whether a requirement is satisfied or not. Thus, the requirements must be specified in a precise manner. Deriving measures from the characteristics of the BPQRM, using the proposed multi-level hierarchy of quality aspects, allows for specifying precise requirements. Since a measure per definition is a variable to which a value resulting from a measurement is assigned, requirements related to the measure can be formulated in the form of mean values or thresholds, for example. Moreover, the BPQRM supports process designers in assessing the quality of a particular BP design and comparing alternative designs comprehensively. On the one hand, potentials for improvement of a certain BP can be identified using measures derived from the BPQRM. This is applicable for BPs already realized, as well as for BPs at design-time. For existing BPs, values related to the measures may be gathered using monitoring techniques or interviews, for example. Thus, potentials for improvement, such as listed in Section 3.5.2, may be identified. At design-time, simulation methods can be applied, as described for performance in this book. The support of simulation methods for the process designer is described later in this section.

On the other hand, alternative BP designs can be compared by comparing values that were gathered using the measures (cf. v. on page 3).

The proposed quality modeling approach also supports business analysts and process designers. Since it represents quality aspects, it supports the early quality requirements elicitation from the BP model. The approach allows for a more complete representation of the overall BP design, which may be relevant for design comparison. Moreover, it also supports requirements engineers in gathering early IS requirements, as BP modeling is a starting point for IS requirements elicitation.

The support of the prediction methods BIIS and IntBIIS for the roles can be condensed by three activities – impact prediction, decision support, and requirements verification. The three activities are performed at design-time, using model-based performance prediction. Requirements engineers are able to check whether a performance requirement on an IS is satisfied for a proposed IS design and a given BP design (cf. i. on page 3). They can conduct a simulation study using the models created by the system designer and the process designer, and compare the simulation results to the require-ments. If a requirement is not satisfied, either the designs or the requirement may be adapted prior to implementation. System designers can create an IS design using the original PCM elements. Then, they are able to analyze its performance considering the BP design, in order to identify bottlenecks and system design flaws. They can also compare alternative designs in or-der to identify an IS design that performs best for a given BP design (cf. ii. on page 3). Thus, even answering "make-or-buy" questions regarding software components, for example, is supported [Koziolek (2008)], although costs are not considered in this book. For example, differences in predicted performance measures between a standard component and a self-designed component can be investigated. Moreover, IS-related "what-if" questions can be answered by the system designer, using the proposed prediction methods. Hardware administrators are able to check the hardware resource utilization for a proposed IS design or BP design by conducting a simulation study using the models created by the system designer and the process designer (cf. iii. on page 3). They can identify overloaded hardware resources or determine the dimensioning of future hardware acquisitions. Process de-signers are able to create a BP design, using the newly introduced model elements. The modeling elements provide a vocabulary to describe BPs and their organizational environment, as well as related performance properties. Then, the process designers can analyze the BP performance considering the IS design in order to identify bottlenecks and process design flaws. They can also compare alternative designs in order to identify a BP design that performs best for a given IS design (cf. v. on page 3). Moreover, BP-related "what-if" questions can be answered by the process designer using the proposed prediction methods. Business analysts are able to check whether a performance requirement on a BP is satisfied for a proposed BP design and a given IS design (cf. iv. on page 3). They can conduct a simulation study using the models created by the process designer and the system designer, and compare the simulation results to the requirements. If a requirement cannot be satisfied, either the designs or the requirement may be adapted before the BP is rolled out in the organization.

The prediction methods allow for identifying whether a BP design and an IS design are misaligned from the BP perspective (meaning that at least one BP requirement is not satisfied). The prediction methods also allow for identifying whether a BP design and an IS design are misaligned from the IS perspective (meaning that at least one IS requirement is not satisfied). In dependence upon the design space, the aforementioned roles can explore whether it is more appropriate to change a certain part of the IS design or a certain part of the BP design. From the BP perspective, they can explore whether a proposed IS redesign is worthwhile to achieve alignment if it is allowed to change the IS design. Alternatively, they are able to investigate whether a proposed BP redesign is worthwhile to achieve alignment. From the IS perspective, they can analyze whether a proposed BP redesign is worthwhile to achieve alignment if it is allowed to change the BP design. For example, in most cases, it will not be possible to change the workload induced by the BP. Alternatively, they are able to explore whether a proposed IS redesign is worthwhile to achieve alignment. The design alternatives can be compared based on the predicted performance measures in order to select an aligned overall design consisting of the BP design and the IS design.

The roles may prefer using prediction methods, because they make their decisions more replicable, compared to expert estimations. The predictions result in quantitative data, which can be used for decision support and requirements verification. Thus, decisions do not have to rely completely on an expert's intuition. This argument is supported by practitioner's feedback from the case study in Section 10.4.2 who stated, for example, that using the prediction methods they had facts which could be assessed objectively and that impact could be identified which possibly could not be identified by expert estimations. Moreover, simulation is expected to be more reliable than expert estimations in general, if the models are adequate. Using simulation also may prevent effort required for creating system prototypes or prototypical process execution for performance estimation. The prediction methods allow for alignment in the early design phases. Aligning the designs early can reduce time and costs for rework, due to poor performance in subsequent phases.

The partial models of the PCM (original as well as newly introduced ones) are reusable for different contexts, due to clearly defined interfaces. One model can be replaced by another quickly. Thus, several design alternatives can be explored with little effort, by changing single parameters or entire partial models.

According to [Koziolek (2008)], only little performance engineering knowledge is required using the Palladio approach, because domain-specific modeling languages are provided. The performance models and their simulators are encapsulated and do not have to be understood by the users. Thus, even non-experts are able to conduct performance predictions. The same applies to the extensions proposed in this book. Therefore, the business analyst, for example, can verify a requirement in a simulation study without understanding, in detail, the models created by the system designer and the process designer, as well as the underlying simulation algorithm.

11.3 Assumptions and Limitations

The contributions proposed in this book rely on assumptions that may bear some limitations, as discussed in this section.

The quality model BPQRM assumes a close relationship between BP quality and IS quality, which is supported by [Osterweil (1987), Osterweil (1997)]. It assumes that quality characteristics from software product quality standards can be adapted to the BP context. Quality characteristics contained in these standards are quite generic. Therefore, they can also be found in quality models and standards of several other domains [Juran & Godfrey (1999)].

Several assumptions and limitations of the original PCM were presented in [Becker (2008)]. Since this book builds upon the PCM, its assumptions and limitations also apply to the contributions proposed in this book. A short description of the most important ones in the context of this book is given in the following.

Static IS architecture: The modeled IS is assumed to be static. This means that software components cannot move from one hardware node to another, and properties of hardware nodes cannot change. Consequently, dynamic binding of services or cloud computing scenarios, for example, are barely supported by the PCM, because infrastructure is adapted dynamically in these scenarios. However, first approaches to self-adaptive system analysis based on the PCM [Becker et al. (2013)] came up recently.

Little algorithm influence: The Palladio approach assumes that IS performance is mainly determined by the system architecture. Algorithms cannot be reflected adequately in the PCM. Hence, the influence of algorithms on performance is largely neglected.

Focus on information systems: The PCM provides limited support for event-based systems. It assumes synchronous, blocking calls, which are common in the IS domain. The PCM does not support event-based systems, which usually rely on asynchronous message passing.

Entity availability: The PCM assumes that required model information is available and was specified in the partial models by the corresponding development role. Further it is assumed that a common abstraction and modeling is agreed among several actors of a specific development role. The same is assumed for the new partial models proposed in this book.

There are several assumptions and limitations regarding the prediction methods proposed in this book, which are listed in the following.

Granularity of events: IntBIIS assumes that for aligning BP designs and IS designs a rough estimation of fine-grained IS events is sufficient. One limitation of IntBIIS is that the different granularities of events, in terms of their duration, might limit the feasibility of the integrated simulation. In cases where many fine-grained IS events occur during a short time-frame (e.g., a second) simulating a week, or even a year, might take a long time. This is because fine-grained simulation (which takes long per simulated second) is required, but also a long simulated time-frame is needed. However, this seems to be a hypothetic limitation, as we focus on IS response times that have a discernible impact on BP performance. It is assumed that cases where the IS simulation has a large number of fine-grained events per second, do not have to be considered in detail. Because fine-grained IS events neither affect the BP performance directly, nor significantly influence the workload burstiness in a BP scenario. Only if IS events get a granularity that is comparable to BP events, they obtain importance from a business perspective Nevertheless, the order picking process example includes IS events in a millisecond range, where it was simulated over a long time-frame (i.e., a year). This demonstrates the feasibility of the integrated simulation, even if fine-grained IS events are included in the simulation study.

Static processing rate of human actors: The proposed PCM extension and simulation behavior assume a static processing rate of human actors, where the processing rate may differ from one actor to the other in reality. Even the processing rate of a certain actor may vary, for example, if the actor is tired or ill. Although a more detailed elicitation and specification of the processing rate of the single actors may be desirable from a performance prediction point of view, it bears a high risk of abuse. Thus, it is not allowed to determine the processing rate of a particular actor in most countries, due to regulations of law or the works councils (e.g., §87 [BetrVG] in Germany).

Static process design: The modeled BP and organizational environment are assumed to be static.

This means that dynamic selection of suppliers or temporary adaptations in the control flow, for example, is not supported.

Information object availability: It is assumed that the BP is designed in a way that information objects are available, when they are required for process execution. This means that a BP instance is never blocked, due to missing information objects.

11.4 Future Work

Future work closely related to the single contributions was discussed already at the end of the corresponding sections in this book. Section 3.7 presents future work on the BPQRM. Future work on the quality modeling approach and the related tooling was described in Section 4.4. Future work on the prediction of the mutual impact between BPs and ISs was presented in Section 9.5. These are further developments of the proposed contributions, which are expected to be realized in a short time-frame. In the following, future work on the alignment of BP quality and IS quality, in a broader sense, is discussed by outlining two areas of extension.

11.4.1 Continuous Alignment and Quality Evolution

The BPQRM is a first step in a quality-aware evolution of BPs and ISs. Based on the BPQRM, continuous alignment and quality control from BP level, down to software architecture and hardware levels could be established. Abstract objectives (e.g., on business level) have to be related to base measures (e.g., on hardware level). Quality control could be built upon techniques, such as process mining, meta-modeling, and simulation. In the following, five steps, building on each other, are described to establish continuous alignment and quality control.

First, a set of relevant base measures suitable for assessing common objectives related to the quality characteristics of the BPQRM has to be identified. Because a wide variety of measures are possible, for selection, common application scenarios and requirements of practitioners may be considered. A defined set of base measures is the prerequisite for applying and/or adapting elicitation techniques.

Second, values related to the selected base measures have to be elicited in the as-is BP or IS. Therefore, techniques, such as process mining (e.g., [van der Aalst (2007)]) and monitoring of component-based software systems (e.g., [Ehlers & Hasselbring (2011)]), can be applied or have to be adapted for the requested measures. Analyzing and adapting existing techniques should be a second step, because the corresponding information must be available for meta-modeling in the following step.

Third, the base measures' values (e.g., resource demands, delays, or failure probabilities) have to be documented in corresponding attributes of the BP and IS model(s) to be available for model-based quality prediction. Therefore, an underlying model covering functional and structural design aspects, as well as quality-related aspects, has to be specified. The PCM and its proposed extensions is a good starting point for developing such an underlying model. The PCM already contains attributes related to base measures of quality characteristics, such as performance, reliability, and maintainability of an IS. BP-specific extensions to the PCM, including attributes related to BP performance, were proposed in this book. In the future, the PCM must be extended by model elements and attributes related to base measures of other quality characteristics. Moreover, the PCM may be extended, in order to reflect the BPQRM component information object (cf. Section 9.5) and related base measures. While extending the PCM, it will become more and more complex. Therefore, approaches to organize and dynamically generate different views, based on a single underlying model, such as Orthographic Software Modeling [Atkinson & Stoll (2008)], may be applied and adapted. For example, a view may show all attributes related to a certain quality characteristic, but may hide attributes of the other quality characteristics. Another view, for example, may show all BP parts related to a certain IS, where other BP parts are hidden. Moreover, it may be useful to rearrange the PCM in several modular models, in order to reduce complexity. Like with a single underlying model, there are approaches to organize and dynamically generate views based on a modular single underlying model [Kramer et al. (2013)]. Constructing a modular single underlying model should be the third step, because values related to the base measures have to be documented before they are composed, as specified by derived measures in the following step.

Fourth, in order to assess abstract objectives, derived measures have to be built upon the base measures. Thus, quality prediction results based on the underlying model can be composed to assess the objectives. Therefore, a second meta-model – the measure meta-model – that describes how the measures are composed to derived measures have to be developed. The separation in two meta-models is required to distinguish the representation of a BP and IS in one model from the specification of the measures in the other model. Existing meta-models related to software measures (e.g., [SMM 1.0 (2012)]) may be a starting point for this. Continuous meta-modeling may enable traceability among the hardware level, the software architecture level, and the BP level. Traceability comprises the relationship between a derived measure and its components (i.e., base measures and/or derived measures) within the measure meta-model. Moreover, traceability comprises the relation between a base measure in the measure meta-model, and the related value in the underlying model, as well as between a derived measure in the measure meta-model, and the related quality prediction result.

As a fifth step, the underlying model has to be applied for quality prediction. The proposed simulation methods currently support the evaluation of BPs and ISs in terms of performance. Prediction methods for other quality characteristics have to be developed, which is discussed in the following section. Thus, designs can be evaluated in terms of diverse quality aspects. Moreover, automated design space exploration including various quality aspects is desirable. The consideration of a variety of quality aspects in simulation must be accompanied by a modularization of the current simulators. This is needed to adequately handle the different quality aspects in simulation and to enable maintainability and further extensibility.

11.4.2 Comprehensive Quality Prediction

Part II of this book focuses on performance prediction, where a comprehensive set of quality characteristics was proposed in Part I. Further quality characteristics have to be included in an integrated quality prediction to enable a quality-aware evolution of BPs and ISs. Besides performance, mutual impact between BPs and ISs in terms of the other quality characteristics of the BPQRM have to be investigated. Especially in terms of reliability and security, there is mutual impact between BPs and ISs. There are approaches to software-architecture-based reliability [Brosch et al. (2012)] and security [Sharma & Trivedi (2007)] prediction based on Discrete-Time Markov Chains [Norris (1998)]. These quality characteristics are also highly relevant in the BP context. For example, there are approaches from the workflow management system community (e.g., [Cardoso et al. (2004)]), which are related to BP reliability. [Rodríguez et al. (2007)] and [Jensen

& Feja (2009)] address security aspects in the BP context. [Brosch et al. (2010)] combines software-architecture-based reliability predictions with calculation of financial impact resulting from cost-relevant BPs. Markov-chain based approaches seem to be a good starting point to include further quality characteristics in an integrated quality prediction. Moreover, a com-bined prediction of different quality characteristics may give insights on interrelations between the single characteristics. For example, performance may be limited by frequent exception handling, due to insufficient reliability. This can provide further possibilities for design improvement.

Bibliography

[van der Aalst (2007)] van der Aalst, W.M.P. *Process Mining: Discovery, Conformance and Enhancement of Business Processes*, Springer, ISBN: 3642193447, 2011. 26, 207

[Adam et al. (2009)] Adam, S., Riegel, N., Dörr, J. *The Role of Quality Aspects for the Adequacy of Business Processes and Business Information Systems*, Journal of Business Process Integration and Management, Vol. 4 Iss. 2, pp. 124–133, Inderscience, 2009. 3, 55, 59, 104

[Aerts et al. (2004)] Aerts, A.T.M., Goossenaerts, J.B.M., Hammer, D.K., Wortmann, J.C. *Architectures in context: on the evolution of business, application software, and ICT platform architectures*, Information and Management, Vol. 41 No. 6, pp. 781–794, Elsevier, 2004. 1

[Al-Gahtani (2001)] Al-Gahtani, S. *The Applicability of TAM Outside North America: An Empirical Test in the United Kingdom*, Information Resources Management Journal, Vol. 14 Iss. 3, pp. 37–46, IGI Global, 2001. 157

[Ammenwerth et al. (2010)] Ammenwerth, E., Breu, R., Paech, B. *User-Oriented Quality Assessment of IT-Supported Healthcare Processes – a Position Paper*, In: BPM 2009 Workshops, Lecture Notes in Business Information Processing, Vol. 43, pp. 617–622, Springer, 2010. 28

[Armbrust (2010)] Armbrust, O. *The SCOPE Approach for Scoping Software Processes*, PhD Theses in Experimental Software Engineering, Band 32, Fraunhofer Verlag, ISBN: 3839601371, 2010. 193

[Atkinson & Stoll (2008)] Atkinson, C., Stoll, D. *An Environment for the Orthographic Modeling of Workflow Components*, In: Proceedings of the Prozessinnovationen mit Unternehmenssoftware (PRIMIUM) Subconference at the Multikonferenz Wirtschaftsinformatik (MKWI), 2008 208

[ABACUS 3.2] Avolution Pty Ltd: ABACUS 3.2, http://www.avolution.com.au/ (Last Access: 2010.11.24). 66, 68

[Ballou et al. (1998)] Ballou, D.P., Wang, R., Pazer, H.L., Tayi, G.K. *Modelling Information Manufacturing Systems to Determine Information Product Quality*, Management Science, Vol. 44 No. 4, pp.462–484, INFORMS, 1998. 36

[Balsamo & Marzolla (2003)] Balsamo, S., Marzolla, M. *A Simulation-Based Approach to Software Performance Modeling*, In: Proceedings of the 9th European Software Engineering Conference, pp. 363–366. ACM Press, 2003. 112

[Bandara et al. (2005)] Bandara, W., Gable, G.G., Rosemann, M. *Factors and measures of business process modelling: Model building through a multiple case study*, European Journal of Information Systems, Vol. 14 No. 4, pp. 347–360, Palgrave Macmillan, 2005. 2, 59

[Banks et al. (2009)] Banks, J., Carson, J.S., Nelson, B.L., Nicol, D.M. *Discrete-Event System Simulation*, Prentice Hall, ISBN: 0136062121, 2009. 142

[Barjis (2008)] Barjis, J. *The importance of business process modeling in software systems design*, Science of Computer Programming, Vol. 71 Iss. 1, pp. 73–87, Elsevier, 2008. 2, 3, 55, 104

[Basili et al. (1994)] Basili, V.R., Caldiera, G., Rombach, H.D. *The Goal Question Metric Approach*, In: Marciniak, J.J. (ed.) *Encyclopedia of Software Engineering*, pp 528–532, Wiley and Sons, ISBN: 0471540048, 1994. 155

[Bause (1993)] Bause, F. *Queueing Petri Nets – A formalism for the combined qualitative and quantitative analysis of systems*, In: Proceedings of the 5th International Workshop on Petri Nets and Performance Models, pp. 14–23, IEEE, 1993. 6, 129

[Becker et al. (2013)] Becker, M., Becker, S., Meyer, J. *SimuLizar: Design-Time Modeling and Performance Analysis of Self-Adaptive Systems*, In: Proceedings of the Software Engineering 2013 conference, Lecture Notes in Informatics, Vol. P-213, pp. 71–84, GI, 2013. 205

[Becker (2008)] Becker, S. *Coupled Model Transformations for QoS Enabled Component-Based Software Design*, PhD thesis, University of Oldenburg, Germany, 2008. 84, 88, 152, 205

[Becker et al. (2009)] Becker, S., Koziolek, H., and Reussner, R. *The Palladio component model for model-driven performance prediction*, Journal of Systems and Software, Vol. 82, pp. 3–22, Elsevier, 2009. 34, 85, 86, 87, 88, 104, 112, 186, 190

[BetrVG] Betriebsverfassungsgesetz, Bundesgesetz, Bundesrepublik Deutschland. 206

[Betz et al. (2012)] Betz, S., Burger, E., Eckert, A., Oberweis, A., Reussner, R., Trunko, R. *An approach for Integrated Lifecycle Management for Business Processes and Business Software*, In: Mistrik, I., Tang, A., Bahsoon, R., Stafford, J.A. (eds.) *Aligning Enterprise, System, and Software Architectures*, pp. 136–154, IGI Global, ISBN: 1466621990, 2012. 113

[ADONIS 3.9] BOC Information Technologies Consulting AG: ADONIS 3.9, http://www.adoniscommunity.com/ (Last Access: 2010.10.26). 68

[Box et al. (2008)] Box, G.E.P., Jenkins, G.M., Reinsel, G.C. *Time Series Analysis : Forecasting and Control*, Wiley Series in Probability and Statistics, Wiley, ISBN: 0470272848, 2008. 93

[Böhme & Reussner (2008)] Böhme, R., Reussner, R. *Validation of Predictions with Measurements*, In: Eusgeld, I., Freiling, F.C., Reussner, R. (eds.) *Dependability Metrics*, pp. 14–18, Springer, ISBN: 9783540689461, 2008. 152, 153, 154

[Brosch et al. (2010)] Brosch, F., Gitzel, R., Koziolek, H., Krug, S. *Combining Architecture-Based Software Reliability Predictions with Financial Impact Calculations*, Electronic Notes in Theoretical Computer Science, Vol. 264 No.1, pp. 3–17, Elsevier, 2010. 210

[Brosch et al. (2012)] Brosch, F., Koziolek, H., Buhnova, B., Reussner, R. *Architecture-Based Reliability Prediction with the Palladio Component Model*, Transactions on Software Engineering, Vol. 38 No.6, IEEE Computer Society, 2012. 209

[Caetano et al. (2007)] Caetano, A., Pombinho, J., Tribolet, J. *Representing Organizational Competencies*, In: Proceedings of the 2007 ACM symposium on applied computing, pp. 1257–1262, ACM, 2007. 18, 39

[McCall et al. (1977)] McCall, J., Richards, P., Walters, G. *Factors in Software Quality – Concepts and Definitions of Software Quality*, Joint General Electric and U.S. Air Force Report No. RADC-TR-77-369, Vol. 1, pp. 3–5, 1977. 22

[Camp (1989)] Camp, R.C. *Benchmarking – The Search for Industry Best Practices that Lead to Superior Performance*, Quality Resources, ISBN: 0527916358, 1989. 27

[Cardoso et al. (2004)] Cardoso, J., Miller, J., Arnold, J. *Modeling Quality of Service for Workflows and Web Service Processes*, Journal of Web Semantics, pp. 281–308, Elsevier, 2004. 28, 209

[Chandy & Martin (1983)] Chandy, K.M., Martin, A.J. *A Characterization of Product-Form Queuing Networks*, Journal of the ACM, Vol. 30 Iss. 2, pp. 286–299, ACM, 1983. 83

[Cho (2009)] Cho, V. *Data Quality on the Internet*, In: Hung, H., Wong, Y.H. Cho, V. (eds.) *Ubiquitous Commerce for Creating the Personalized Marketplace: Concepts for Next Generation Adoption*, pp. 171–176, IGI Global, ISBN: 1605663786, 2009. 36

[McClelland (1973)] McClelland, D. *Testing for competence rather than for intelligence*, American Psychologist, Vol. 28 No. 1, pp. 1–14, American Psychological Association, 1973. 39

[Crosby (1979)] Crosby, P.B. *Quality is Free: The Art of Making Quality Certain*, McGraw-Hill, ISBN: 0070145121, 1979. 22

[Dale (2003)] Dale, B.G. *Managing Quality*, Wiley-Blackwell, ISBN: 0631236147, 2003. 22, 27

[Davenport (1993)] Davenport, T.J. *Process Innovation: Reengineering Work through Information Technology*, Harvard Business School Press, ISBN: 1422160661, 1993. 1, 6, 18, 27, 54, 103

[Davenport & Short (1990)] Davenport T.H., Short, J.E. *The New Industrial Engineering: Information Technology and Business Process Redesign*, Sloan Management Review, Vol. 31 No. 4, pp. 11–27, MIT Sloan School of Management, 1990. 17, 27

[Davis et al. (1989)] Davis, F.D., Bagozzi, R.P., Warshaw, P.R. *User Acceptance of Computer Technology: A Comparison of two Theoretical Models*, Management Science, Vol. 35 No. 8, pp. 982–1003, INFORMS, 1989. 8, 157

[DeLone & McLean (1992)] DeLone, W.H., McLean, E.R. *Information Systems Success: The Quest for the Dependent Variable*, Information Systems Research, Vol. 3 No. 1, pp. 60–95, INFORMS, 1992. 104

[Deming (1982)] Deming, E.W. *Out of the Crisis*, MIT Press, ISBN: 0911379010, 1982. 22

[Ehlers (2004)] Ehlers, F. *Das Prozess-Potential-Screening: ein Verfahren zur Identifikation von Verbesserungsmöglichkeiten in Krankenhaus-*

prozessen, PhD thesis, University of Heidelberg, 2004 (in German). 31, 38, 39

[Ehlers et al. (2006)] Ehlers, F., Ammenwerth, E., Haux, R. *Process Potential Screening – An Instrument to Improve Business Processes in Hospitals*, Methods of Information in Medicine, Vol. 45 Iss. 5, pp. 506–514, Schattauer Publishers, 2006. 28, 45

[Ehlers & Hasselbring (2011)] Ehlers, J., Hasselbring, W. *A Self-Adaptive Monitoring Framework for Component-Based Software Systems*, In: Proceedings of the 5th European Conference on Software Architecture, Lecture Notes in Computer Science Vol. 6903, pp. 278–286, Springer, 2011. 207

[Eatock et al. (2002)] Eatock, J., Paul, R.J., Serrano, A. *Developing a Theory to Explain the Insights Gained Concerning Information Systems and Business Processes Behaviour: The ASSESS-IT Project*, Information Systems Frontiers, Vol. 4 No. 3, pp. 303–316, Springer, 2002. 112

[Feigenbaum (1991)] Feigenbaum, A.V. *Total Quality Control*, McGraw-Hill, ISBN: 9780071126120, 1991. 22

[Fischermanns (2009)] Fischermanns, G. *Praxishandbuch Prozessmanagement*, Verlag Dr. Götz Schmidt, ISBN: 3921313732, 2009 (in German). 28, 31, 39

[Fishbein & Ajzen (1975)] Fishbein, M., Ajzen, I. *Belief, Attitude, Intention and Behavior: An Introduction to Theory and Research*, Addison-Wesley, ISBN: 0201020890, 1975. 8, 157, 158

[Franks (2011)] Franks, G. *Simulating Layered Queueing Networks with Passive Resources*, Proceedings of the 2011 Symposium on Theory of Modeling & Simulation: DEVS Integrative M&S Symposium, pp. 8–15, ACM, 2011. 129

[Fujimoto (1990)] Fujimoto, R.M. *Parallel Discrete Event Simulation*, Communications of the ACM, Vol. 33 No.10, pp.30–53, ACM, 1990. 126, 127

[Gabriel et al. (2002)] Garbiel, R., Knittel, F., Taday, H., Reif-Model, A. *Computergestützte Informations- und Kommunikationssysteme in der Unternehmung*, Springer, ISBN: 3540665137, 2002 (in German). 31, 39

[Gagne & Trudel (2009)] Gagne, D., Trudel, A. *Time-BPMN*, In: Proceedings of the 2009 IEEE Conference on Commerce and Enterprise Computing, pp. 361–367, IEEE Computer Society, 2009. 63, 65, 70, 75

[Giaglis et al. (1999)] Giaglis, G.M., Paul, R.J., O'Keefe, R.M. *Research note: integrating business and network simulation models for IT investment evaluation*, Logistics Information Management, Vol. 12 No. 1–2, pp. 108–117, Emerald, 1999. 113

[Giaglis et al. (2005)] Giaglis, G.M., Hlupic, V., Vreede, G.J., Verbraeck, A. *Synchronous design of business processes and information systems using dynamic process modelling*, Business Process Management Journal, Vol. 11 No. 5, pp. 488–500, Emerald, 2005. 112

[Gladwin & Tumay (1994)] Gladwin, B., Tumay, K. *Modelling Business Processes with Simulation Tools*, In: Proceedings of the 26th conference on Winter simulation, pp.114–121, Society for Computer Simulation International, 1994. 112

[Graupner et al. (2008)] Graupner, S., Rolia, J., Edwards, N. *Deriving IT Configurations from Business Processes*, In: Proceedings of the 5th IEEE Conference on Enterprise Computing, E-Commerce and E-Services, pp. 317–322, IEEE, 2008. 129

[Grigori et al. (2001)] Grigori, D., Casati, F., Dayal, U., Shan, M. *Improving Business Process Quality through Exception Understanding*,

Prediction, and Prevention, In: Proceedings of the 27th International Conference on Very Large Data Bases, pp. 159–168, Morgan Kaufmann Publishers Inc., 2001. 25

[Guceglioglu & Demirors (2005)] Guceglioglu, A.S., Demirors, O. *Using Software Quality Characteristics to Measure Business Process Quality*, In: Proceedings of the 3rd International Conference on Business Process Management, Lecture Notes in Computer Science Volume 3649, pp. 374–379, Springer, 2005. 2, 29, 54

[Gulla (2007)] Gulla, J. *Using Models in Enterprise Systems Projects*, In: Krogstie, J., Opdahl, A.L., Brinkkemper, S. (eds.) Conceptual Modelling in Information Systems Engineering, pp. 107–122, Springer, ISBN: 3540726764, 2007. 61, 62, 64, 65, 70, 75

[Hammer & Champy (1993)] Hammer, M., Champy, J. *Reengineering the Corporation, A Manifesto for Business Revolution*, HarperBusiness, ISBN: 0887306403, 1993. 17, 27

[Hammer (2007)] Hammer, M. *The Process Audit*, Harvard Business Review, Vol. 85 Iss. 4, pp. 111–123, Harvard Business Publishing, 2007. 27

[Harrington et al. (1997)] Harrington, H.J., Esseling, E.K.C., van Nimwegen, H. *Busiess Process Improvement Workbook*, McGraw-Hill, ISBN: 0070267790, 1997. 27

[Harzallah & Lecrere (2002)] Harzallah, M., Lecrere, M. *CommOnCV: Modelling the Competencies Underlying a Curriculum Vitae*, In: Proceedings of the 14th International Conference on Software Engineering and Knowledge Engineering, pp. 65–71, ACM, 2002. 39

[Heckl & Moormann (2010)] Heckl, D., Moormann, J. *Process Performance Management*, In: vom Brocke, J., Rosemann, M. (eds.) *Handbook on Business Process Management 2*, pp. 115–135, Springer, ISBN: 3642019811, 2010. 26

[Heidari et al. (2011)] Heidari, F., Loucopoulos, P., Kedad, Z. *A Quality-Oriented Business Process Meta-Model*, In: Proceedings of the 7th International Workshop on Enterprise and Organizational Modeling and Simulation, Lecture Notes in Business Information Processing Volume 88, pp. 85–99, Springer, 2011. 2, 29, 54

[Heidrich (2009)] Heidrich, J. *Goal-oriented Quantitative Software Project Control*, PhD Theses in Experimental Software Engineering, Band 24, Fraunhofer Verlag, 2009. 193

[Henderson & Venkatraman (1993)] Henderson, J.C., Venkatraman, N. *Strategic alignment: Leveraging information technology for transforming organisations*, IBM Systems Journal, Vol.32 No.1, pp. 4–16, IBM, 1993. 4

[Heravizadeh (2009)] Heravizadeh, M. *Quality-aware Business Process Management*, Ph.D. thesis, Queensland University of Technology, 2009. 25

[Heravizadeh et al. (2009)] Heravizadeh, M., Mendling, J., Rosemann, M. *Dimensions of Business Processes Quality (QoBP)*, In: Business Process Management Workshops 2008, Lecture Notes in Business Information Processing Volume 17, pp. 80–91, Springer, 2009. 2, 4, 29, 31, 39, 53, 59

[Herbst et al. (1997)] Herbst, J., Junginger, S., Kühn, H. *Simulation in Financial Services with the Business Process Management System ADONIS*, In: Proceedings of the 9th European Simulation Symposium, pp. 491–495, 1997. 112, 125, 134, 147, 153, 154

[Hiekkanen et al. (2013)] Hiekkanen, K., Helenius, M., Korhonen, J.J., Patricio, E. *Aligning Alignment with Strategic Context: A Literature Review*, In: Proceedings of the 5th International Conference on Digital Enterprise Design and Management, Advances in Intelligent Systems and Computing Volume 205, pp 81–98, Springer, 2013. 4

[Hlupic & Robinson (1998)] Hlupic, V. Robinson, S. *Business Process Modelling and Analysis Using Discrete-Event Simulation*, In: Proceedings of the 30th Conference on Winter Simulation, pp.1363–1369, IEEE Computer Society Press, 1998. 112

[Hopcroft et al. (2006)] Hopcroft, J.E., Motwani, R., Ullman, J.D. *Introduction to Automata Theory, Languages, and Computation*, Prentice Hall, ISBN: 0321455363, 2006. 136

[Horus 1.2.1] Horus software GmbH: Horus Business Modeler 1.2.1, http://www.horus.biz/ (Last Access: 2010.12.17). 68

[ARIS Design Platform 7.1] IDS Scheer AG: ARIS Design Platform 7.1, http://www.idsscheer.com/en/ARIS_ARIS_Platform/ 3730.html (Last Access: 2010.11.21). 66, 67

[IEEE Std. 1061-1992] IEEE Std. 1061-1992 Standard for Software Quality Metrics Methodology, 1992. 22

[IEEE Std. 1516] Simulation Interoperability Standards Committee, IEEE standard for modeling and simulation High Level Architecture (HLA) – Framework and Rules, 2000. 127

[Imai (1986)] Imai, M. *Kaizen: The Key to Japan's Competitive Success*, Mcgraw-Hill, ISBN: 007554332X, 1986. 26

[GRADE 4.1] INFOLOGISTIK GmbH: GRADE 4.1, http://www. infologistik.com/grade/ (Last Access: 2010.11.21). 68

[COBIT 5 (2012)] ISACA: Control Objectives for Information and Related Technology 5, 2012. 27

[ISO/IEC 9126-1] ISO/IEC 9126-1: Software engineering – Product quality – Part 1: Quality model, First edition, 2001. 2, 3, 22, 23, 31, 55

[ISO/IEC 25000] ISO/IEC 25000: Software engineering – Software product Quality Requirements and Evaluation (SQuaRE) – Guide to SQuaRE, First edition, 2005. 22, 23, 30

[ISO/IEC 25012] ISO/IEC 25012: Software engineering – Software product Quality Requirements and Evaluation (SQuaRE) – Data quality model, First edition, 2008. 22, 23, 37

[ISO/IEC TR 25021] ISO/IEC TR 25021 Software engineering – Software product Quality Requirements and Evaluation (SQuaRE) – Quality measure elements, First edition, 2007. 34, 42, 47

[ISO/IEC 15939] ISO/IEC 15939: Systems and software engineering – Measurement process, Second edition, 2007. 40

[Jensen & Feja (2009)] Jensen, M., Feja, S. *A Security Modeling Approach for Web-Service-Based Business Processes*, In: Proceeedings of the 16th IEEE International Conference and Workshop on the Engineering of Computer Based Systems, pp. 340–347, IEEE Computer Society, 2009. 61, 63, 64, 65, 210

[Juran (1986)] Juran, J.M. *The Quality Trilogy: A Universal Approach to Managing for Quality*, Quality Progress, Vol. 9 No. 8, pp. 19–24, American Society for Quality, 1986. 22

[Juran & Godfrey (1999)] Juran, M.J., Godfrey A.B. *Juran's Quality Handbook*, McGraw-Hill, ISBN: 007034003, 1999. 22, 205

[Johnson et al. (1993)] Johanson, H.J. McHugh, P., Pendlebury, A.J., Wheeler W.A. *Business Process Reengineering: Breakpoint Strategies for Market Dominance*, Whiley, ISBN: 0471950882, 1993. 27

[Kahn et al. (2002)] Kahn, B., Strong, D., Wang, R. *Information Quality Benchmarks: Product and Service Performance*, Communication of the ACM, Vol. 45 No.4, pp. 184–192, ACM, 2002. 38

[Kaplan & Norton (1993)] Kaplan, R.S., Norton, D.P. *Putting the Balanced Scorecard to Work*, Harvard Business Review, Vol. 71 No. 5, pp. 134–147, Harvard Business Publishing, 1993. 26

[Kappe (2011)] Kappe, A. *Entwicklung und Umsetzung eines Konzepts zur Modellierung von Qualitätsinformationen in einem Geschäftsprozessmodell*, Master Thesis, Software Engineering Heidelberg, 2011. 60, 67, 70, 72

[Kern Process 2.6] Kern AG: Kern Process 2.6, http://www.kern.ag/ (Last Access: 2010.12.17). 68

[King & Xia (2004)] King, W.R., Xia, W. *Assessing the Organizational Impact of IT Infrastructure Capabilities*, Katz Graduate School of Business, University of Pittsburgh, 2004, available online: http://www.inst-informatica.pt/v20/ersi/11_ersi/documentos/King.pdf (Last Access: 2013.03.19). 1, 104

[Kounev (2006)] Kounev, S. *Performance Modeling and Evaluation of Distributed Component-Based Systems Using Queueing Petri-Nets*, IEEE Transactions on Software Engineering, Vol. 32 No. 7, pp. 486–502, IEEE, 2006. 129

[Kounev & Dutz (2009)] Kounev, S., Dutz, C. *QPME – A Performance Modeling Tool Based on Queueing Petri Nets*, ACM SIGMETRICS Performance Evaluation Review, Vol. 36 No. 4, pp. 46–51, ACM, 2009. 129

[Kounev et al. (2011)] Kounev, S., Spinner, S., Meier, P. *QPME 2.0 – A Tool for Stochastic Modeling and Analysis Using Queueing Petri Nets*, In: Sachs, K., Petrov, I., Guerrero, P. (eds.) *From Active Data Management to Event-Based Systems and More*, Lecture Notes in Computer Science Volume 6462, pp 293–311, Springer, ISBN: 9783642172267, 2011. 129

[Korherr (2008)] Korherr, B. *Business Process Modelling: Languages, Goals, and Variabilities*, VDM Verlag, ISBN: 3836487160, 2008. 59, 62, 65

[Koziolek et al. (2011)] Koziolek, A., Koziolek, H., Reussner, R. *PerOpteryx: Automated Application of Tactics in Multi-Objective*

Software Architecture Optimization, In: Proceedings of the 2nd International ACM Sigsoft Symposium on Architecting Critical Systems, pp. 33–42, ACM, 2011. 112, 149

[Koziolek (2008)] Koziolek, H. *Parameter Dependencies for Reusable Performance Specifications of Software Components*, PhD thesis, University of Oldenburg, 2008. 85, 152, 153, 154, 202, 204

[Koziolek & Reussner (2008)] Koziolek H., Reussner, R. *A Model Transformation from the Palladio Component Model to Layered Queueing Networks*, In: Kounev, S., Gorton, I., Sachs, K. (eds.) *Performance Evaluation: Metrics, Models and Benchmarks*, Lecture Notes in Computer Science Volume 5119, pp. 58–78, Springer, 2008. 129

[Koziolek et al. (2013)] Koziolek, H., Schlich, B. Becker, S., Hauck, M. *Performance and reliability prediction for evolving service-oriented software systems*, Industrial experience report, Empirical Software Engineering, Vol. 18 Iss. 4, pp 746–790, Springer, 2013. 7, 151, 156, 171

[Kramer et al. (2013)] Kramer, M.E., Burger, E., Langhammer, M. *View-centric engineering with synchronized heterogeneous models*, In: Proceedings of the 1st Workshop on View-Based, Aspect-Oriented and Orthographic Software Modelling, ACM, 2013. 208

[Kueng (2000)] Kueng, P. *Process Performance Measurement System: A Tool to Support Process-Based Organizations*, Total Quality Management, Vol. 11 No 1., pp. 67–85, Carfax Publishing, 2000. 26

[Law & Kelton (2000)] Law, A.M., Kelton, W.D. *Simulation Modeling and Analysis*, McGraw-Hill series in industrial engineering and management science. McGraw-Hill, ISBN: 007329411, 2000. 83, 84, 85, 137, 138, 142

[Lazowska et al. (1984)] Lazowska, E., Zahorjan, J., Graham, G.S., Sevcik, K.C. *Quantitative System Performance – Computer System Analysis Using Queueing Network Models*, Prentice-Hall, ISBN: 0137469756, 1984. 6, 82, 83, 87, 97

[Lee et al. (2006)] Lee, Y.W., Pipino L.L., Funk. J.D., Wang, R.Y. *Journey to Data Quality*, The MIT Press, ISBN: 0262122871, 2006. 36

[Lenz (2012)] Lenz, H. *Applying Performance Prediction in Practice in order to Align Business Process and IT Design*, Master Thesis, Software Engineering Heidelberg, 2012. 157, 165, 166, 182

[Likert (1932)] Likert, R. *A Technique for the Measurement of Attitudes*, Archives of Psychology, Vol. 22 No. 140, pp. 1–55, 1932. 160

[Lin & Song (2011)] Lin, H. Song, C. *Simulation of Hydraulic Anti-lock Braking System Control Based on a Co-simulation Model by AMESim and Simulink*, In: Proceedings of the 2011 International Conference on Transportation, Mechanical, and Electrical Engineering, pp. 775–778, IEEE, 2011. 125

[Liu (2011)] Liu, J. *Parallel Discrete-Event Simulation*, In: Cochran, J.J. et al. (eds.) *Wiley Encyclopedia of Operations Research and Management Science*, Wiley & Sons, ISBN: 9780470400630, 2011. 126, 127

[Lohrmann & Reichert (2013)] Lohrmann, M., Reichert, M. *Understanding Business Process Quality*, Studies in Computational Intelligence Volume 444, In: Glykas, M. (ed.) *Business Process Management – Theory and Applications*, pp 41–73, Springer, ISBN: 3642284086, 2013. 29, 54

[Luftman (2000)] Luftman, J. *Assessing Business-IT Alignment Maturity*, Communications of the Association for Information Systems, Vol. 4 Article 14, AIS, 2000. 4

[Malone et al. (2003)] Malone T.W., Crowston, K., Herman, G.A. *Organizing Business Knowledge: The MIT Process Handbook*, The MIT Press, ISBN: 0262134292, 2003. 25

[Martens (2007)] Martens, A. *Empirical Validation of the Model-driven Performance Prediction Approach Palladio*, Master Thesis, University of Oldenburg, 2007. 152, 154, 190

[Martens et al. (2011)] Martens, A., Koziolek, H., Prechelt, L., Reussner, R. *From monolithic to component-based performance evaluation of software architectures*, Epirical Software Engineering, Vol. 16 Iss. 5, pp.587–622, Springer, 2011. 186

[Mayer et al. (1992)] Mayer. R.J., Cullinane. T.P., deWitte P.S., Knappenberger. W.B., Perakath. B., Wells. M.S. *IDEF3 Process Description Capture Method Report*, AL-TR-1992-0057, Infomlation Integration for Concurrent Engineering Project, 1992. 112

[Meier (2010)] Meier, P. *Automated Transformation of Palladio Component Models to Queueing Petri Nets*, Diploma Thesis, Karlsruhe Institute of Trechnology, 2010. 129

[Meier et al. (2011)] Meier, P., Kounev, S., Koziolek, H. *Automated Transformation of Component-based Software Architecture Models to Queueing Petri Nets*, In: Proceedings of the 19th International IEEE/ACM Symposium on Modeling, Analysis and Simulation of Computer and Telecommunication Systems, pp. 339–348, IEEE, 2011. 129

[Melao & Pidd (2003)] Melao, N., Pidd, M. *Use of business process simulation: A survey of practitioners*, Journal of the Operational Research Society, Vol. 54 No. 1, pp. 2–10, Palgrave Macmillan, 2003. 7, 151

[Melenovsky (2005)] Melenovsky, M.J. *Business Process Management's Success Hinges on Business-Led Initiatives*, Gartner Note G00129411, Gartner Inc., 2005. 2

[Melling (1994)] Melling, W.P. *Enterprise Information Architectures – They're Finally Changing*, ACM SIGMOD Record, Vol. 23 Iss. 2, pp. 493–504, ACM, 1994. 104

[MEMOCenterNG] MEMOCenterNG build 2010-10-18, University of Duisburg-Essen, Chair of Information Systems, http://www.wi-inf.uni-duisburg-essen.de (Last Access: 2010.12.19). 66

[Mendling (2008)] Mendling, J. *Metrics for Process Models*, Lecture Notes in Business Information Processing Volume 6, Springer, ISBN: 9783540892243, 2008. 2, 26, 54

[Menzel (2012)] Menzel, I. *Optimizing the Completeness of Textual Requirements Documents in Practice*, PhD Thesis, Dept. of Computer Science, University of Kaiserslautern, 2012. 193

[Merkle & Henss (2011)] Merkle, P., Henss, J. *EventSim – an Event-driven Palladio Software Architecture Simulator*, In: Palladio Days 2011 Proceedings, Karlsruhe Reports in Informatics 32, pp. 15–22, KIT, 2011. 88, 139, 140, 143

[Mevius (2008)] Mevius, M.: *A Novel Modeling Language for Tool-based Business Process Engineering*, In: Proceedings of the 2008 ACM symposium on Applied computing, pp.590–591, ACM, 2008. 62, 63, 64, 65

[Mi et al. (2008)] Mi, N., Casale, G., Cherkasova, L., Smirni, E. *Burstiness in Multi-Tier Applications: Symptoms, Causes, and New Models*, In: Proceedings of the 9th International Conference on Middleware, pp. 265–286, Springer, 2008. 96, 108

[de Miguel et al. (2000)] de Miguel, M., Lambolais, T., Hannouz, M., Betge-Brezetz, S., Piekarec, S. *UML Extensions for the Specification and Evaluation of Latency Constraints in Architectural Models*, In: Proceedings of the 2nd international workshop on Software and performance, pp. 83–88, ACM Press, 2000. 112

[Mooney et al. (1996)] Mooney, J.G., Gurbaxani, V., Kraemer, K.L. *A process oriented framework for assessing the business value of information technology*, The DATA BASE for Advances in Information Systems, Vol. 27 Iss. 2, pp. 68–81, ACM, 1996. 1, 18, 104

[Neely et al. (2001)] Neely, A., Adams, C., Crowe, P. *The performance prism in practice*, Measuring Business Excellence, Vol. 5 No. 2, pp.6–12, Emerald, 2001. 26

[Norris (1998)] Norris, J.R. *Markov chains*, Cambridge University Press, ISBN: 0521481813, 1998. 209

[O'Brien & Marakas (2010)] O'Brien, J., Marakas, G. *Introduction to Information Systems*, McGraw-Hill, ISBN: 0072823119, 2010. 18

[BPMM 1.1 (2008)] Object Management Group, Business Process Maturity Model (BPMM), Version 1.1, formal/2008-01-17, 2008. 27

[BPMN 2.0 (2011)] Object Management Group, Business Process Model and Notation (BPMN), Version 2.0, formal/2011-01-03, 2011. 42, 61, 72

[SMM 1.0 (2012)] Object Management Group, Structured Metrics Metamodel (SMM), Version 1.0, formal/2012-01-05, 2012. 209

[UML 2.0 (2005)] Object Management Group, Unified Modeling Language (UML), Version 2.0, formal/2005-07-05, 2005. 87, 100, 136

[SPTP 1.1 (2005)] Object Management Group, UML Profile for Schedulability, Performance, and Time (SPTP), Version 1.1, formal/2005-01-02, 2005. 4

[QFTP 1.1 (2008)] Object Management Group, UML Profile for Modeling Quality of Service And Fault Tolerance Characteristics And Mechanisms (QFTP), Version 1.1, formal/2008-04-05, 2008. 4

[Oppenheim (2000)] Oppenheim, A.N.: *Questionnaire Design, Interviewing and Attitude Measurement*, Continuum International Publishing Group Ltd, ISBN: 0826451764, 2000. 44

[Osterweil (1987)] Osterweil, L.J. *Software Processes are Software Too*, In: Proceedings of the 9th International Conference on Software Engineering, pp. 2–13, IEEE Computer Society, 1987. 29, 204

[Osterweil (1997)] Osterweil, L.J. *Software Processes are Software Too*, Revisited: An Invited Talk on the Most Influential Paper of ICSE 9, In: Proceedings of the 1997 International Conference on Software Engineering, pp.540–548, IEEE Computer Society, 1997. 30, 204

[Painter et al. (1996)] Painter, M.K., Fernandes, R., Padmanaban, N., Mayer, R.J. *A Methodology for Integrating Business Process and Information Infrastructure Models*, In: Proceedings of the 28th conference on Winter simulation, pp. 1305–1312, IEEE Computer Society, 1996. 112, 113

[Paul & Serrano (2004)] Paul, R.J., Serrano, A. *Collaborative information systems and business process design using simulation*, In: Proceedings of the 37th International Conference on System Sciences, IEEE Computer Society, 2004. 112

[Pavlovski & Zou (2008)] Pavlovski, C.J., Zou, J. *Non-functional requirements in business process modeling*, In: Proceedings of the 5th Asia-Pacific conference on Approachual Modelling, pp. 103–112, Australian Computer Society, 2008. 2, 3, 59, 60, 61, 73, 75

[Pidd & Castro (1998)] Pidd, M., Castro, R.B. *Hierarchical modular modelling in discrete simulation*, In: Proceedings of the 28th conference on Winter simulation, pp. 383–389, IEEE Computer Society, 1998. 127

[Pipino et al. (2002)] Pipino, L.L., Lee, Y.W., Wang, R.Y. *Data Quality Assessment*, Communications of the ACM, Vol. 45 No. 4, pp. 211–218, ACM, 2002. 38

[Pohl & Rupp (2011)] Pohl, K., Rupp, C. *Requirements Engineering Fundamentals*, Rocky Nook, ISBN: 1933952814, 2011. 40

[Powell et al. (2001)] Powell, S.G., Schwaninger, M., Trimble, C. *Measurement and Control of Business Processes*, System Dynamics, Vol. 17 Iss. 1, pp. 63–91, Wiley & Sons, 2001. 2

[Pyzdeh & Keller (2009)] Pyzdeh, T., Keller, P. *The Six Sigma Handbook*, McGraw-Hill, ISBN: 0071623388, 2009. 26

[Rech & Schmitt (2009)] Rech, J., Schmitt, M. *Embedding Information about Defects, Decisions, Context, Quality, and Traceability in*

CIM- and PIM-level Software Models, Information and Software Technology, pp. 21, Elsevier, 2009. 2

[Redman (1996)] Redmann, T.C. *Data Quality for the Information Age*, Artech House Publishers, ISBN: 0890068836, 1996. 36

[Reijers (2005)] Reijers, H.A. *Process Design and Redesign*, In: Dumas, M., van der Aalst, W.M.P., ter Hofstede, A.H.M. (eds.) *Process-Aware Information Systems – Brindging People and Software through Process Technology*, Wiley-Interscience, ISBN: 9780471663065, 2005. 25, 27, 35

[Rodríguez et al. (2006)] Rodríguez, A., Fernández-Medina, E., Piattini, M. *Security Requirement with a UML 2.0 Profile*, In: Proceedings of the 1st International Conference on Availability, Reliability and Security, pp. 670–677, IEEE Computer Society, 2006. 61, 63

[Rodríguez et al. (2007)] Rodríguez, A., Fernández-Medina, E., Piattini, M. *A BPMN Extension for the Modeling of Security Requirements in Business Processes*, IEICE Transactions on Information and Systems, Vol.E90-D No. 4, pp. 745–752, Oxford University Press, 2007. 61, 63, 209

[Rolia & Sevcik (1995)] Rolia J., Sevcik, K. *The method of layers*, IEEE Transactions on Software Engineering, Vol. 21 No. 8, pp. 689–700, IEEE, 1995. 6, 129

[Rosemann & vom Brocke (2010)] Rosemann, M., vom Brocke, J. *Handbook on Business Process Management 1: Introduction, Methods, and Information Systems*, Springer, ISBN: 3642004156, 2010. 2

[Rubner et al. (1998)] Rubner, Y., Tomasi, C., Guibas, L. *A metric for distributions with applications to image databases*, In: Proceedings of the 6th International Conference on Computer Vision, pp. 59–66, IEEE Computer Society, 1998. 188

[Runeson et al. (2012)] Runeson, P., Host, M., Rainer, A., Regnell, B. *Case Study Research in Software Engineering: Guidelines and Examples*, Wiley&Sons, ISBN: 1118104358, 2012. 191, 192, 193

[Saeedi et al. (2010)] Saeedi, K., Zhao, L., Sampaio, P.R.F. *Extending BPMN for Supporting Customer-Facing Service Quality Requirements*, In: Proceedings of the 2010 IEEE International Conference on Web Services, pp. 616–623, IEEE Computer Society, 2010. 3, 59, 60, 61, 62, 64, 65, 70

[Sánchez-González et al. (2012)] Sánchez-González, L., García, F., Ruiz, F., Mendling, J. *Quality indicators for business process models from a gateway complexity perspective*, Information and Software Technology, Vol. 54 Iss. 11, pp. 1159–1174, Elsevier, 2012. 30

[Serrano & den Hengst (2005)] Serrano, A., den Hengst, M. *Modelling the Integration of BP and IT Using Business Process Simulation*, Enterprise Information Management, Vol. 18 No. 6, pp. 740–759, Emerald, 2005. 112

[Sharma & Trivedi (2007)] Sharma, V. Trivedi, K. *Quantifying Software Performance, Reliability and Security: An Architecture-Based Approach*, Journal of Systems and Software, Vol. 80 Iss. 4, pp. 493–509, Elsevier, 2007. 209

[Shumway (2011)] Shumway, R.H. *Time Series Analysis and Its Applications : With R Examples*, Springer Texts in Statistics, Springer, ISBN: 144197864X, 2011. 93

[Smith (1990)] Smith, C.U. *Performance Engineering of Software Systems*, Addison-Wesley, ISBN: 0201537699, 1990. 6

[Standish Group International Inc. (2004)] Standish Group International Inc., 2004 Third Quarter Research Report, West Yarmouth, 2004. 2

[Stewart (2011)] Stewart, W.J. *Probability, Markov Chains, Queues, and Simulation: The Mathematical Basis of Performance Modeling*, Princeton University Press, ISBN: 0691140626, 2011. 164

[Tan & Takakuwa (2007)] Tan, Y., Takakuwa, S. *Predicting the Impact on Business Performance of Enhanced Information System Using Business Process Simulation*, In: Proceedings of the 39th conference on Winter simulation, pp. 2203–2211, IEEE Computer Society, 2007. 112

[Tolk & Muguira (2003)] Tolk, A., Muguira, J.A. *The Levels of Conceptual Interoperability Model (LCIM)*, In: Proceedings of the IEEE Fall Simulation Interoperability Workshop, IEEE CS Press, 2003. 127

[Tsai et al. (2010)] Tsai, W., Chen, S., Hwang, E.T.Y., Hsu, J. *A Study of the Impact of Business Process on the ERP System Effectiveness*, Journal of Business and Management, Vol. 5 No. 9, pp. 26–37, Canadian Center of Science and Education, 2010. 104

[Vanderfeesten et al. (2007)] Vanderfeesten, I., Cardoso, J., Mendling, J., Reijers, H.A., van der Aalst, W.M.P. *Quality Metrics for Business Process Models*, In: Fischer, L. (ed.) BPM and Workflow Handbook 2007, Lighthouse Point: Future Strategies, pp. 179–190, ISBN: 9780977752713, 2007. 26, 54

[Varga & Hornig (2008)] Varga, A., Hornig, R. *An overview of the OMNeT++ simulation environment*, In: Proceedings of the 1st international conference on Simulation tools and techniques for communications, networks and systems, Article No. 60, ICST, 2008. 112

[Venkatesh & Davis (2000)] Venkatesh, V., Davis, F. D. *A theoretical extension of the technology acceptance model: Four longitudinal field studies*, Management Science, Vol. 46 No. 2, pp 186–204, INFORMS, 2000. 157

[Verbesselt et al. (2010)] Verbesselt, J., Hyndman, R., Zeileis, A., Culvenor, D. *Phenological change detection while accounting for abrupt and gradual trends in satellite image time series*, Remote Sensing of Environment, Vol. 114 No. 12, pp. 2970–2980, Elsevier, 2010. 93

[Wand & Wang (1996)] Wand, Y., Wang, R.Y. *Anchoring Data Quality Dimensions in Ontological Foundations*, Communication of the ACM, Vol. 39 No. 11, pp. 86–95, ACM, 1996. 36

[Wang & Strong (1996)] Wang, R.Y., Strong, D.M. *Beyond accuracy: What data Quality means to data consumers*, Journal of Management Information Systems, Vol. 12 No. 4, pp. 5–34, M.E. Sharpe Inc., 1996. 36, 38

[Warren et al. (1995)] Warren, J.R., Crosslin, R.L. MacArthur, P.J. *Simulation Modeling for BPR: Steps to Effective Decision Support*, Information Systems Management, Vol. 12 No. 4, pp. 32–42, Inderscience, 1995. 112

[Weske (2007)] Weske, M. *Business Process Management: Concepts, Languages, Architecutes*, Springer, ISBN: 3540735224, 2007. 17

[WMC (1999)] Workflow Management Coalition, W. M. C. Specification, Terminology & Glossary (Document No. WFMC-TC-1011), Workflow Management Coalition Specification, Feb. 1999. 17, 18, 91, 92

[Wieringa et al. (2003)] Wieringa, R.J., Blanken, H.M., Fokkinga, M.M., Grefen, P.W.P.J. *Aligning Application Architecture to the Business Context*, In: Proceedings of the 15th international conference on Advanced information systems engineering, Lecture Notes in Computer Science Vol. 2681, pp. 209–225, Springer, 2003. 2

[WinterGreen Research (2012)] WinterGreen Research, Business Process Management (BPM) Market Shares, Strategies, and Forecasts, Worldwide, 2012 to 2018, 2012-09-05. 1, 2

[W3C (2003)] W3C: QoS for Web Services: Requirements and possible Approaches, W3C Working Group Note, 2003, `http://`

`www.w3c.or.kr/kr-office/TR/2003/ws-qos` (Last Access: 2013.09.24). 29

[Yang (2003)] Yang, G. *Towards a library for process programming*, In: Proceedings of the 2003 international conference on Business process management, pp. 120–135, Springer, 2003. 30

[Zeigler (1984)] Zeigler, B.P. *Multifacetted modelling and discrete event simulation*, Academic Press, ISBN: 0127784500, 1984. 127